Jacqueline Humphries

LUND HUMPHRIES | CONTEMPORARY PAINTERS

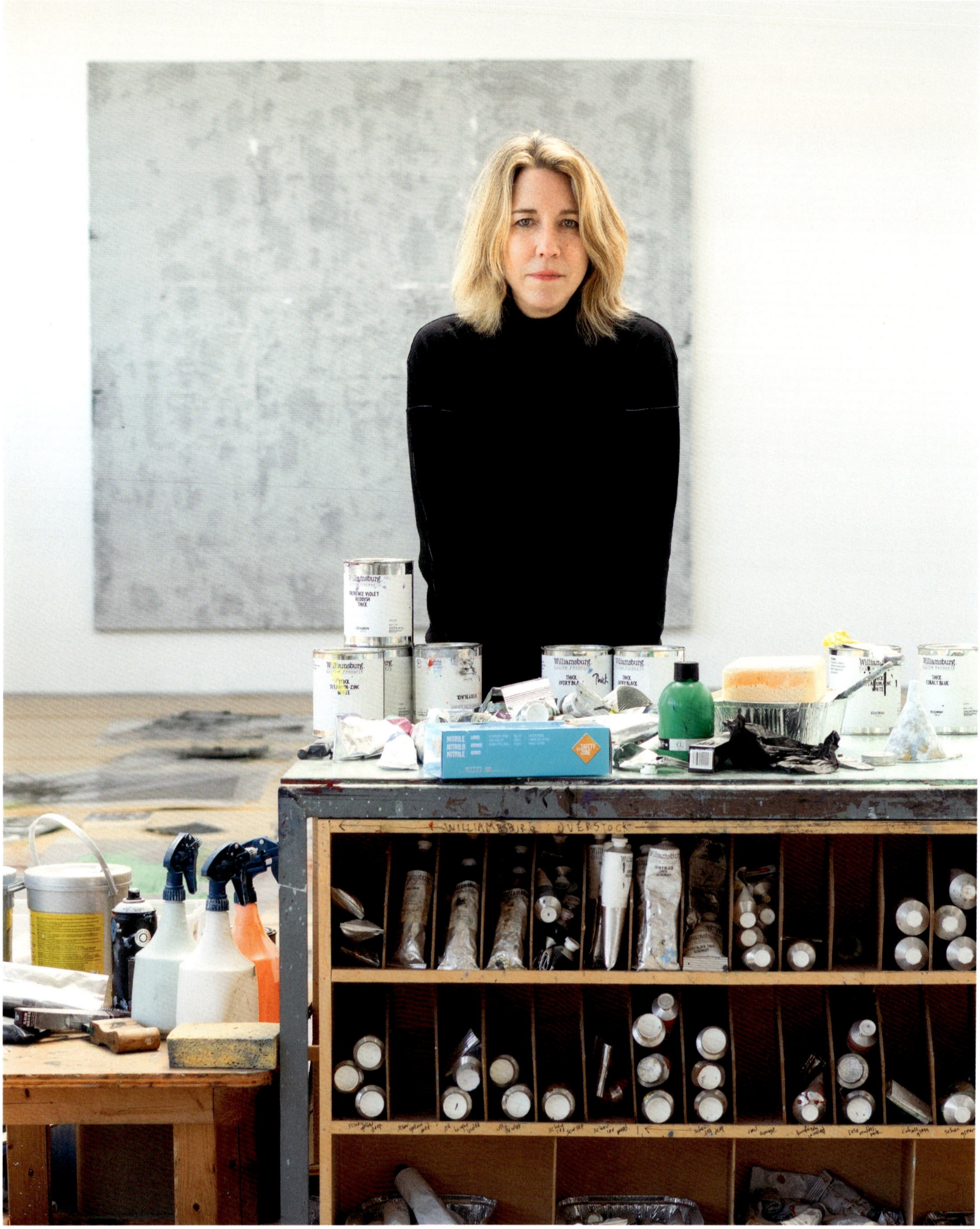
Williamsburg
THICK IVORY BLACK
THICK COBALT BLUE

Frances Guerin

Jacqueline Humphries

LUND HUMPHRIES | CONTEMPORARY PAINTERS

Contemporary Painters Series
Series Editor: Barry Schwabsky

The Contemporary Painters Series is a curated series of accessible, authoritative and highly illustrated monographs on the world's leading living painters, which locates painting as a vibrant and vital part of contemporary art.

The series is edited by American art critic Barry Schwabsky, supported by an international advisory board with a specialist interest in contemporary painting. It aims to redefine 'painting' in the contemporary context as work that is done within the conventions and history of painting, but which may incorporate other materials or techniques.

Also available in the series:
Amy Sillman by Valerie Smith
Bernard Frize by David Rhodes
Ding Yi by Tony Godfrey and Kaimei Wang
Ellen Gallagher by Caoimhín Mac Giolla Léith
Etel Adnan by Kaelen Wilson-Goldie
Gillian Carnegie by Barry Schwabsky
Guillermo Kuitca by Raphael Rubinstein
Hurvin Anderson by Michael J. Propokow
Jim Shaw by David Pagel
Katharina Grosse by Gregory Volk
Liu Xiaodong by John Yau
Lois Dodd by Faye Hirsch
Mary Weatherford by Suzanne Hudson
Neo Rauch by Michael Glover
Nicole Eisenman by Dan Cameron
Philip Taaffe by John Yau
Stanley Whitney by Matthew Jeffrey Abrams
Tal R. by Martin Herbert
Thomas Nozkowski by John Yau
Verne Dawson by John Hutchinson

Contents

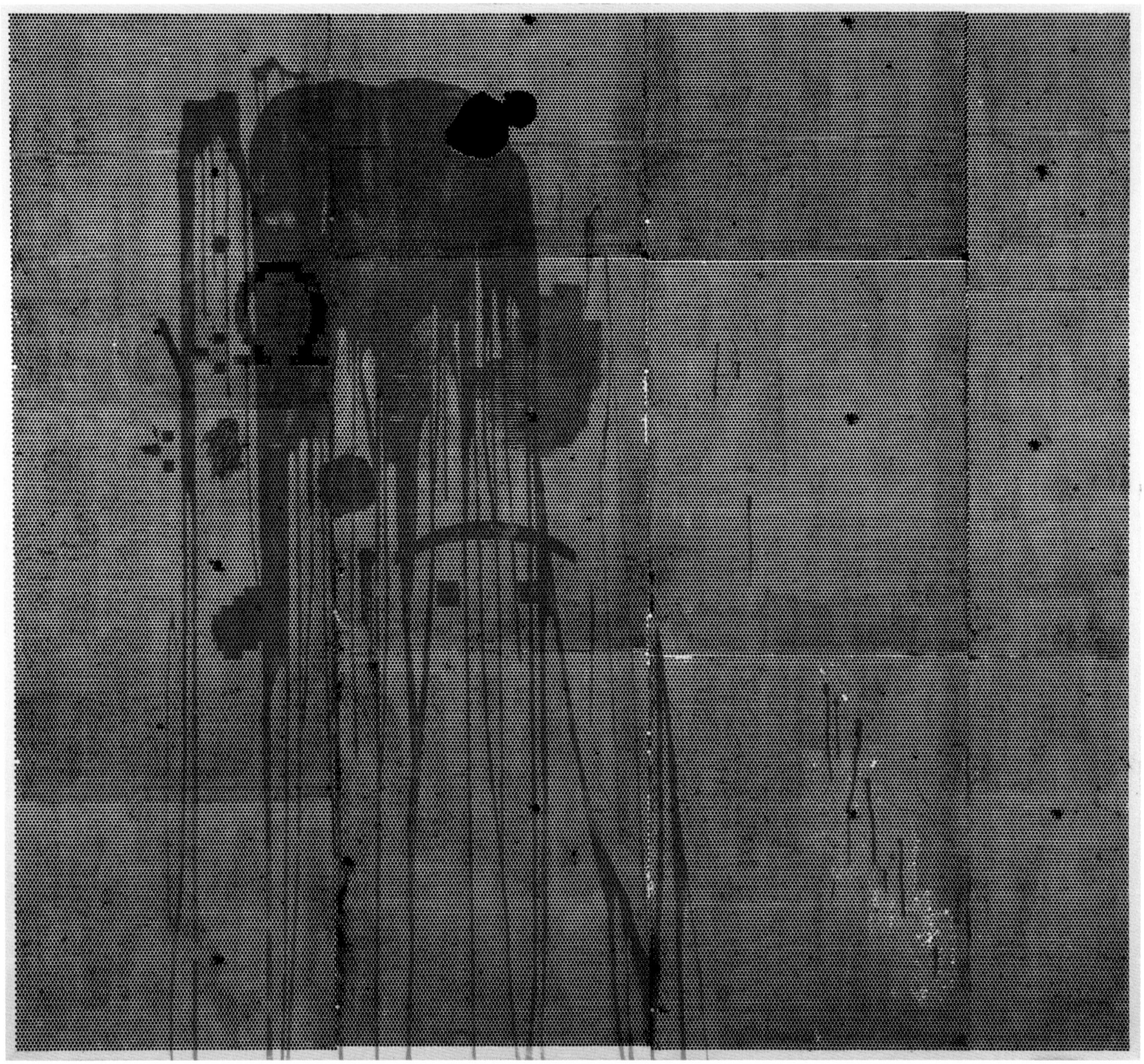

1. One Cat 2017

Oil on linen
254 × 281.9 cm (100 × 111 in)
Albright-Knox Art Gallery, Buffalo, New York;
bequest of Arthur B. Michael, by exchange, 2018

Foreword

Painting has transformed 'into something beyond painting as we once knew it', writes Frances Guerin in her revelatory study of the work of Jacqueline Humphries. I couldn't help thinking back to the late nineteenth century, and the words of my favourite poet, Stéphane Mallarmé: '*On a touché au vers*' – often translated, rather melodramatically, as 'they've done violence to poetry.' Better simply to say, it had been transformed beyond familiarity. Mallarmé, in saying this, compares himself to a breathless traveller unburdening himself of news from afar, testimony of something he's witnessed firsthand and can't forget. Guerin writes with a similar sense of urgency. For unprecedented times, painting has new tasks and therefore new means. Humphries's work may be immediately recognizable *as* painting in ways that would have been familiar to her forebears in modernist abstraction – Barnett Newman, Jackson Pollock, Robert Ryman, among others, whose tactics she imagines herself 'pilfering' more than emulating – but she is involved in her times, aware of the tasks, and in command of the means. Contrary to artists who employ new technologies to reflect the era in which those technologies have arisen, Humphries proceeds, as Guerin explains, by using the specific physical qualities of her painterly art as 'gestures towards the immersive spaces of technological images' – discoursing on the technological from a critical distance. Painting itself is changed in the process, the experiences it offers called into question: 'Paint of different intensities, viscosities, and modes of application coexist in an experience that reinstates the "presentness" of painting and simultaneously causes us to question what we are seeing.' Some might consider this a violence done to painting – a wound inflicted on a beautiful old verity. But no: Humphries changes painting to keep it alive, to render it more responsive to our everyday life in the present. Guerin explores the myriad ways she does this, in what are sometimes 'paintings that refuse to identify as paintings'. But the pleasures they offer, however unprecedented, are ones that can't be experienced anywhere else than in painting.

Barry Schwabsky

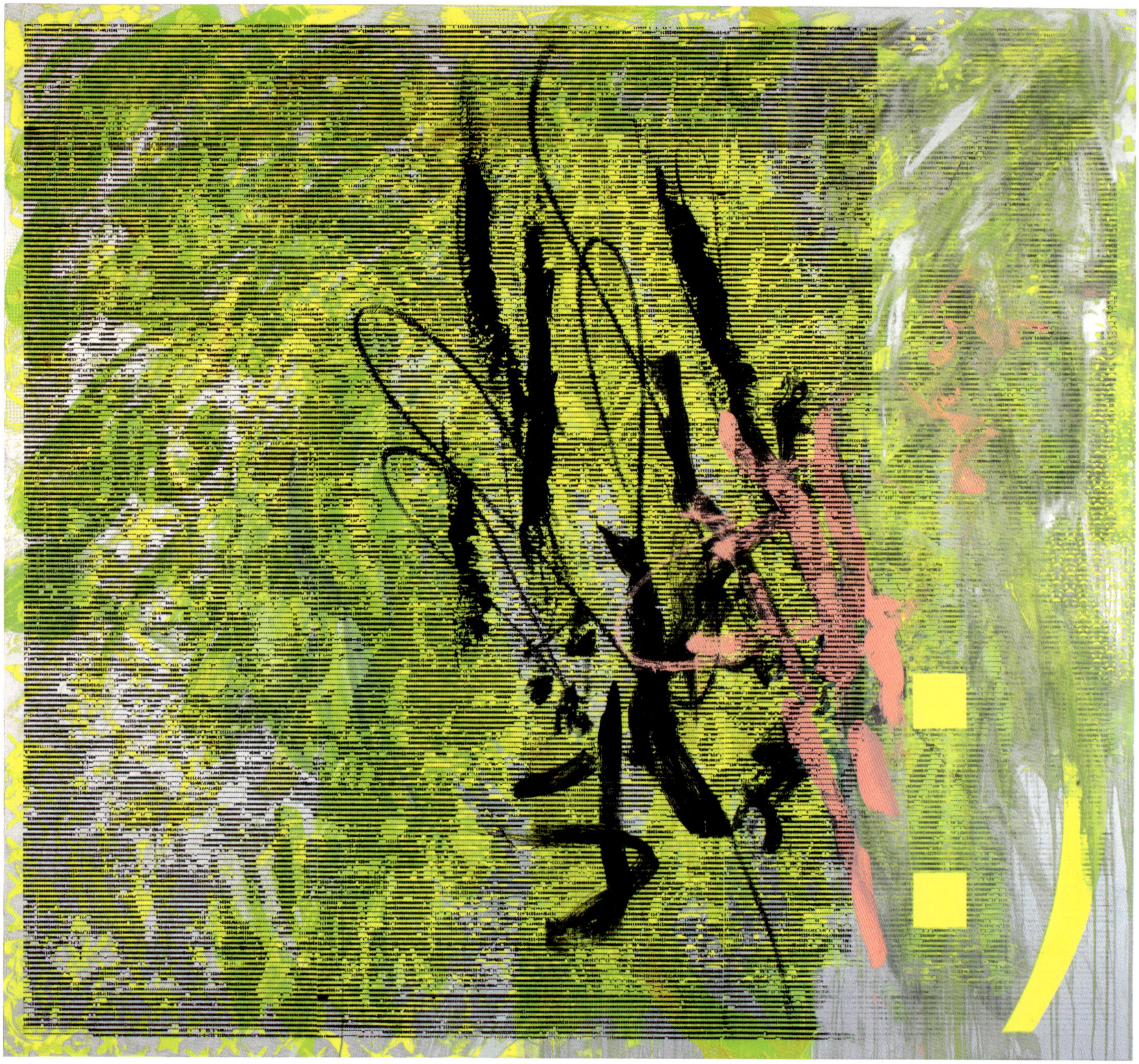

2. (#J^^) :)   2017

Oil on linen
254 × 281.9 cm (100 × 111 in)
Glenstone Museum, Potomac, Maryland

1 The Democracy of Images

In a 2009 interview, Jacqueline Humphries states, 'There doesn't seem to be any available way to effectively discuss or make sense of issues in [contemporary] painting, or even to make judgments about it.' She goes on to say that 'what painters have done in the past 20 years calls for a reinvention of the discourse'.[1] Critics grappling with precisely what Humphries is doing often resort to defining her painting in relation to abstract expressionism.[2] Alternatively, they turn to European modernism to explain Humphries's vision for painting, even as they signal the ambivalence of its relationship to this history.[3] Despite Humphries's painting being filled with the tropes of modernism – repetition, rigorous structure, play with surface and depth, insistence on framing, consciousness of the spectator – she is not looking to solve the same 'problem' of painting. Humphries is not on a teleological quest for the purity of painting.[4] She references the diversity of early and mid-twentieth-century modernism's strategies, but her work moves beyond that of her predecessors. Artists such as Humphries, together with contemporaries such as Charline von Heyl, Laura Owens, Wade Guyton, Christopher Wool, and Mary Weatherford, engage with historical forms of painting. Yet, through their integration of the contemporary visual cultural environment into abstract painting, they do something different. These artists do not arrive at the end of the hallowed halls of American abstract painting. Rather, they move beyond it, seeking to transform painting from within.

Humphries's paintings make sense through a lateral, not a linear historical, logic. The paintings do not pick up where abstract expressionism left off on the trajectory towards the end of painting. Instead, they develop through processes of exchange and interaction within the frameworks given by modernist painting. Simultaneously, Humphries develops a new visual language that places painting as one among many forms of late twentieth- and early twenty-first-century images. On Humphries's canvases, painting discourses, debates, and takes on new personalities at the interface with other visual languages and viewers' responses. This engagement with the contemporary context is what makes them democratic.

Humphries's works are riddled with paradoxes. On the one hand, they strive to break with the history of art. On the other hand, they are indebted to this same history. Humphries's abstract paintings are conceptual, soliciting an intellectual and culturally conditioned response from the viewer. They are simultaneously committed to an aesthetics of painting that invites a corporeal consciousness. They tease and confront their viewers by departing from assumptions and expectations, and at the same time they inspire wonder and awe, as painting has done for centuries.

The works are intellectually detached and yet accessible to all, often appearing both laconic and playful. In another level of irony, Humphries pilfers liberally from the visual languages of contemporary popular culture – computer graphics, video games, cinema, amusement parks, and nightclub visuals – to create works that hang on the walls of museums and galleries. She might be working 'beyond painting', but she has achieved success through applying paint to a canvas. Like Marcel Duchamp's readymades a century ago, Humphries transforms the everyday into high art. Unlike the readymades, though, Humphries's repurposing of the popular takes the most traditional of fine art forms: painting.

Beyond abstraction

'Pushing abstraction forward – or grabbing it out of the future – is what attracted me.' – Jacqueline Humphries [5]

Humphries's trajectory as a painter is well documented. She was born in New Orleans in 1960, educated at Bennington College and on the streets of New York City in the late 1970s. In 1980, she spent a year in Paris where she created her 'own history of art'.[6] Back in the United States, she completed her education at Parsons School of Design in 1985, followed by a year in the Whitney Independent Study Program in 1986. However, the question that is rarely asked of Humphries is, 'Why abstraction?' It is as though abstraction is in her DNA and there is no need to ask the question. Humphries admits that she made self-portraits when teaching herself to paint; but these remedial exercises are never exhibited.[7] However, looking at the works she has painted since, we can surmise that she is not interested in painting as a depiction of anything: painting for her is an object in the material world. As she says in a recent interview, and as becomes increasingly obvious when looking at and thinking about her work, painting is one component in a 'set of new relations that arise[s]' from its place in the world.[8] Painting is a thing, a visual entity that exists together with movies, photographs, and computer and smartphone screens. Painting does not represent that world.

Crucially, abstraction is the language with which Humphries explores 'beyond' the shifting conception and reception of painting in the late twentieth century.[9] When Humphries and her American contemporaries were maturing in the 1980s, she says that 'everyone was obsessed with "the end of painting"'.[10] Likewise, she claims that painting was not a wise choice for an artist when she was at the Whitney ISP.[11] Yet, while Humphries's fellow students were exploring highly charged work in mixed-media, video, and performance, painting was certainly not dead. Painting, and abstraction, were undergoing radical revision.[12] Indeed, the 1980s are defined by neo-expressionist and related painting movements featuring the work of artists such

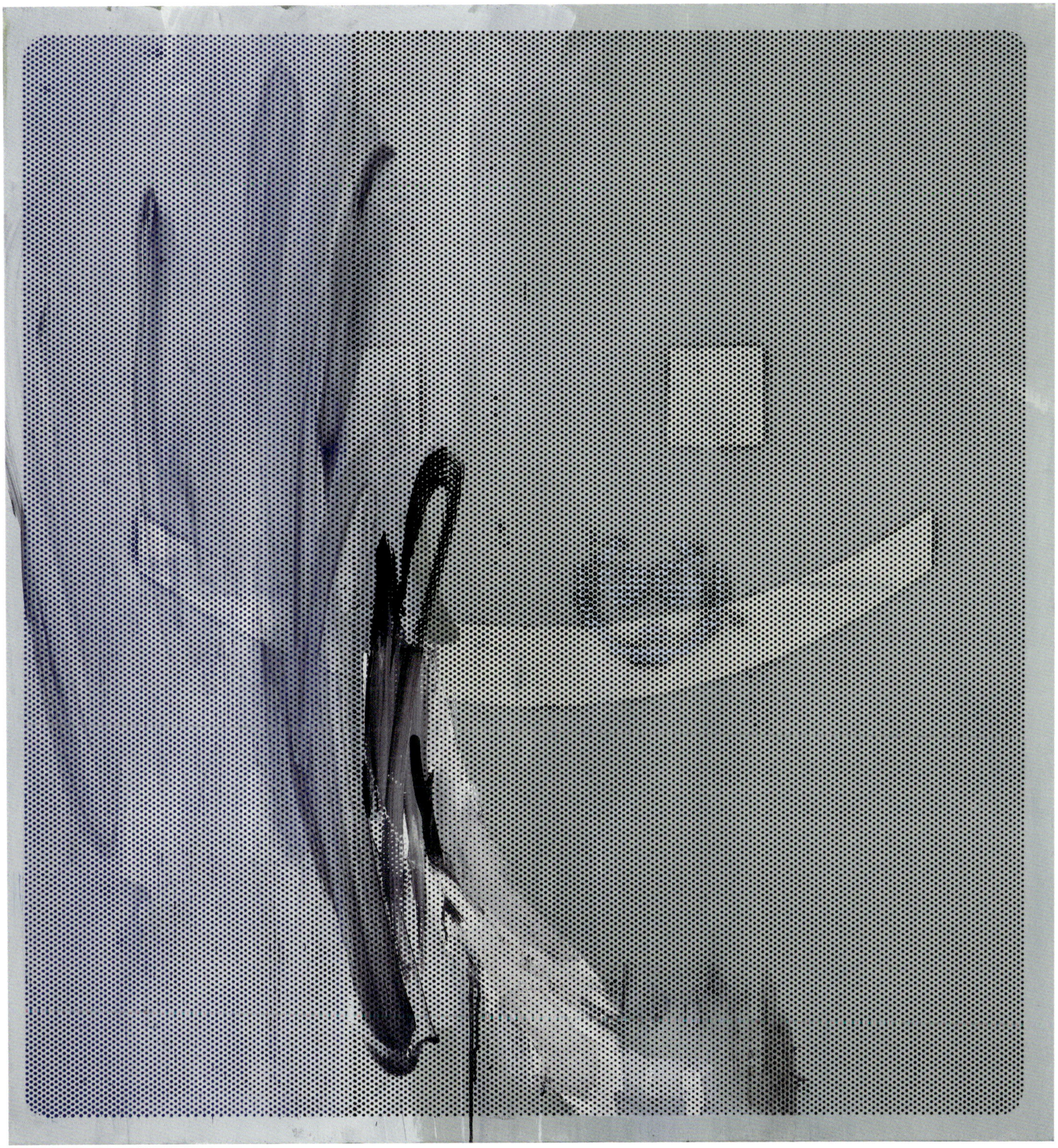

3. 🥺 :) 2020

Oil on linen
152.4 × 144.8 cm (60 × 57 in)

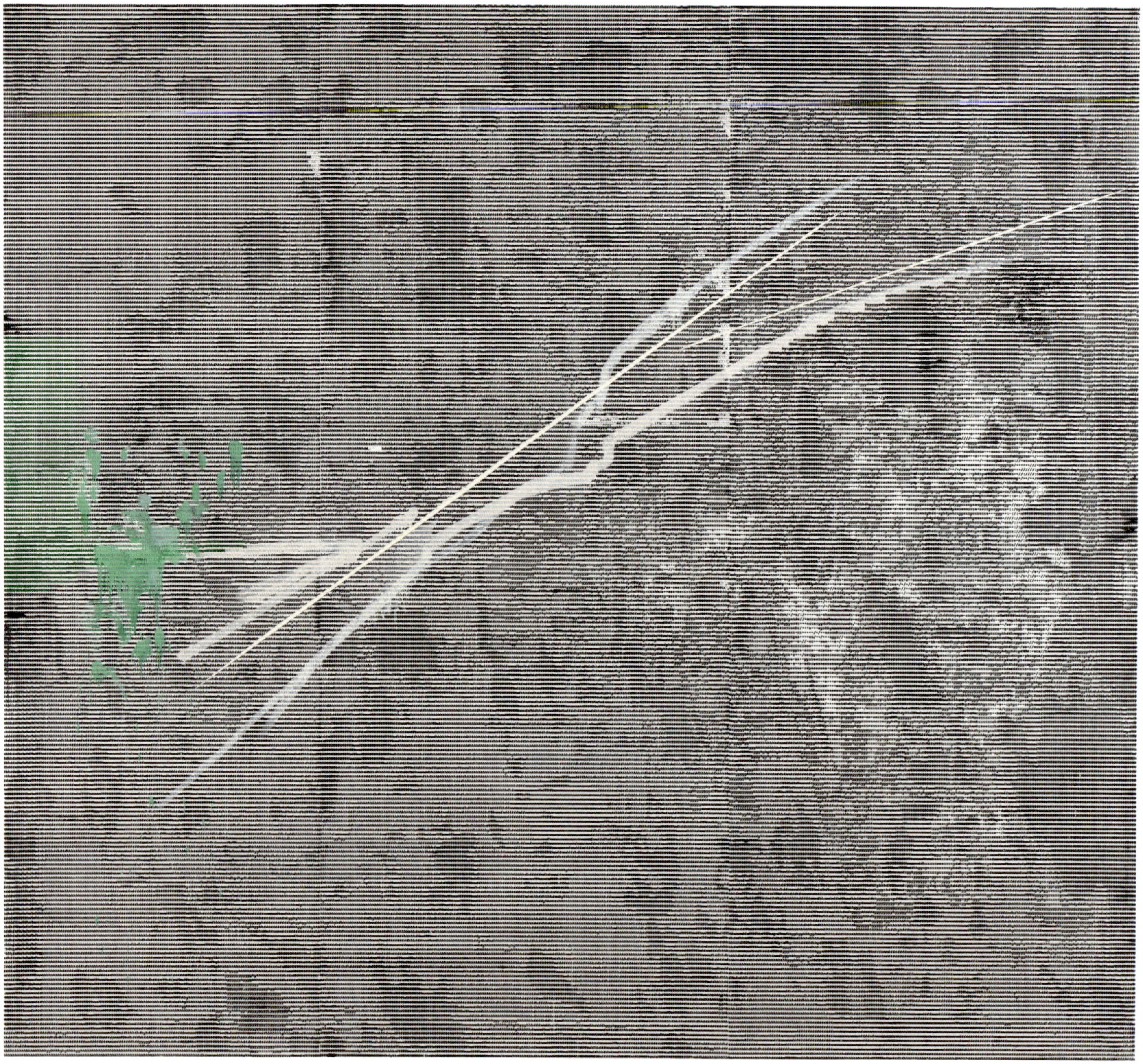

4. Untitled 2021

Oil on linen
254 × 281.9 cm (100 × 111 in)

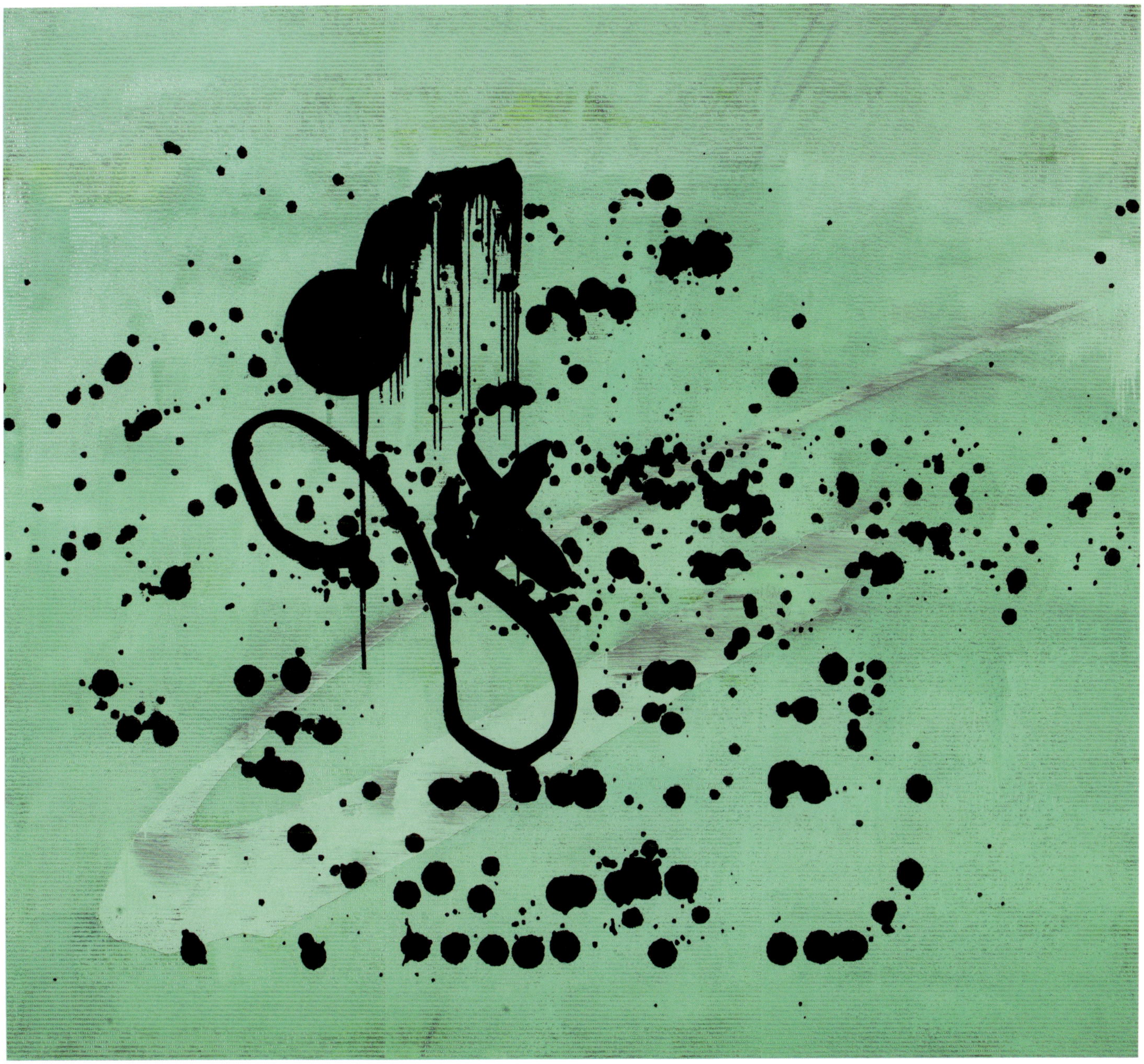

5. •SX 2020

Oil on linen
254 × 281.9 cm (100 × 111 in)

as Julian Schnabel, David Salle, and Eric Fischl. Distinct from American and European trends of neo-geo, neo-expressionism, *figuration libre*, or *transavanguardia*, Humphries and her generation were concerned with a new kind of abstract painting.[13] They were in pursuit of a 'beyond abstraction'. Humphries uses the familiar visual language of abstraction – surface and depth, frame and centre, colour and line – while refusing to respect the boundaries established by this language. She does what she wants with the modernist toolkit and then adds elements and effects of popular culture. Her use of popular cultural icons and images extends to the point where one might wonder if what she paints is 'abstraction' at all.

In recent years, Humphries has used emoticons and emojis, cat images and video-game icons. Thus, she disrespects the rules and history of abstraction. She freely appropriates signs and images designed for instantaneous digital communication and consumption, and, on her canvases, the visual language becomes a figurative representation. Her refusal to respect the language of abstraction leaves art critics in a quandary. How are we meant to talk about Humphries's paintings? Her insistence on 'grabbing' abstraction 'out of the future' suggests that we do not yet have the

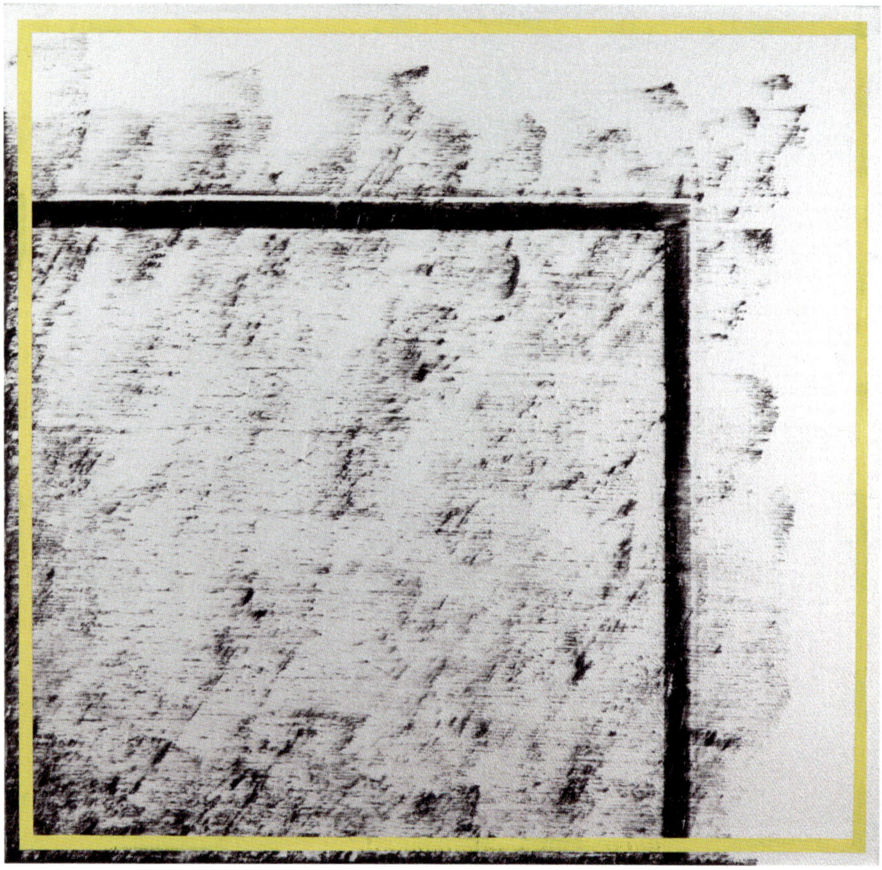

6. Untitled 2012

Oil and enamel on linen
97.2 × 101.9 cm (38¼ × 40⅛ in)

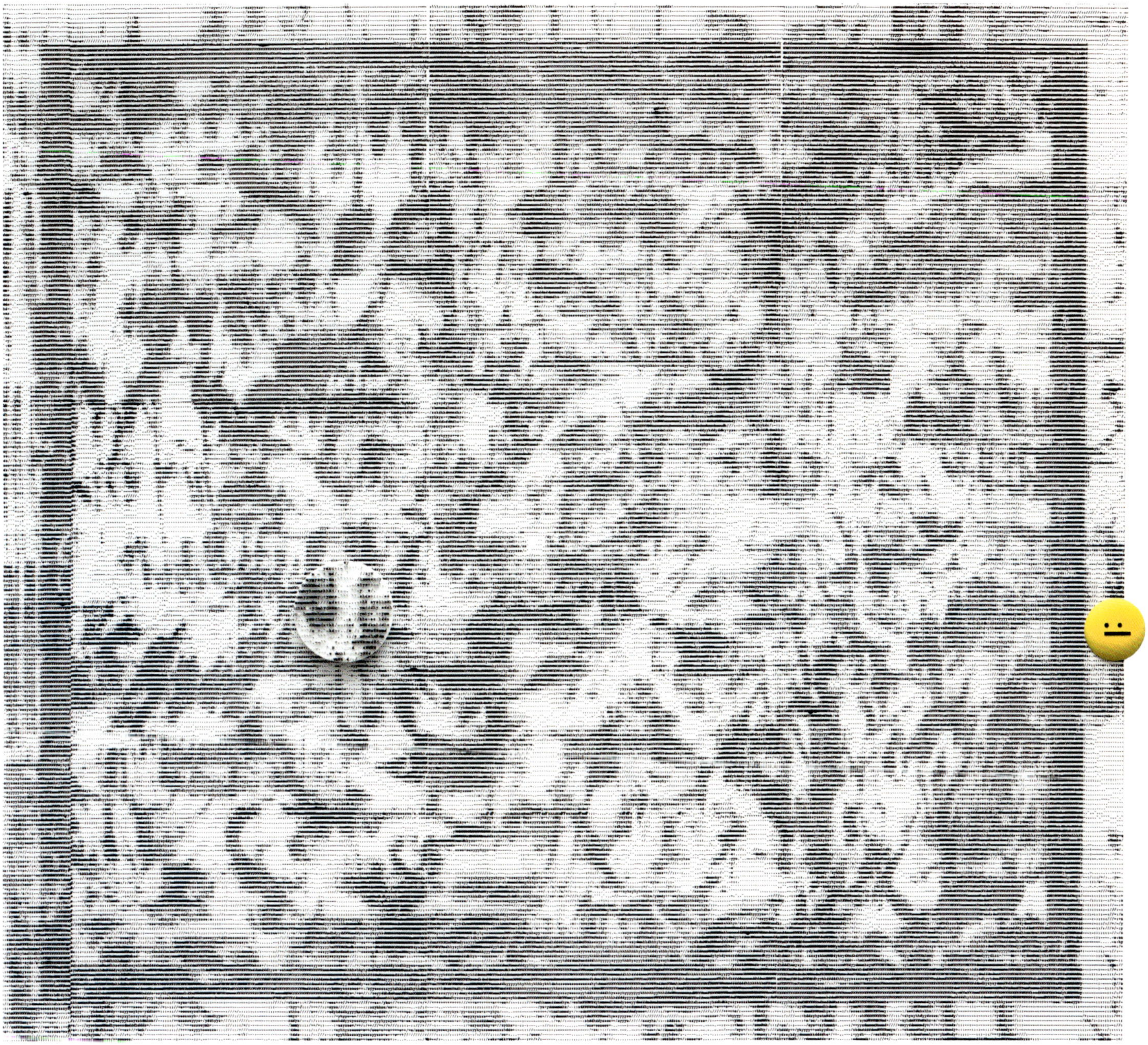

7. sysysy/ :| 2018

Oil on linen with Poly-Optic Resin objects
289.6 × 322.6 cm (114 × 127 in)

language with which to discuss what she is doing. And yet, various elements of her process are familiar because they adapt the gestures used by modernist artists for over a century. For example, instead of appropriating Brillo boxes, soup cans, and comics, as Pop artists such as Andy Warhol and Roy Lichtenstein did in the mid-twentieth century, Humphries uses emojis and video-game icons. While Jasper Johns repeatedly painted American flags and targets, Humphries paints images of nested windows on computer screens as seen in *Untitled*, 2012 (fig.59). Like Johns, Humphries pursues questions of painting's relationship to the world through popular cultural and visual forms. Likewise, her paintings engage with those forms, but are still paintings within a rectangular frame. Similarly, cubist painters appropriated the modes of seeing and affect of contemporaneous visual cultural phenomena in the early twentieth century. While Pablo Picasso and Georges Braque fragmented the picture plane to harness the multiple perspectives and kineticism of the industrial world, Humphries draws on the virtual windows of technological images. Thus, she does what abstract artists have always done: her work remains tethered to form and reference, even if these references are springboards to moving beyond abstraction.

Despite Humphries's violation of the principles of twentieth-century modernism and American abstract expressionism, these past artistic forms provide reference points for understanding her work. On the canvas, Humphries may shirk the rigid demands made on painting in the past, but her consciousness of its achievements is vital to understanding her vision.

Forty years after first seeing Édouard Manet's late flower paintings in Paris, Humphries still mentions the influence of Manet on her process and aesthetic.[14] She does not elaborate on what specifically about Manet is important to her. In conversation, she often does this, leaving her interlocutor to fill in the gaps. Manet was one of a generation of European painters to make painting feel alive by making it tactile. After Manet, painters set out on a path to flat surfaces and the dominance of form over material. As if in a gesture of 'criticise me if you dare', Humphries's paint can be thick, sensuous, textured. It is, on the one hand, the epitome of all that post-modernism rejected: highly gestured, three-dimensional, executed by an artist who is fully present to the material of the painting. On the other hand, her handling of paint is a 'catch me if you can' game with the history of art. For example, there are times when the paintings move closer in texture and visual appearance to stone sculpture. At other times, as I will demonstrate, the paintings can be explained through the language given us for understanding the cinema. This pilfering of one aspect of painting's history, only to say, 'I'm going to do with it as I please,' recurs across the oeuvre, and thus becomes a motivating force behind the work in the pages to come. Humphries's innovation lies here: in a debt to her predecessors and simultaneous disregard for their intentions.

Artist, painting, and viewer

Humphries belongs to a generation of American painters whose work grew from the tilled soil of abstract expressionism's preoccupation with the interior self. Distinct from their self-reflection, Humphries's paintings make sense not as expressions of the artist's inner life, but for their conversations with the contemporary visual environment. Consistent with today's fluid distinctions between representation and abstraction, Humphries's abstract paintings are as figurative as ever. Hers is a controlled, graphic practice that does not distinguish between public and private, internal and external, individual and historical experiences of painting. This is in keeping with the contemporary visual and technological forms that she appropriates: computer-generated icons, photographs, digital prints, stencils, algorithms, and disco imagery. Eventually, Humphries removes herself from the painterly process through manipulating these gleaned forms and creating new viewing effects. Abstract expressionism may be the ground zero, but any residual traces driven by romantic notions of the artist as visionary are removed from Humphries's canvases.

Accordingly, unlike her mid-century American predecessors, Humphries does not layer expressive gestures in search of an authentic emotional core. Her highly structured canvases explore conceptual ideas that encourage transient viewing experiences. Typically, the viewer's experience is familiar, though not always from being in the presence of paintings. Rather, before her works, viewers are ushered into modes of looking more familiar from movies, video games, computer imagery, and smartphone screens. The paintings reference the experiences and viewing habits forged in the contemporary visual environment.

Simultaneously, the paintings can inspire us to have a sensuous, bodily experience. At a distance, we are reminded of the flickering reflections on a turned-off 1950s television screen when looking at the shifting greys of *Horizontal #15*, 1998 (fig.10). We are pulled forward to examine the work up close in an attempt to clarify what we are looking at. From Humphries's earliest paintings, we are drawn to examine the places on the canvas where colours change, truncate, and melt into the support. Humphries's paintings never sit still: on the one hand, the viewer is invited to experience conceptual ideas encouraging intellectual and culturally determined responses. On the other, the same painting will prompt exploration through the viewer's physical movement around the gallery space. Humphries thus reformulates the multiple perspectives of illusory and virtual moving images on a screen by situating the viewer within real space and historical time. Added to these multiple responses, the works can also be deeply romantic thanks to their aesthetic handling of colour, light, and paint. They boldly unfurl paint on a canvas, inviting the 'absorption' of their viewer, away from the world of things.[15] This is and always has been, according to Michael Fried, the purpose of painting.[16]

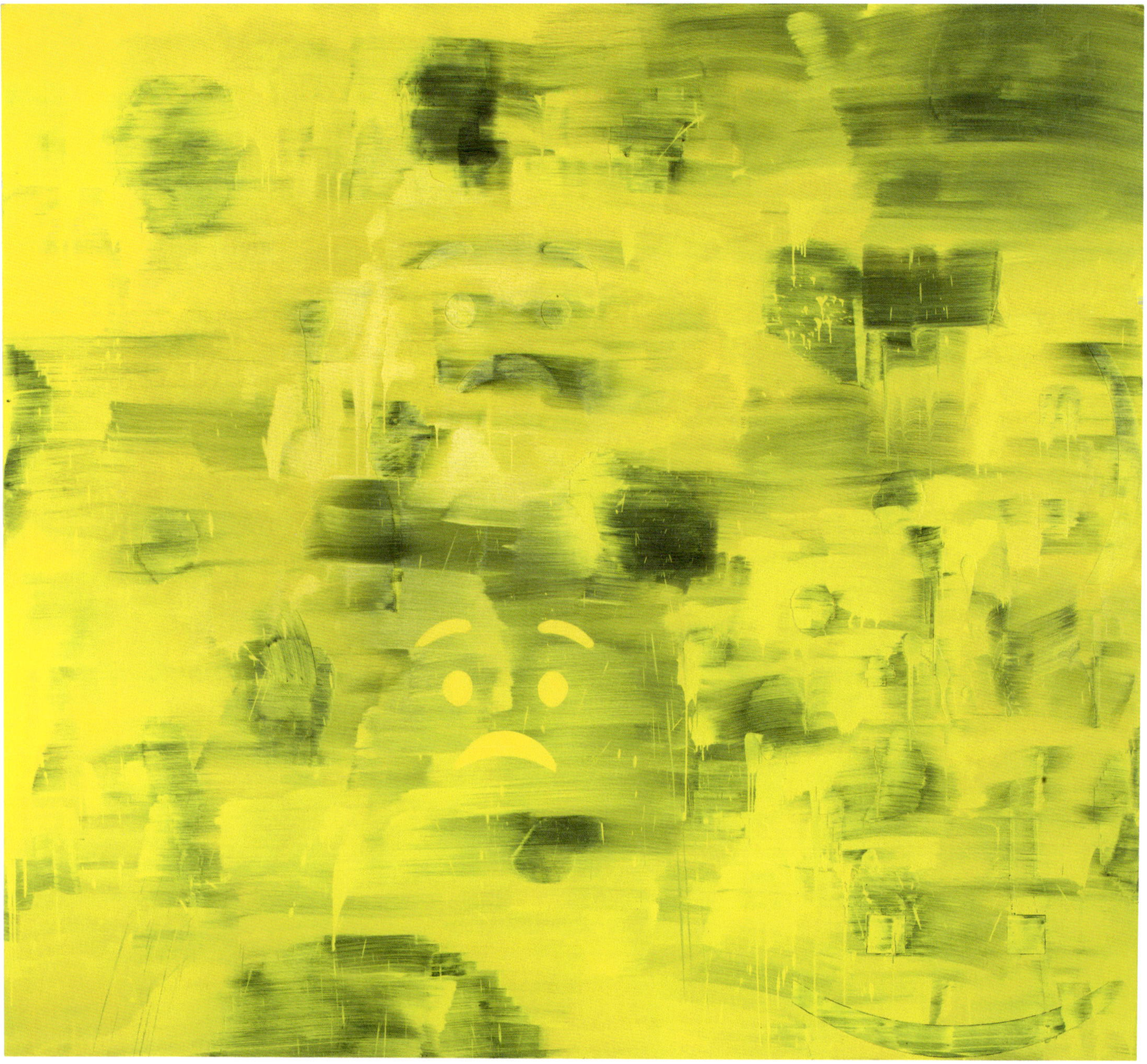

8. 😟:) 2017

Oil on linen
254 × 281.9 cm (100 × 111 in)

9. ???~ 2017
Oil on linen
254 × 281.9 cm (100 × 111 in)

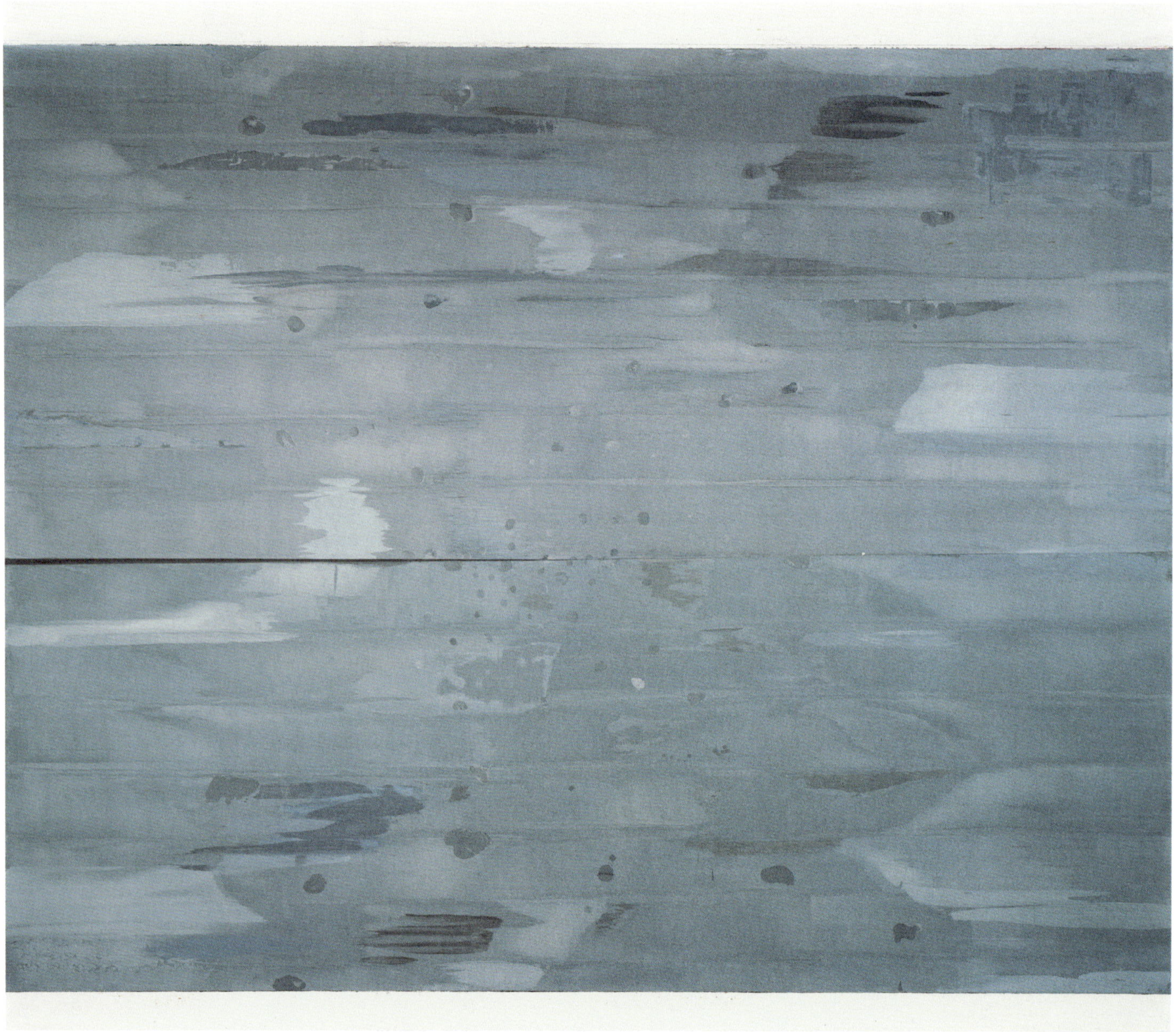

10. Horizontal #15 1998

Oil on linen
228.6 × 259.1 cm (90 × 102 in)

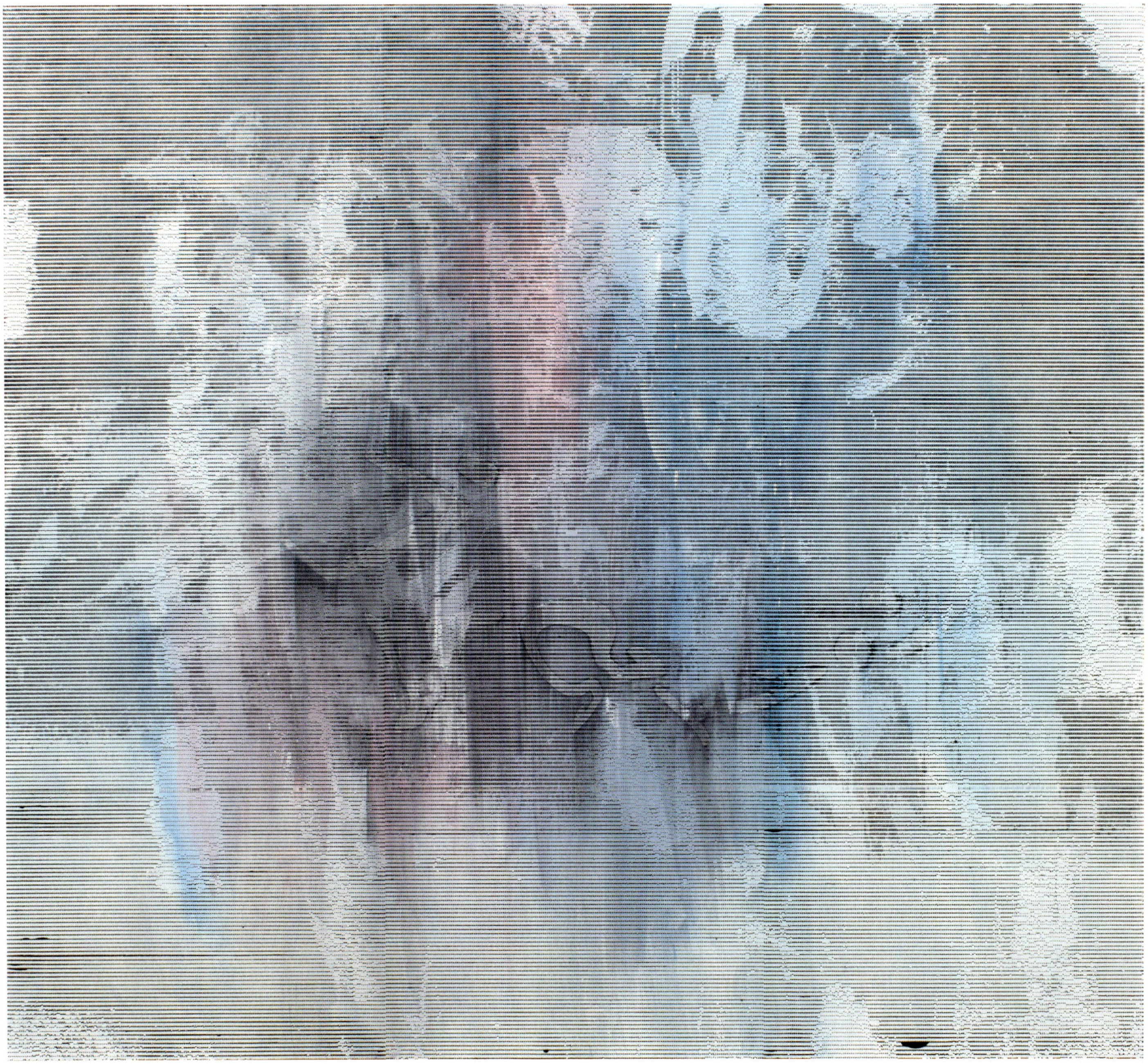

11. ××× ★× 2019

Oil on linen
289.6 × 322.6 cm (114 × 127 in)

The democracy of images

Humphries moves beyond abstract painting by creating a democracy of images. David Joselit describes Jackson Pollock's abstractions as polyphonic in their embrace of multiple visual languages.[17] Humphries similarly adopts myriad visual languages, and also fashions text into images to create a new language for abstract painting. Beyond colour-field abstraction, Humphries uses emoticons, screen images, anachronistic computer codes, symbols, and encoding systems. Recently, she has transformed white noise, CAPTCHA symbols, emoticons, and emojis into bases for stencils. As Joselit says, these visual languages often erupt onto the picture surface.[18] While they burst out of other layers and onto the surface, they also recede. Diverse visual languages hover under the painted surface and, at times, multiple signs, symbols, and codes are remediated into the same painting. This detail is important because it highlights the radicality of Humphries's vision. Unlike Pollock, Humphries does not explore the return of an unconscious language of images through the use of polyphonic visual languages. Her brand of multiplicity is always reaching for democracy on the canvas. It is not, again in distinction from Pollock, one language coming into focus before fading out to make room for the next. For Humphries, the canvas offers a coexistence of different signs and images, from high and low art forms past and present. Such is its reach for democracy.

Humphries uses and invokes multiple types of images and texts as a playful reminder of the contemporaneity and everydayness of painting. Specifically, her paintings discourse on the disposability of the signs that clutter our vision. In turn, her work might be seen as an annexation and simultaneous dethroning of painting from its one-time privileged place in the (nineteenth-century) hierarchies of art history. For Humphries, painting begins as a translation of machine- or technologically produced signs, and at the same time is the only medium adequate to this process of transformation. In contrast to Pollock's gestural expression, her surface is meticulously worked and comes alive before the viewer in a physical and emotional experience. Pollock dripped paint onto a canvas to challenge its four sides, orientation, and the assumptions about both as a given. For Humphries, the frame is only ever a pictorial reference, one of multiple modernist tropes to be negotiated. Likewise, scale, surface, depth, and the other familiar features of modernist painting are mere tools in the service of her brand of painterly expression.

This, in turn, leads to another, coexistent, layer of democracy. Humphries's paintings are best seen in the flesh. In reproduction, they seem like different images altogether. They are made for an encounter with a physical viewer, to be looked at in person, at different distances, over time, hung on a wall. We know this about painting in general, but for Humphries the imperative to be before the artwork appears non-negotiable. The physical experience is crucially woven into the discourse of her paintings' democracy. Elsewhere, in his discussion of Humphries's silver paintings

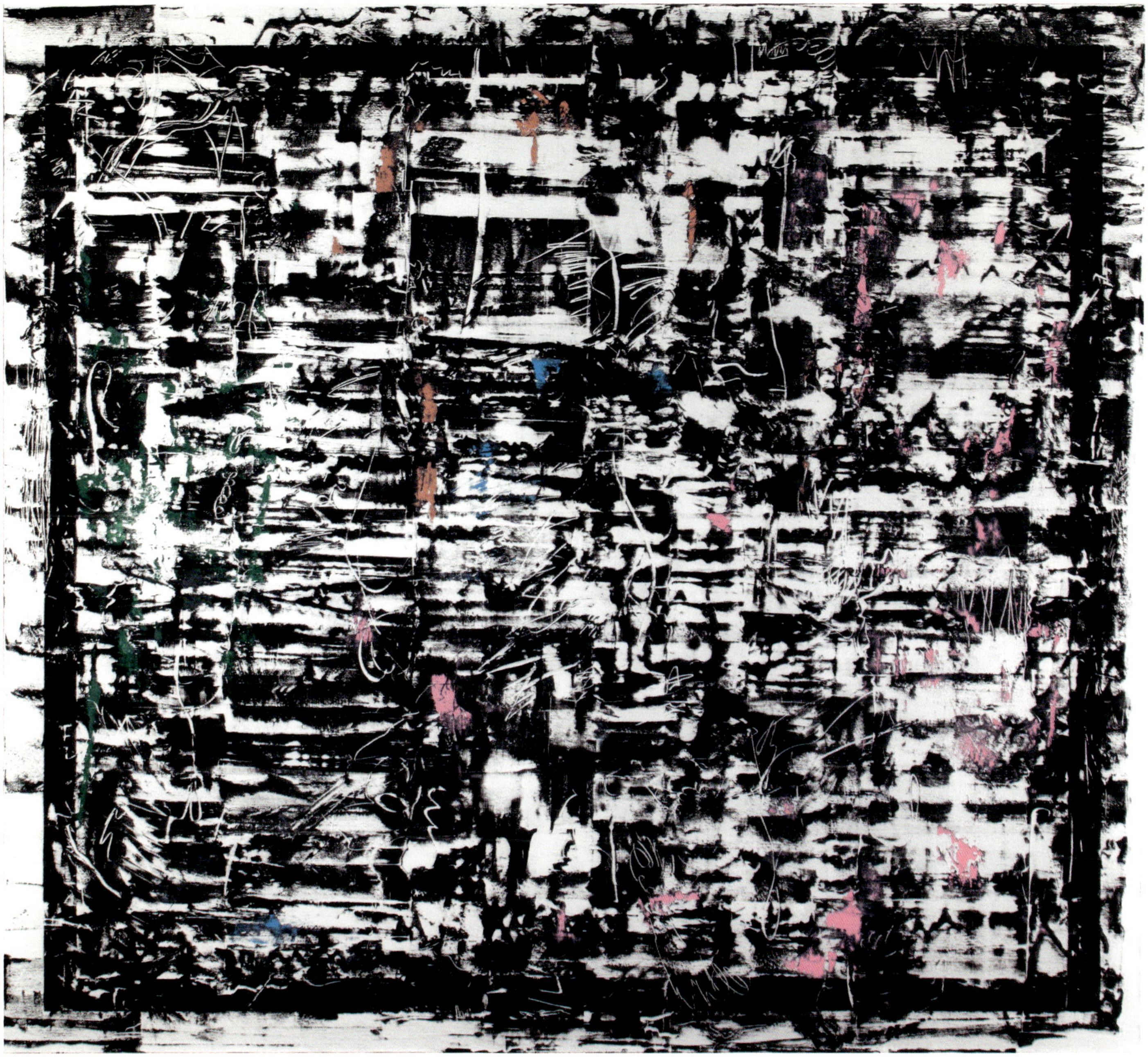

12. Untitled 2014

Oil on linen
289.6 × 322.6 cm (114 × 127 in)

Tate; Presented by Tate Americas Foundation, courtesy of the North American Acquisitions Committee with additional assistance from Komal Shah and Gaurav Garg 2015, accessioned 2021

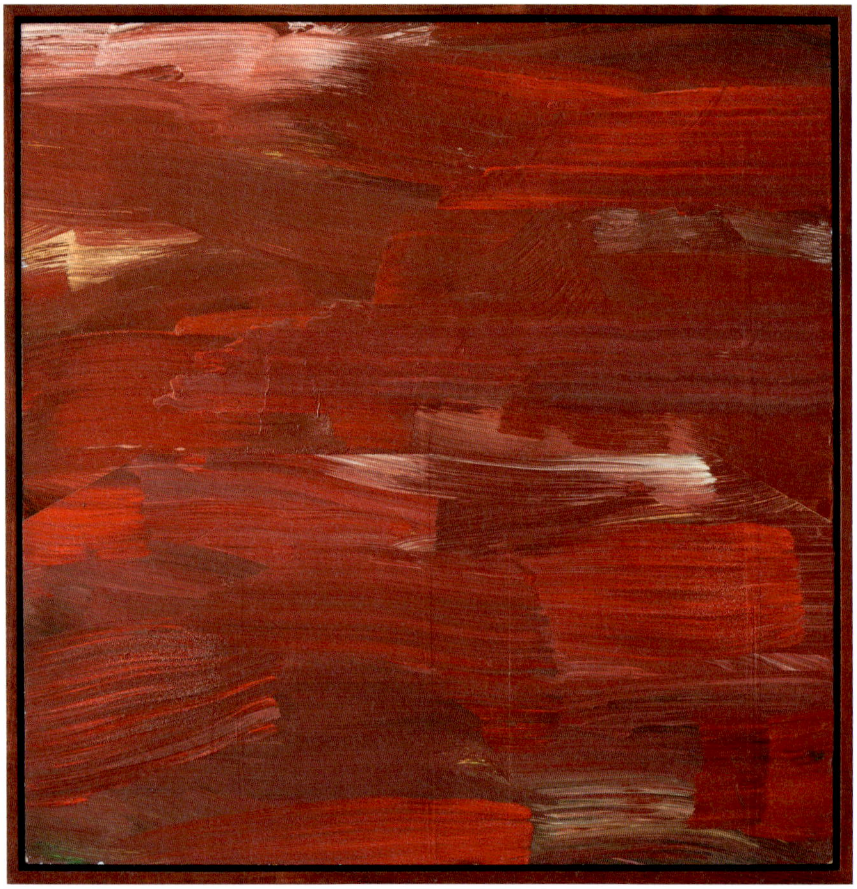

13. Horizontal #4 ½ 1997

Oil on board
76.2 × 76.2 cm (30 × 30 in)
The Metropolitan Museum of Art, New York;
gift of Barbara Nicholson, 2016

from the 2010s, Joselit explores the viewer's kinetic experience over time with the painting as three-dimensional object. He attributes this kineticism to the Cézanne-like 'disruptive passage[s] of bright color', often concentrated in isolated sections of Humphries's canvases.[19] To extend Joselit's comments to Humphries's entire oeuvre reveals that this kineticism is also distinct from that of a Cézanne painting because it is transient and infinite. Cézanne's fruit appears to roll off the table on its way into our space. But for Humphries, the fruit changes direction, stops in its tracks and transforms into a calcified layer of paint without representation, depending on where the viewer stands in relationship to the painting. Unlike the motion through space of Cézanne's fruit, it is not simply the viewer's experience of the painting that is ephemeral. Rather, on a single canvas, the painted form – the apple equivalent – appears and disappears over time and the viewer's position in front of the painting.

The physical and often unpredictable experience before Humphries's paintings leads to a process of discovery that rewards the viewer with ownership – albeit temporary – of the work's meaning. Unlike the experience of Mark Rothko's

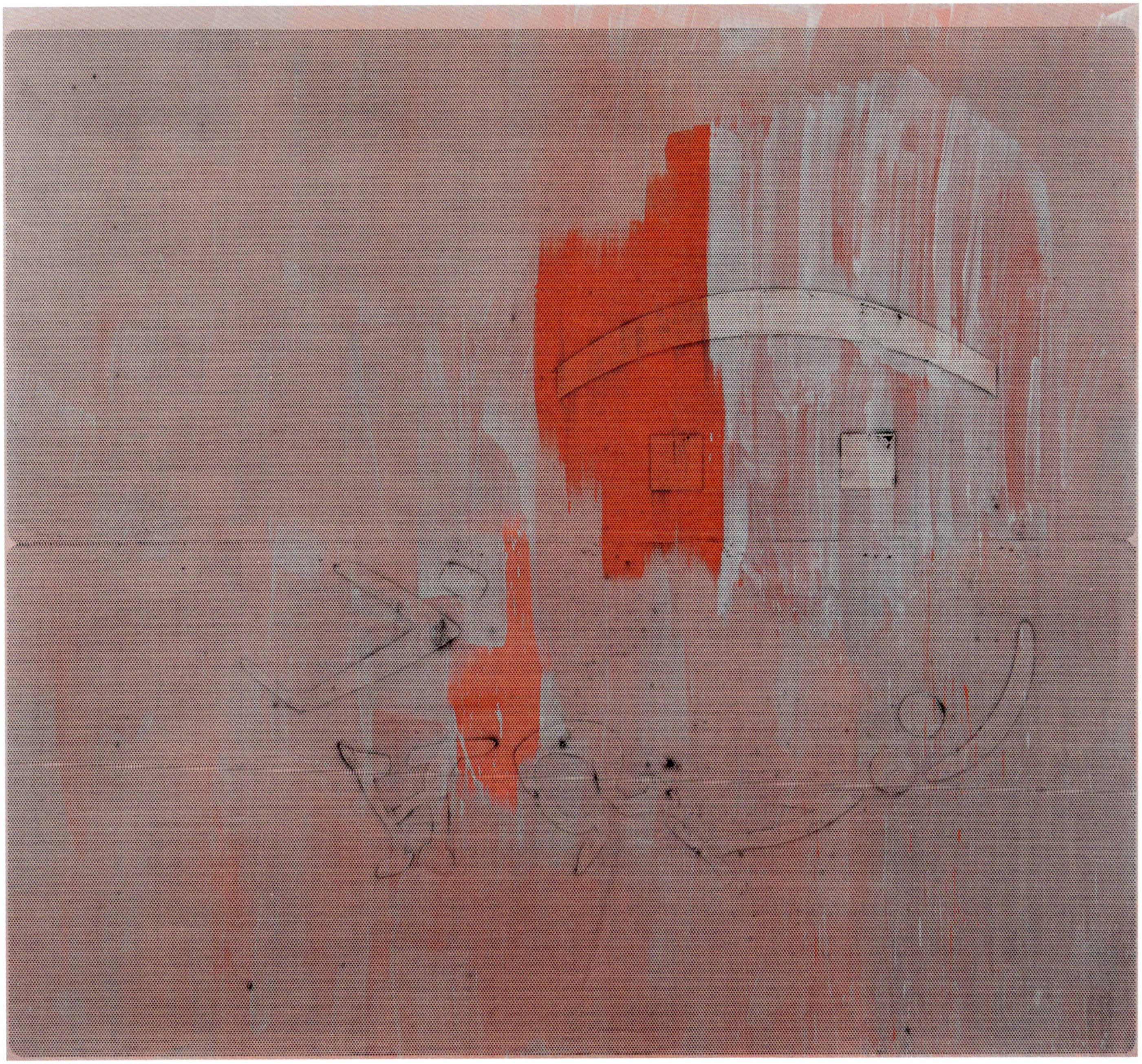

14. Untitled 2019

Oil on linen
254 × 281.9 cm (100 × 111 in)

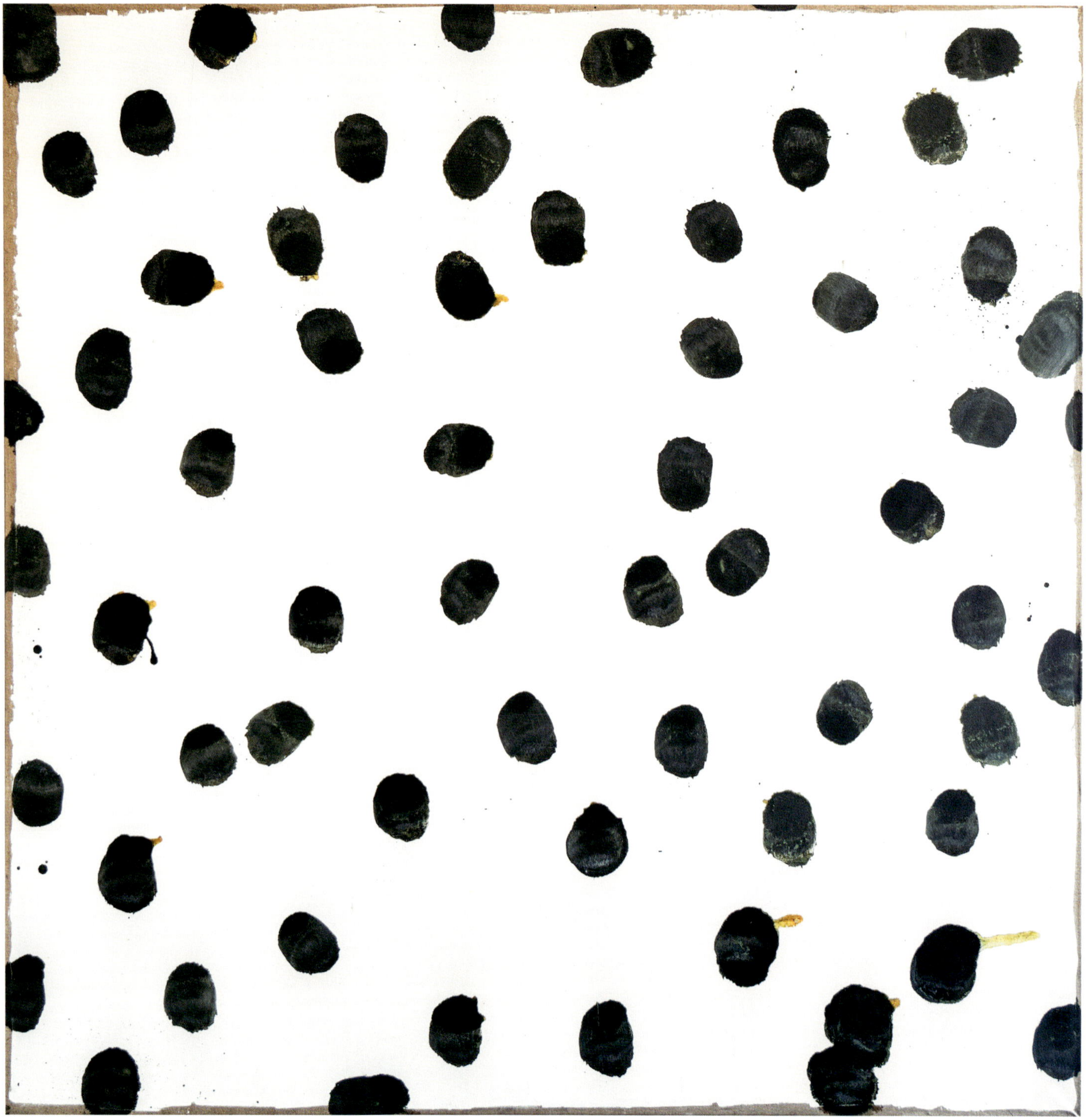

15. Untitled 1989

Oil on linen
182.9 × 182.9 cm (72 × 72 in)

paintings, for instance, we are not drawn to the work in an ultimate deification of its depths. By extension, we do not retreat into our emotional depths in front of her paintings. Neither are we enticed to follow the movement of paint across a surface announcing itself as an illusion, as happens in the physical encounter with, for example, Frank Stella's work.[20] Humphries does play with this interface between taking pleasure in illusion and drawing attention to its history, but her paintings do both in order to arrive at a place that is characterised by neither. The viewer enjoys an emotional and physical encounter with the painting, but typically as a way to discover its relationship to contemporary visual culture. Humphries repurposes, and hence transforms, technological, mechanical, and art historical signs, codes, and symbols into a painterly process. In turn, this process results in layers of paint on a canvas, effecting a challenge to the viewer's expectations, understanding, and experience of painting, as well as their navigation of the contemporaneous visual cultural environment.

Unlike the presentness of a modernist painting, we do not (only) engage in a transcendent experience. Rather, in our search for meaning, we recognise something that is not visualised in the paintings, something drawn from our everyday experience of signs, symbols, codes, and other images. Put differently, through looking at the paintings over time, the overdeterminedness of the signs and symbols of the contemporary visual environment is revealed. In a curious process of self-recognition, the viewing experience is consequently tinged with a pathos for the present. This handing over to the viewer is the ultimate democratic gesture of Humphries's painting.

In one final democratic turn, even though the paintings offer a particular temporal experience in the flesh, in reproduction they are still visually compelling. As seen in the illustrations for this book, in reproduced form, they have aesthetic merit. To argue otherwise would necessitate a return to the notion that there is a correct way of experiencing the paintings as objects. The irony of paintings made to be seen and experienced through multiple senses – paintings that nevertheless reveal an aesthetic expression on the page or digital screen – is yet another argument for their democracy. Their value as objects and images is multilayered, and their underlying intention is to be seen, irrespective of the format of exhibition, and irrespective of Humphries's claim for the paintings.

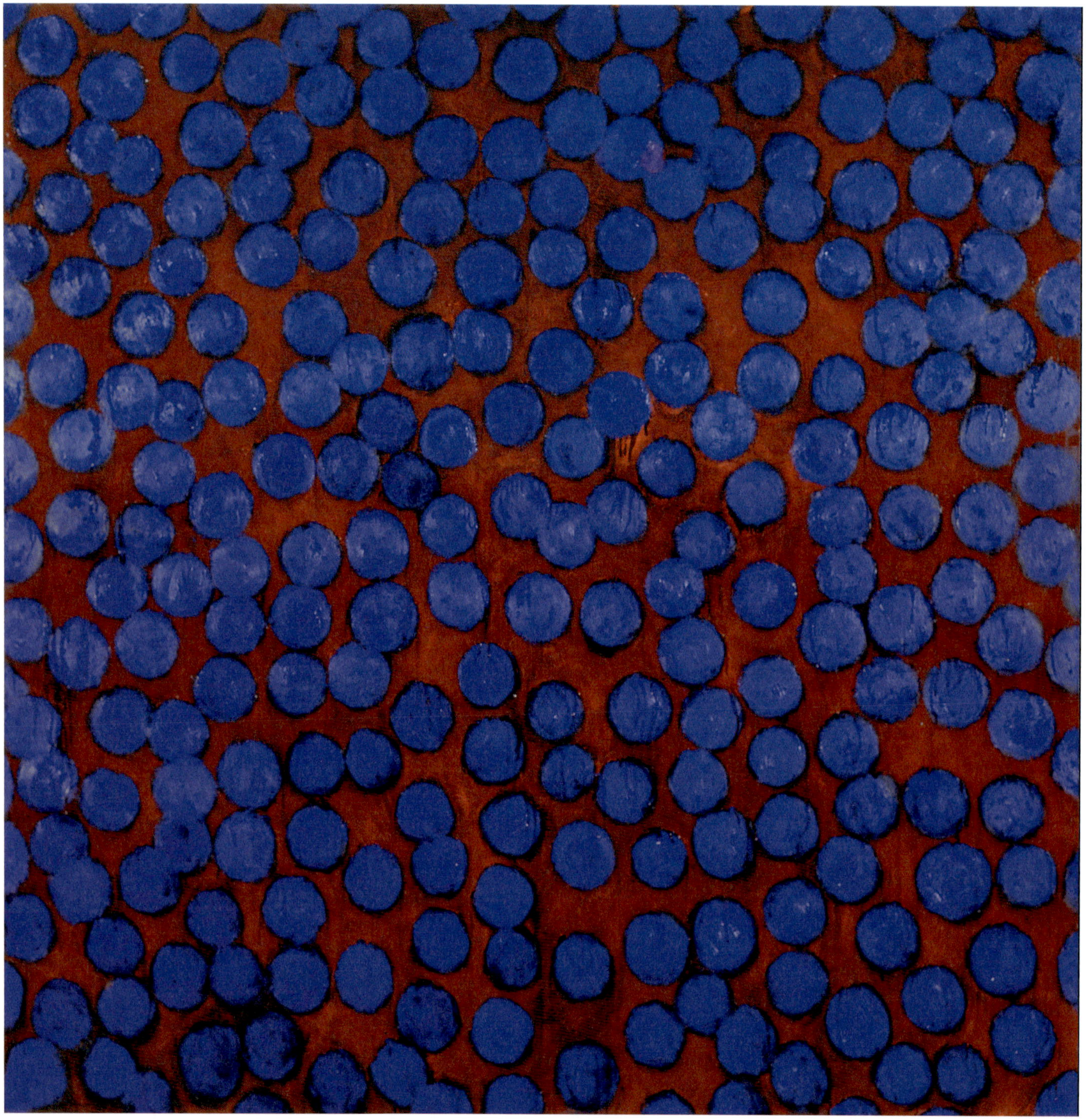

16. Untitled 1988

Oil on canvas
182.9 × 182.9 cm (72 × 72 in)

2 The Translation of Images

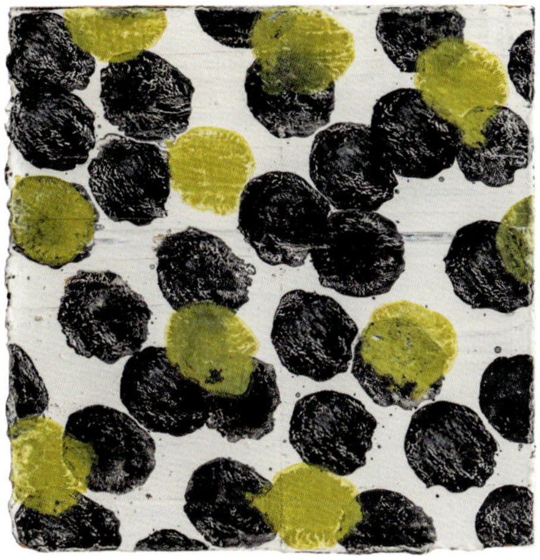

17. Untitled 1989

Oil on wood
15.2 × 15.2 cm (6 × 6 in)

Humphries speaks of her paintings as screen spaces, surfaces onto which anything can be projected.[21] What, then, does she project onto this surface-as-screen? As a painter, Humphries liberally appropriates and repurposes other visual languages. She often chooses signs, idioms, and symbols that are not essentially imagistic: they are foreign – even unsuited – to painting. Through her complex painterly process, they are transformed into images. In the 1980s, she used the shape of holes cut by a mechanical keypunch, an early method of encoding and storing data. The keypunch mark was perfect for inspiring novel forms of repetition and abstraction on canvas. Thus, she made a rapid punching or pressing motion with a paintbrush to create the visual impression of machine-punched holes (see figs 17, 18, 20, 21).[22]

Over thirty years, Humphries has continued to reinvent her process to test the existing limits of painting. Her work of the 1990s and 2000s depended on the languages of cinema, television, photography, and video. Since then, Humphries's appropriations have become explicit: the structure, aesthetic, meaning, and viewing experiences of her works are visibly determined by their translation of commonly used technological languages and signs. Most recently, her earlier use of paint to mimic keypunch marks has evolved to incorporate the actual outputs of machines and technologies.

Process and effect

Thirty years ago, Humphries painted the shape of a keypunch hole on a predominantly monochromatic background. Somewhere between a painted Lucio Fontana perforation, an enlarged pop art pixellation, and an op art pattern painting, Humphries repeated the gesture of the hole filled with paint across single canvases with varying intensities. The blue, black, and brown paint was volatile as colours appeared and disappeared in seemingly random patterns. As the viewer moves around, the patterns made by dots, holes, and circles appear to shimmer and shiver over the surface of the paintings. They change form, colour, and meaning over time and space. Their irregularity evidences painted, not machine-made, dots. In works such as *Untitled*, 1988 (fig.21), optical illusions swirl and swell, inviting a complex visual experience reminding us of paintings by op artists such as Victor Vasarely. We follow patterns and circles, search for beginnings and endings in what is, ultimately, a frustrated quest for stability within the frame. Over time, as our eyes continue to dance around the canvas, we begin to see afterimages and experience glare, effects more

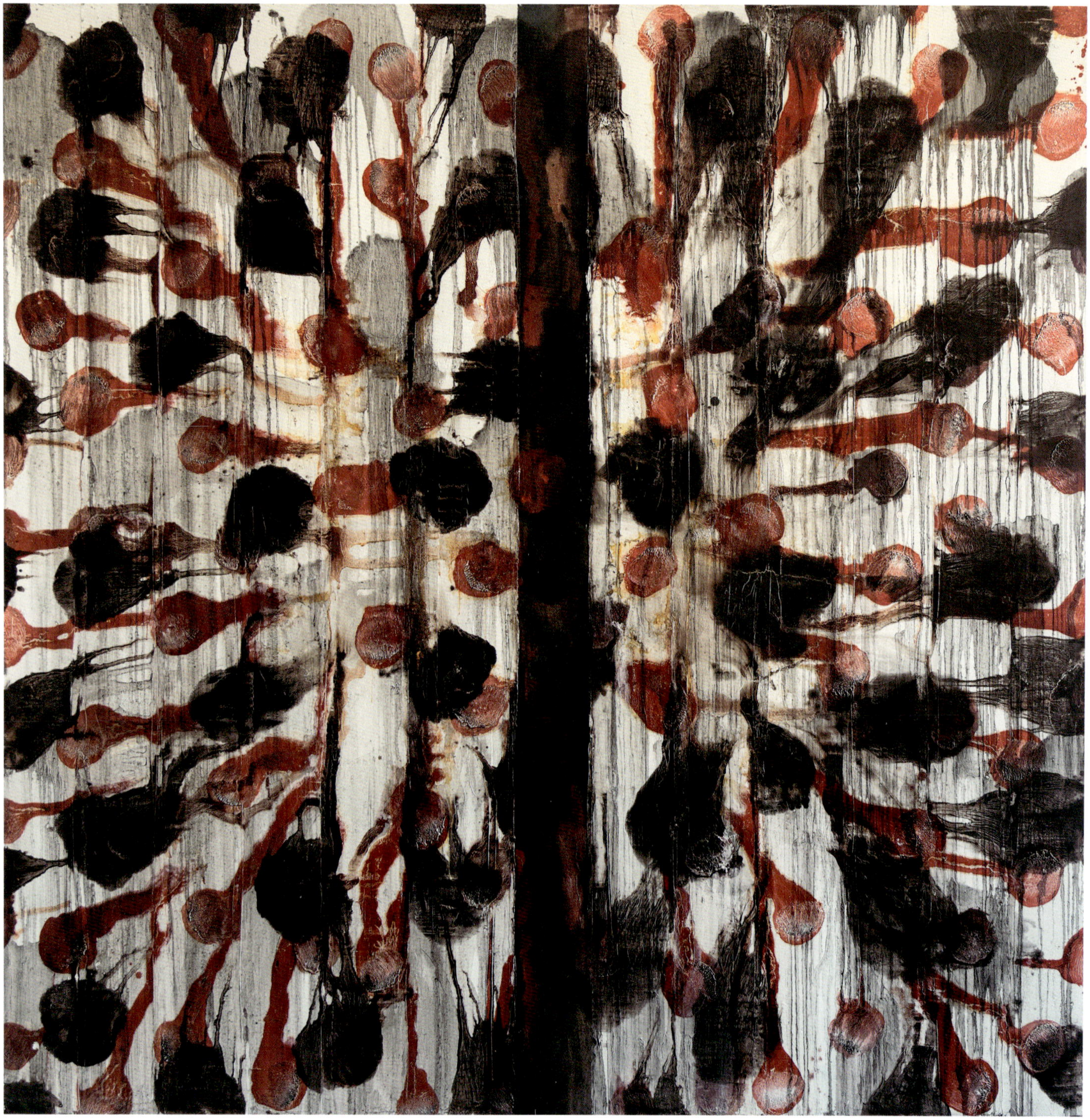

18. Untitled 1990

Oil on linen
203.2 × 203.2 cm (80 × 80 in)

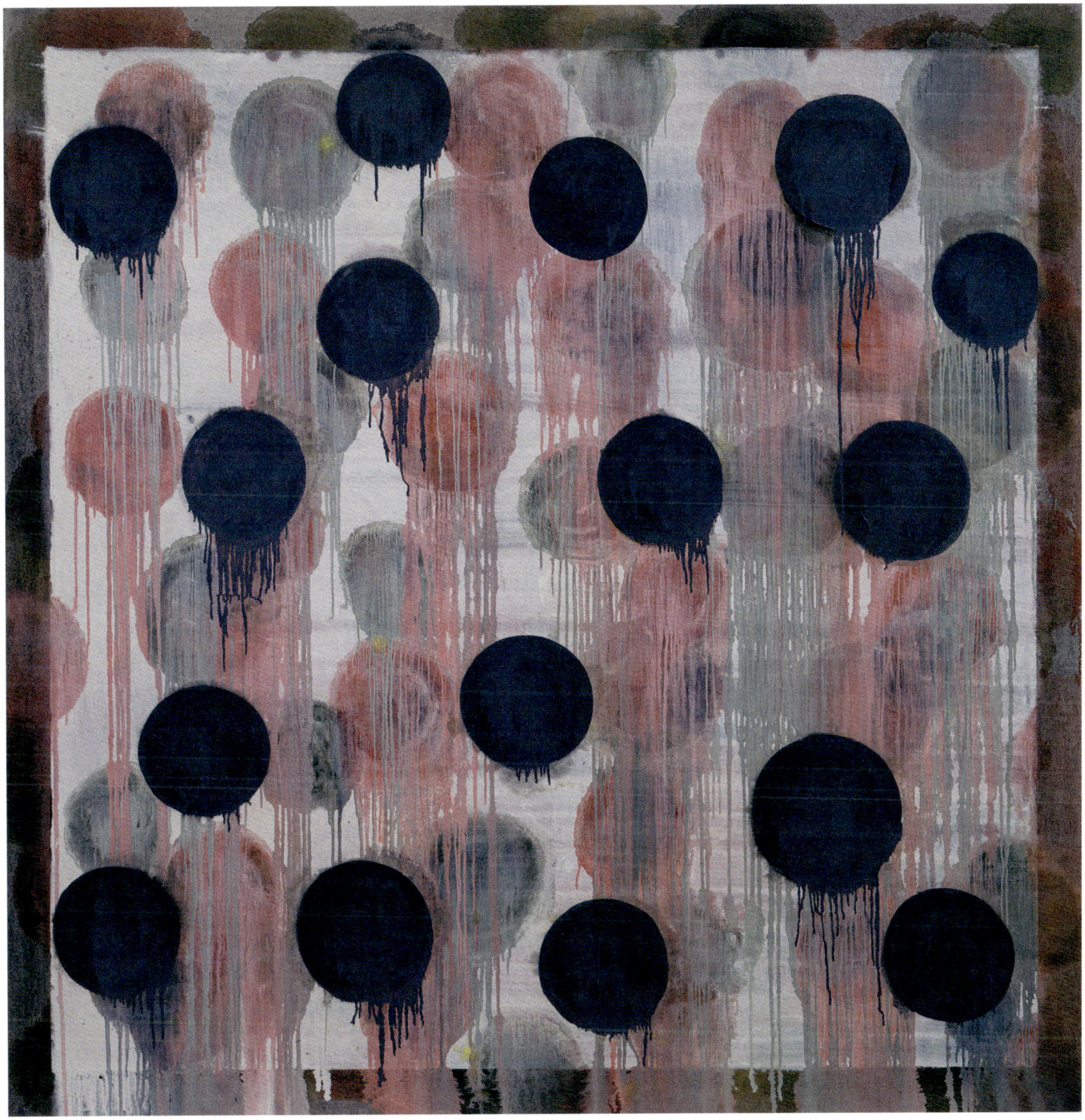

19. Untitled 1989

Oil on linen
152.4 × 152.4 cm (60 × 60 in)

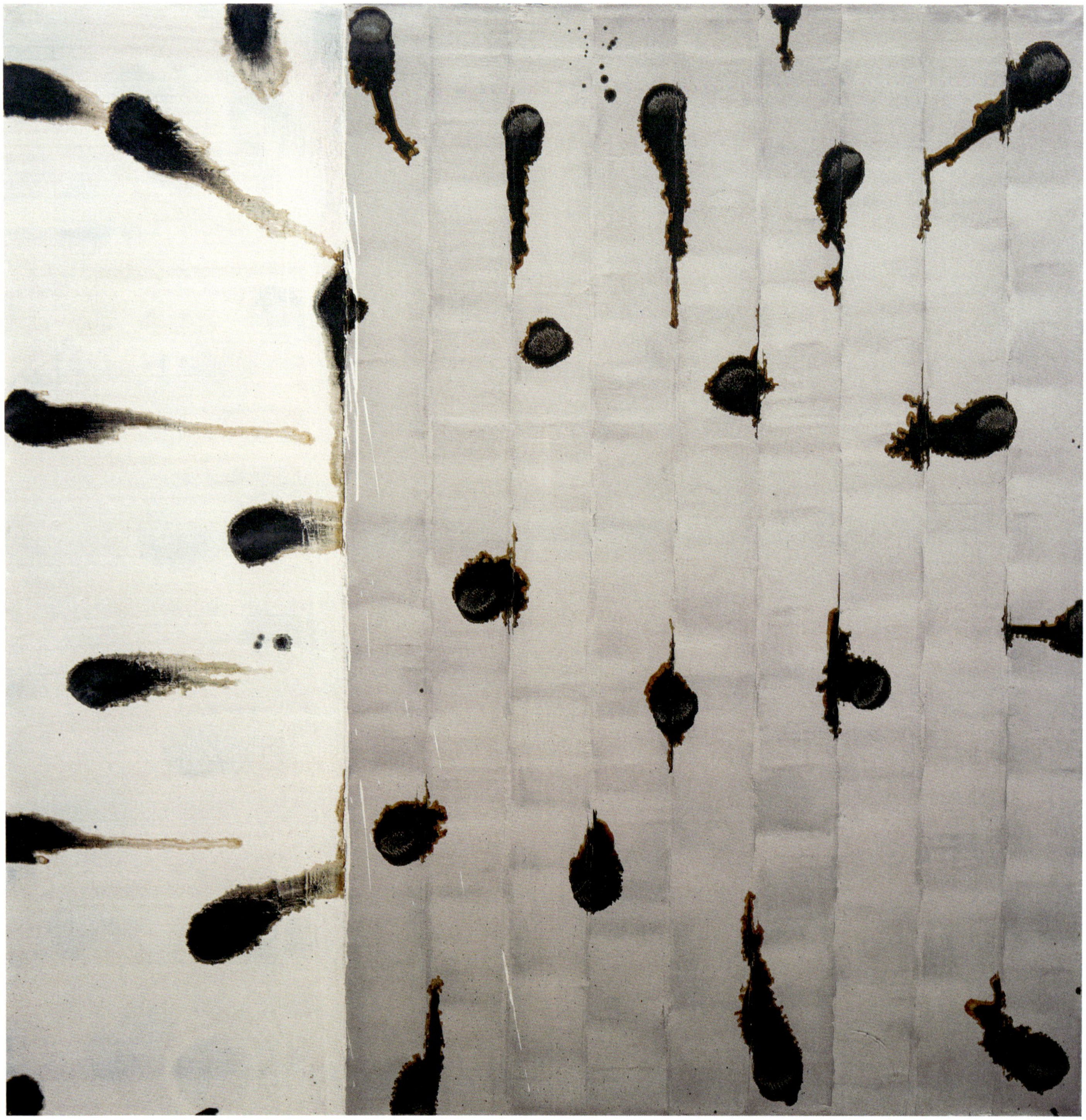

20. Out 1989

Oil on linen
203.2 × 203.2 cm (80 × 80 in)

commonly associated with staring at the television for too long. While artists began to depart from the expressive gestures of abstraction, giving way to smooth minimalist surfaces in the late 1970s, Humphries innovated on these strategies through developing a kinetic abstraction.

Thus, Humphries challenges painting by putting dots into motion. In *Out*, 1989 (fig.20), for example, black dots fly across the canvas, leaving brown smudges in their wake. We start to see an explosion in process. In a characteristic response to abstract painting, the longer we stand before the image, the more figurative alternatives appear and disappear.[23] We see tadpoles rushing away from a disturbance, or microbes bursting out of the space of the painting into ours. Concurrent with the search for something recognisable, divisions in the ground stop us from finding meaning and metaphor. The right two-thirds of the canvas are covered in strips of aluminium-grey paint, while, to the left, a white ground gives momentum and dimensionality to sepia-toned, amphibian-like dots. On closer inspection of the right two-thirds, we see the dots in the middle emerging from the seams between the grey strips. Thus, the apparent explosion of inky-black dots swimming across and out of the painting is no longer possible; the dots are stopped by the structure of the vertical fields, one white, the other nine slender repetitions in grey. In what becomes a familiar Humphries motif, the support and paint are in a conflict that is never resolved, no matter how long we stand before the painting. This tension becomes further complicated when we move backwards and forwards, searching for an explanation. Instead, a proliferation of abstract possibilities dominates our vision. We are no longer looking at perforations on a punch card. The holes on cards as data to be processed for telling a computer of its next operation are transformed through Humphries's painterly process into unpredictable flying dots. The coded language of data is translated into painting and, simultaneously, meaning becomes dispersed and ephemeral.

This translation from static to mobile, from actual holes on paper card into animated painted spheres, takes place before our eyes. Humphries's viewer is invited to become mesmerised, entranced by the patterns and movement in and around the surface before these are abruptly stopped by the vertical striations or, in the case of a work like *Untitled*, 1989 (fig.19), the frame. Through Humphries's process, what was the ground suddenly becomes the painted subject. Thus, at this early stage in her career, Humphries already uses a language foreign to painting in order to move the medium to unfamiliar territory, while still drawing on the history of abstract painting. The blurring of the distinction between figure and ground, subject and support, is precisely a pursuit of modernist painting. Humphries simply introduces gestures that mimic holes made by keypunches into the mix. This coming together of different 'languages', techniques, material states, and art historical references on a painted canvas is early evidence of her push to find a democracy of painting. It is also testimony to her debt and commitment to the precedents of modernist abstraction.

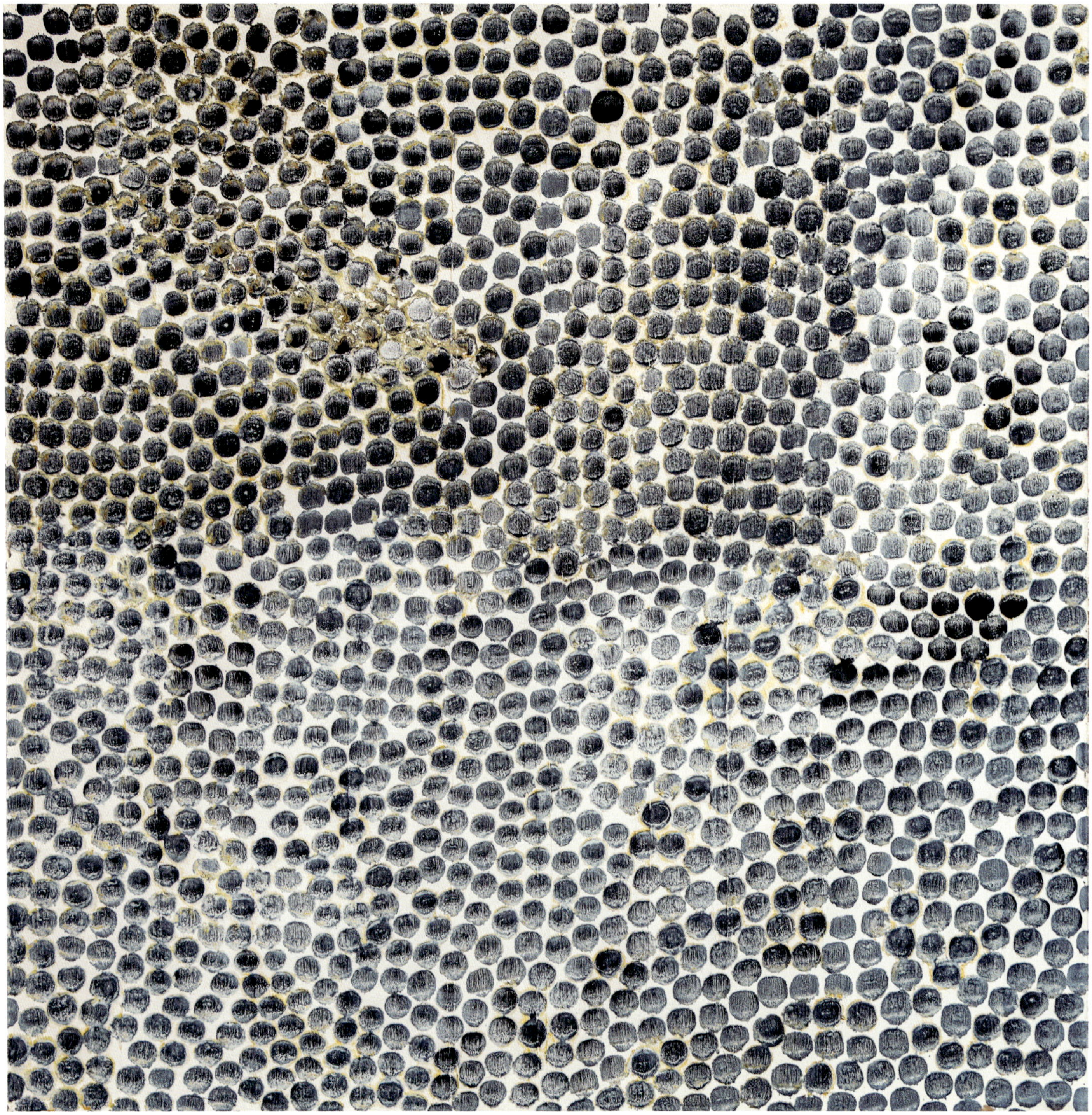

21. Untitled 1988

Oil on linen
182.9 × 182.9 cm (72 × 72 in)

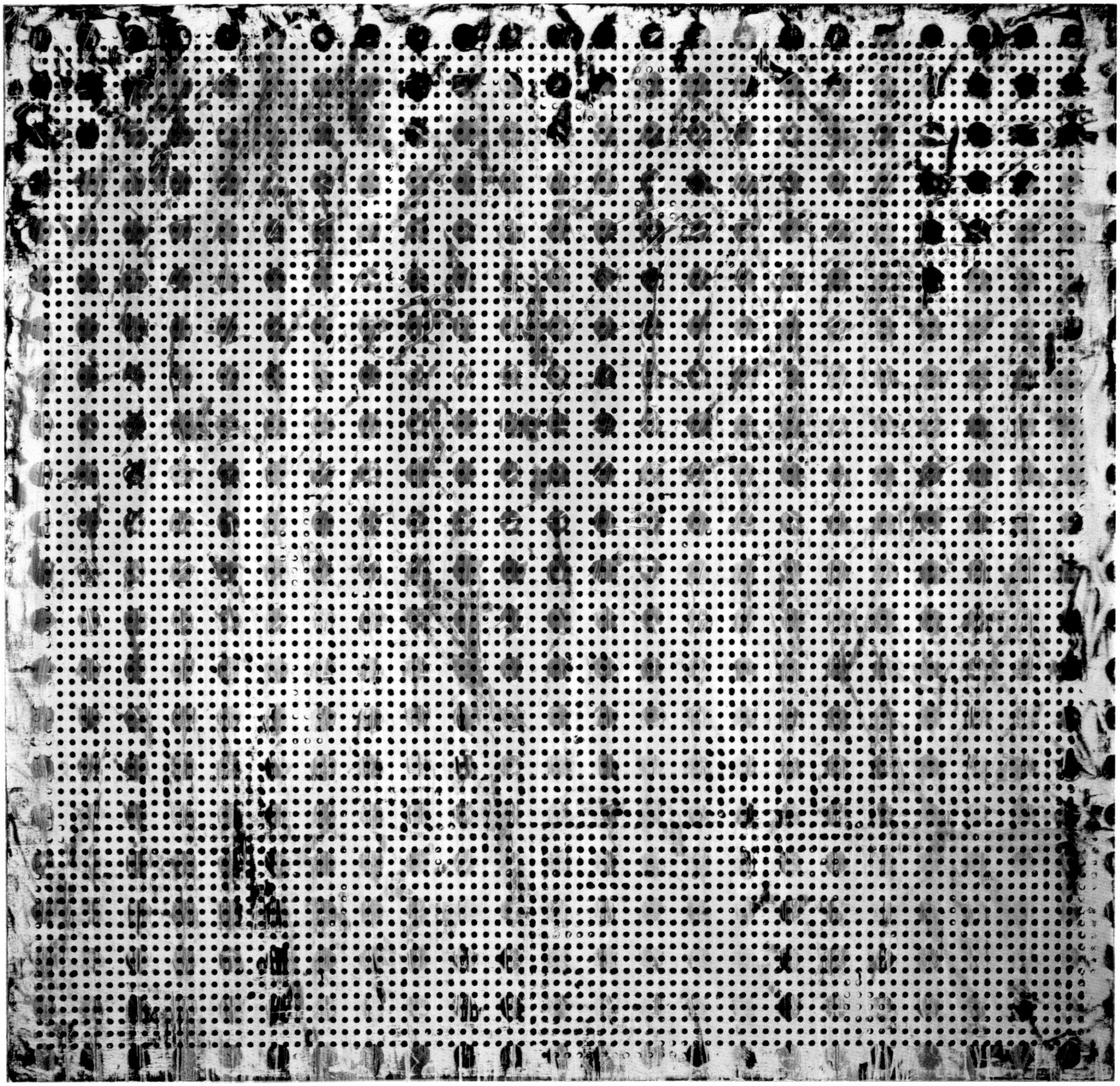

22. Alpha 2014

Oil on linen
228.6 × 254 cm (90 × 100 in)

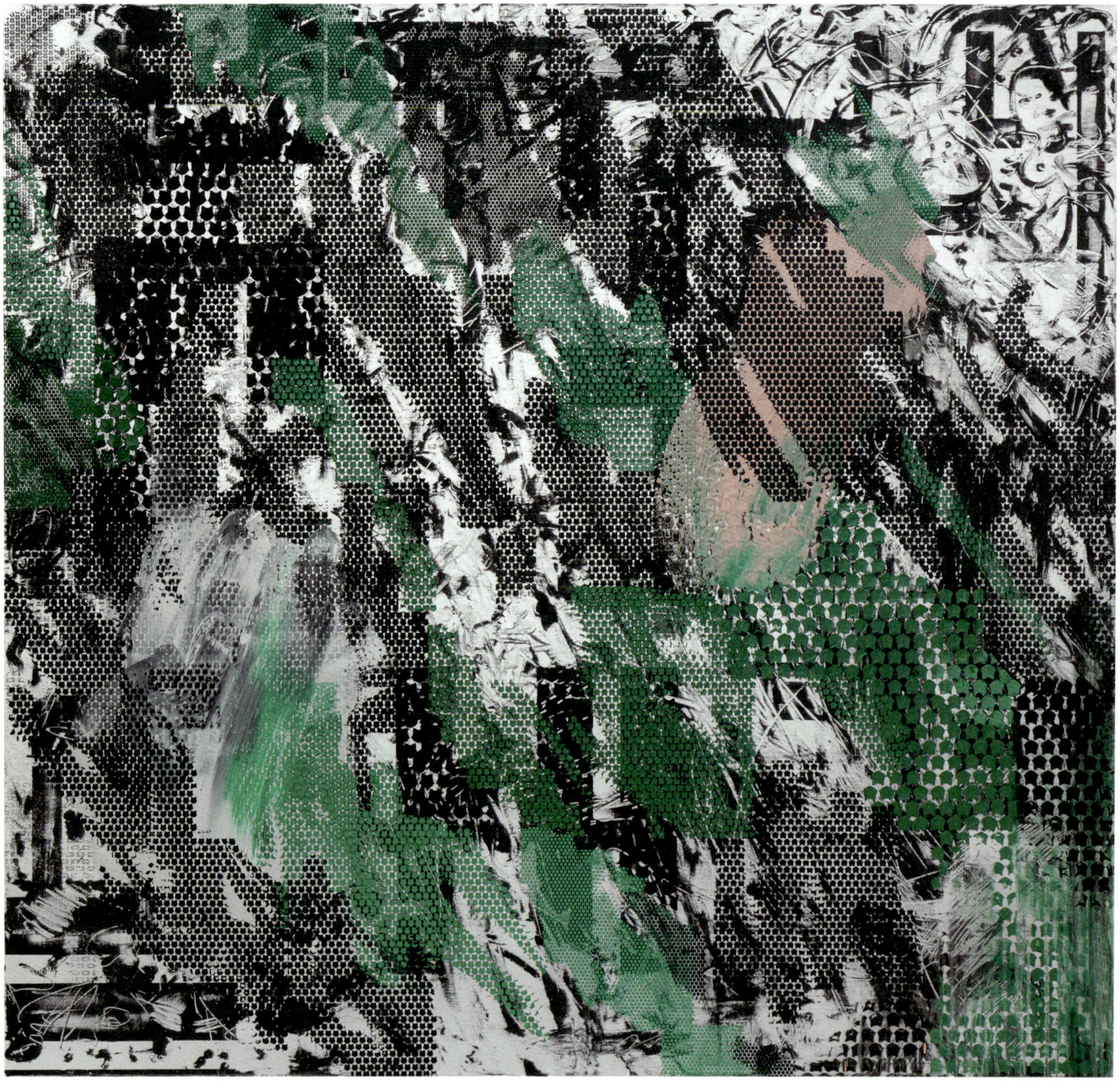

23. :cat: 2016

Oil on linen
228.6 × 243.8 cm (90 × 96 in)

24. :cat: 2016 (detail)

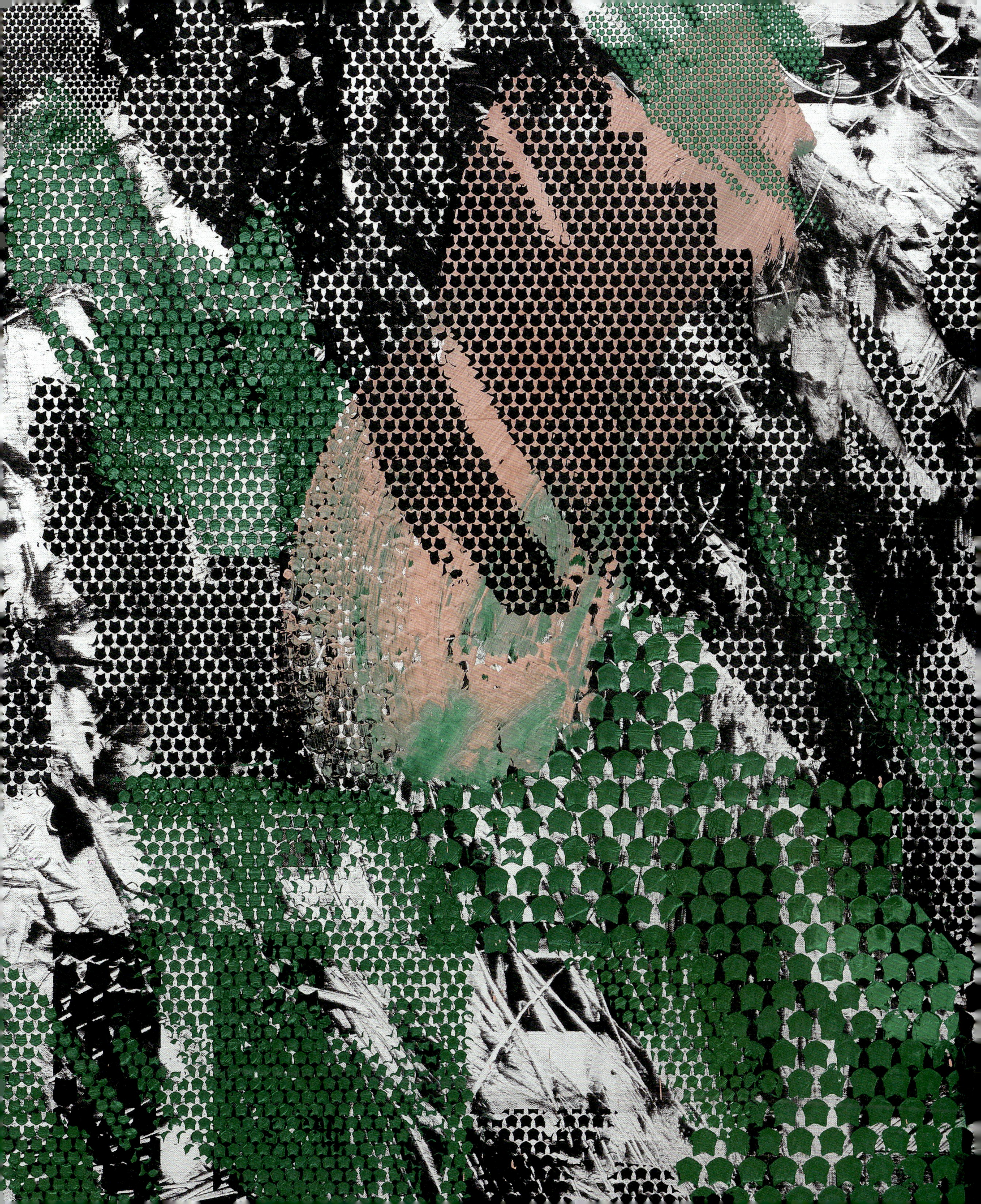

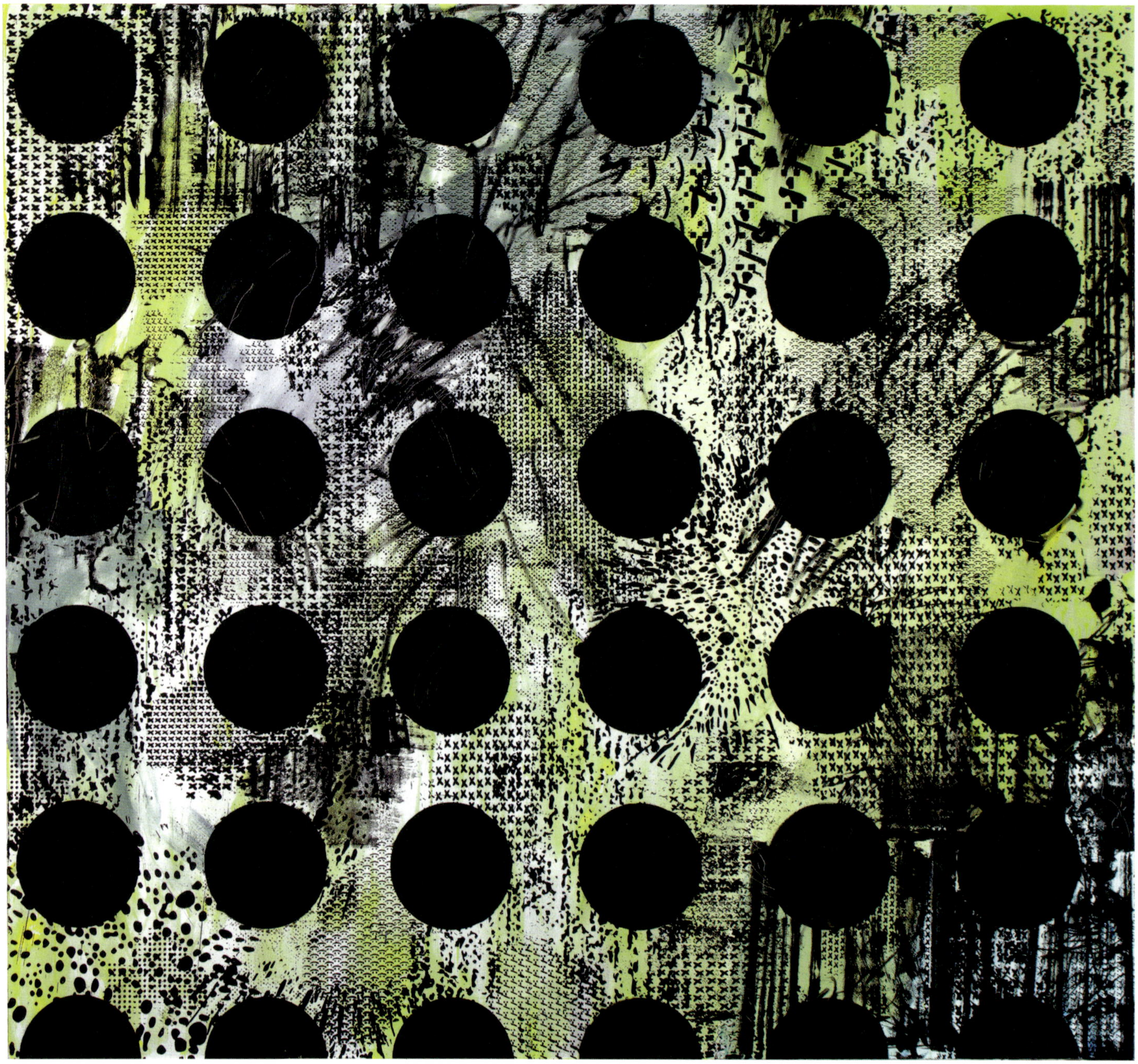

25. O 2015

Oil on linen
254 × 281.9 cm (100 × 111 in)

Hirshhorn Museum and Sculpture Garden, Smithsonian Institution, Washington, DC; museum purchase with funds provided by the Basil Alkazzi Purchase Fund, 2017

If, in these works, Humphries brings together two different visual forms – mechanical keypunch holes and modernist abstraction – a multiplicity of different languages often coexist. In *:cat:*, 2016 (fig.23), for example, she utilises elements from an early MS-DOS design tool, translated into painting through the application of a stencil. In turn, this is layered in with silver paint. In *:cat:*, different-sized cat emojis disintegrate in the stencilled layer. Painting then recomposes in the transparent layer, like a fresco. Here, the interface with technology is optically transferred to the painting as well as its effect on the viewer through the proliferation of visual languages in concert and contrast, dialogue and struggle.

Screen as interface

Humphries repeatedly reaches for superseded encoding systems and outmoded methods of communication. Multiple languages from different historical periods come together as images on the painting as screen or interface. In his work on the transition to digital representation and its status as a cultural form, Alexander R. Galloway references the screen as a 'mysterious [zone] of interaction that mediate[s] between different realities'.[24] If Humphries's paintings function as screens, this is a useful lens through which to see them. The concept of painting as screen which, in turn, can be understood as an interface, is realised in Humphries's ASCII (American Standard Code for Information Interchange) paintings from the 2010s onwards.

The ASCII works probe the space between word and image, painting and historical forms of computer-generated images, past and present technologies. This 'between' is not an either/or, but an interface. Following Galloway's conception, the paintings create a new language drawing from either side of the divide to create a representational form and effect. By extension, according to Galloway, the reality of a cultural cathexis to mediation is shown in this concept of painting-as-interface. In probing the interstitial space where signs and coded languages are transformed into painting, Humphries finds a material representation of the non-visual and incomprehensible. To do this, her paintings revitalise an anachronistic medium (ASCII), infuse painting with a new dynamism, and afford it a tactile realm. Thus, these paintings exceed the logic of painting while also being distinctly painterly. Nowhere is this excess – the democracy of signs and images – more articulately rendered than in the repetitions, doublings, and enlargements of her ASCII paintings.

ASCII is a system of encoding in which symbols on a keyboard – letters, numbers, punctuation marks – are translated into characters for digital representation. Simply put, ASCII is a language through which computers talk to each other. Humphries herself explains it: 'You know when you were a kid and you went on a trip to NASA?

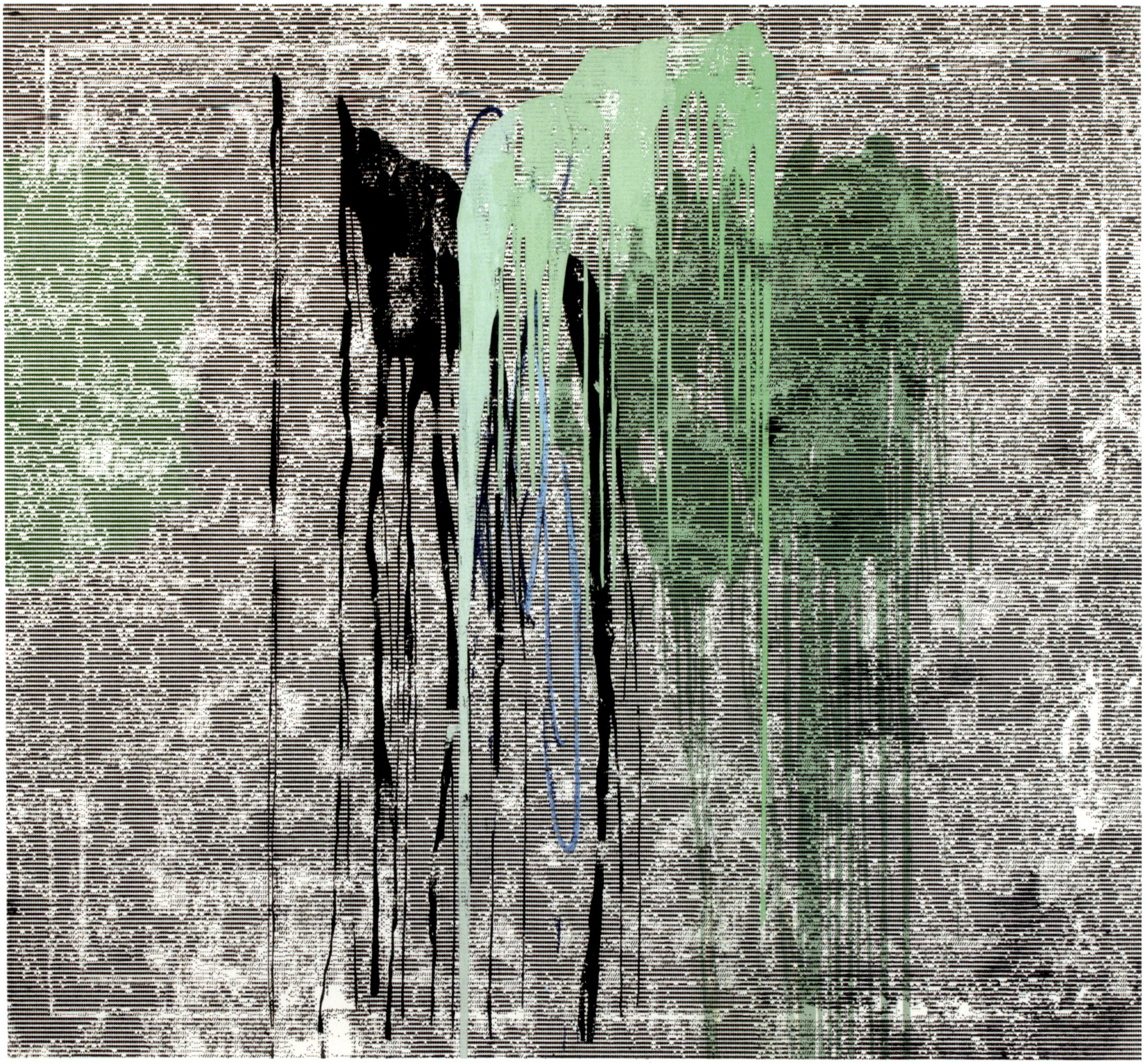

26. s/ssyM+ 2020

Oil on linen
254 × 281.9 cm (100 × 111 in)

It was like they had these huge telex machines and they'd printed a portrait of the president entirely in machine characters.'[25] That is ASCII code made into an image.

In the 2010s, Humphries started translating her earlier paintings into ASCII code on the computer. Accordingly, an earlier painting or painted gesture disintegrates into computer-generated code. That is, the painting is transformed into a new medium – computer code – that has no material existence. The code is then transferred to custom stencils: long panels of plastic sheet, the same height as the painting onto which their pattern will be imprinted.[26] Humphries then works with her familiar process of pushing paint through the stencilled sheets placed over the canvas. Thus, disintegrated images are re-created where none previously existed, serving as a screen through which we look at the painting. Simultaneously, the screen is the painting. In a typical modernist gesture, the works can be vibrant, dynamic depictions eliciting a conceptual response and surfaces of colourful shapes and patterns on canvases inviting an aesthetic experience. The paintings oscillate ambiguously between a play with aesthetic expectation and objects (screens) that negate painting altogether. Thus, these paintings are only as democratic as they are modernist.

Although Humphries's process of production is similar from painting to painting, no two works are alike – even when the same stencil is used to create two or more paintings. Consequently, when incompatible and mutually exclusive media are brought together, the eventual painting is unpredictable. The layering process is done with paints of different viscosities, different rates of drying, different thicknesses. Thus, when the stencil is pulled away from the canvas, there is no knowing in advance which paint will come to the surface: it depends on the behaviour of paints and colours, their degree of wetness, viscosity, and density. White, for example, is always slightly drier than the colours underneath.[27] Thus, when Humphries pushes and pulls the stencilled white around the surface with a thick brush, the wetter colours make their appearance in unpredictable places and patterns across the white surface.

Further variations occur as we approach these paintings. Like the language into which one of the original paintings or painted motifs is translated, akin to the process of reading a hybrid of two or three invented languages, the viewer is removed multiple times from the image that they are supposedly seeing.[28] Thus, despite the repetitive process of creating a painting, many layers of translation and interpretation ensure that viewers always see anew before each work. Moreover, viewing and cognising take place over time, inviting shifts in perception of colours and structural elements of a given work. Each is explored within the frame, at the interface, playing with the expectations of painting as a medium. Its uniqueness is enabled by Humphries' manipulation and mixing of different paints, together with her introduction of elements foreign to painting.

Thus, in *sysysy/:|*, 2018 (fig.7), following the artist's transformation of a gesture into ASCII code, making it into a stencil, clay-like paint is applied to a primed canvas. What we may conventionally recognise as a painting has been covered over, replaced by three-dimensional stencilled horizontal sequences of keyboard characters. An

27. i\Ω.. 2017

Oil on linen
289.6 × 322.6 cm (114 × 127 in)
The Art Institute of Chicago, Chicago;
Kate S. Buckingham Endowment Fund, 2019.889

emoji button is stuck to the side, in what might be seen an exclamation point to the painting. Humphries often then overpaints her stencilled areas with more white. The result is that the fast-drying white of the painting and the black stencilled ASCII overlay exist on the same level. The white is both underneath and painted over the stencilled black. Figure and ground are interchangeable, on the surface, confusing the priority for viewing. The eye moves around and across what, over time, becomes pulsating patterns until, as viewers, we move forward. Close to one such canvas, the painting takes on a dense white and black, substance-like appearance. It is reduced (or elevated, depending on the perspective) to the stuff of painting. Then, in *sysysy/:|*, we are challenged by the emoji button. Is it looking at us? Is it frowning? Smiling? What are we supposed to do with this onlooker, this observer of our movements around the canvas? Perhaps the emoji means nothing at all? Perhaps it is there, looking back, enticing us into seeing meaning in an empty button, just as we do when using emojis in a text message?

For Humphries, this movement and play repeats the relationship between painting and how we see it. Like the screens to which we cathect day and night, the painted image shifts as we move around it, and according to the value that we give the fluctuating details inside the frame. Hyperdetail collapses into a neutral field, reminding us of an image on a screen, only it is different: up close, face to face with the painting, it emerges as a real, three-dimensional object. The painting is a thing with a materiality occupying a space. It is a thing with which we have a physical and sensual relationship. We are pulled by a desire to touch the surface, even if we resist. The authenticity of this relationship is distinct from our interaction with technological screens. It is an aesthetic experience. Yet, the minute we recognise that we are being watched by an emoji pinned to the side of the canvas, we are back engaging with a painting as though from inside an illusory technological world, responding as though the button had emotions and senses. Our experience before a painting such as *sysysy/:|* reminds us of our immersive relationship with technological screens and data. It is also a relationship experienced at a distance in which we are urged to step back and acknowledge that we are looking at a painting. Thus, *sysysy/:|* is a painting inviting us to reflect on our relationship with and behaviour before screens, rather than fully replicating that experience.

In this reflexivity at the interface of painting and screen, image and computer code, Humphries's abstractions offer insight into our contemporary condition. Her paintings may result in a dialogue with the experience of technological screens, but they are something else again when seen on a screen. On screens, the works no longer behave as paintings, but rather become photographic reproductions of paintings. Humphries maintains that, for a painting to be painting, it must be in a room, somewhere, physically present. When seen in reproduction, the multiplicity of languages cohabiting the painting is erased, the democracy of painting removed. The activation of our senses, particularly touching and smelling the thick, clay-like paint, is denied when engaging with an image on screen. If the ASCII works constitute

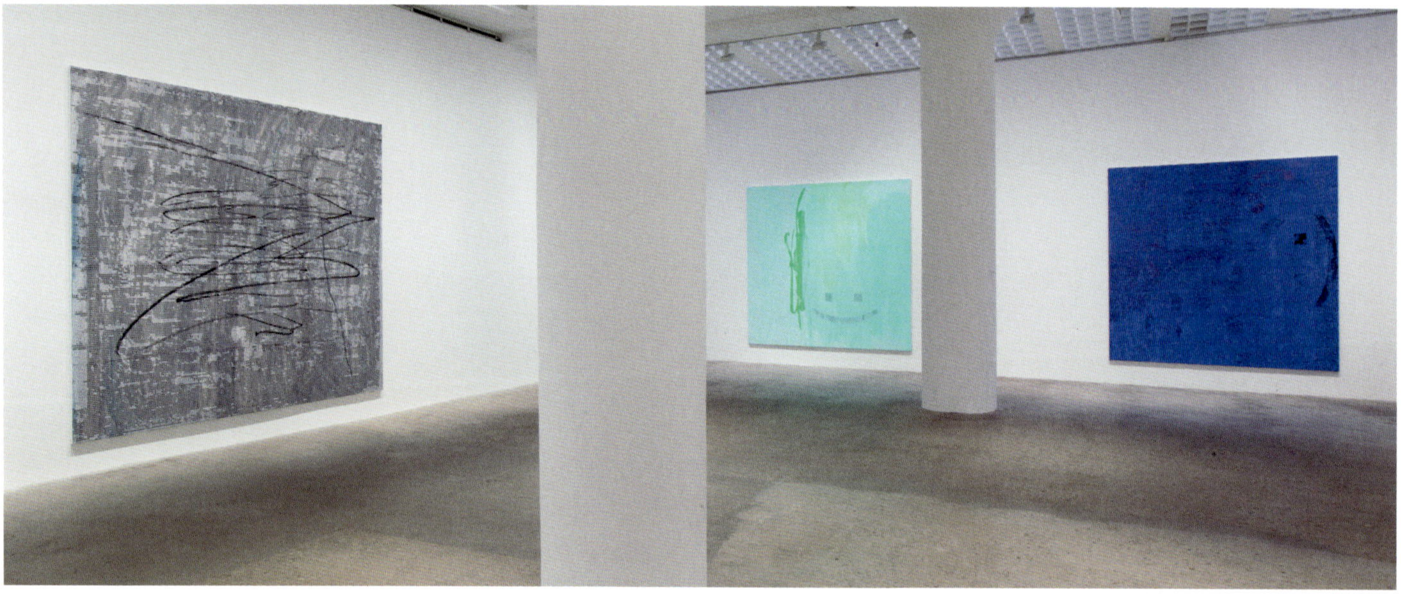

28. Installation view
Greene Naftali, New York, 2017

an interface with the digital world in their representation of the digital network's translation of objects into code, then they do so to explore the very phenomenology of that code as it is defined by the loss of the object.

And yet an image is reinstated just as the painting is erased through the transformational process. *Prima facie*, the painting transformed into an image on a screen becomes a new image. However, Humphries's paintings still invite an aesthetic experience: in reproduction, they are gorgeous. The same is true for the degradation of the image in the ASCII paintings. From painting to code to stencil to painting to reproduction, new images are produced at each stage of the transformational process. As Galloway argues, the interface aesthetic must have an image for it to have an effect. Even if that image is transformed from an informational algorithm, it still has substance.[29]

In the case of *?????h%*, 2018 (fig.29), Humphries's pilfered gesture – translated into ASCII code, transposed to a stencil where it is repeated, forming the pattern for application of paint – is drawn from an earlier work. The gesture that now behaves as a screen began as a Humphries painting. By culling from her own paintings, the repetition works temporally as well as spatially, across the surface of one image and onto the next. Up close, we see thick dashes, symbols, letters and punctuation marks as they have been pushed through the stencil, struggling with the other layers of paint. Standing back, we see the brushstrokes as if they are painted over the top of the earlier work. Our view at a distance is dominated by a density and scaling of patterns that are subsequently layered on a single field to create a sense of colour.[30] Colour appears where we least expect it, where it does not belong, where it surprises even the artist herself. Thus, she re-produces her own work, but in doing so, creates another painting

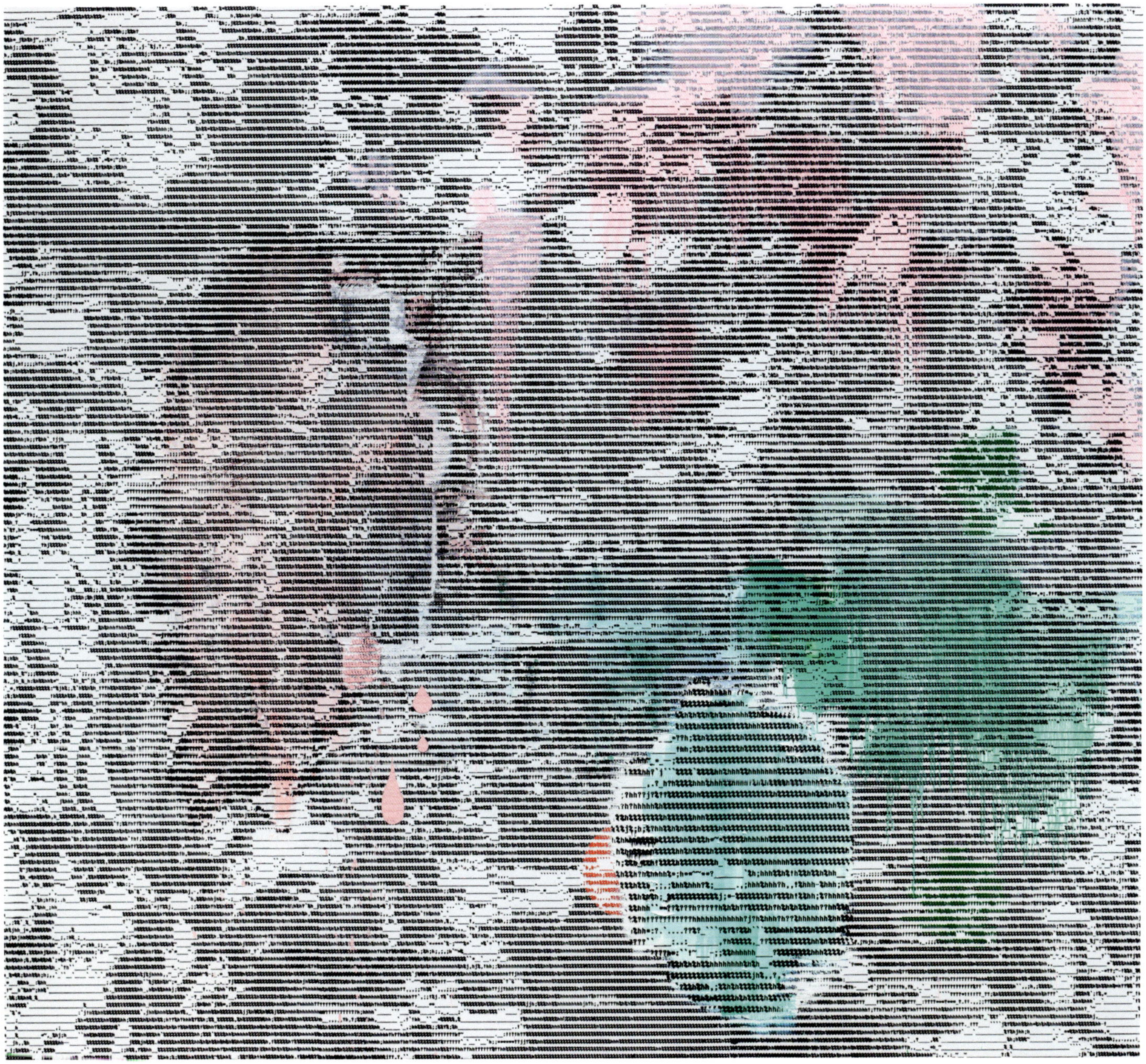

29. ??????h% 2018

Oil on linen
254 × 281.9 cm (100 × 111 in)

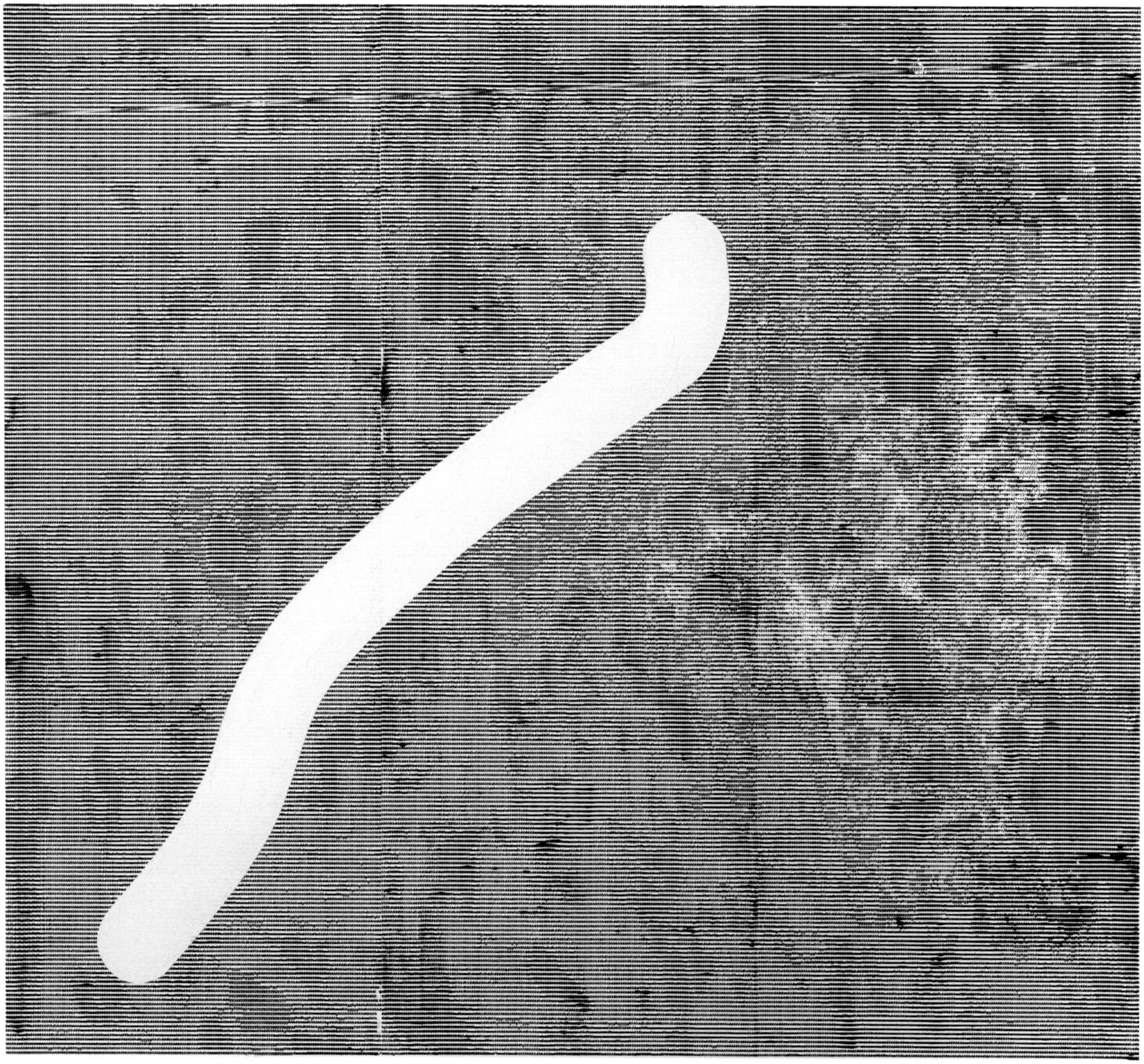

30. MMNddy+ 2020

Oil on linen
254 × 281.9 cm (100 × 111 in)

31. MMNddy+ 2020 (detail)

that she does not recognise. The mutating transformations created by the painter produce a plethora of images at the interface.

When the ASCII code layer is overlaid with a white gesture – a spill, a glitch, the trace of a technological hiccup – as seen in *MMNddy+*, 2020 (fig.30), the paint becomes thick like plaster, appearing as dense impasto. It looks to be even more calcified over an ASCII layer that has spread underneath the stencil. The paint is smudged, makes no sense, and appears as mistakes on the surface. The imperfections of the painting are as surprising as the emergence of colours through the viewer's movement over time. There is no definitive interpretation of these marks. They may be produced by a carefully managed technical process, but they cannot be rationalised. Like painting as a medium, the marks are traces of uniqueness, individuality, the breakdown of technological systems. Thus, the sculptural element of Humphries's paintings is also part of their authenticity and singularity.

In another ironic layer, Humphries's pushing of paint through screens and adding of emojis produce a discourse defined by the artist's removal of her authority. When she sets the process of transformation in motion, she paints, but is not acting like a painter. Rather, Humphries hands over her authority to the computer. And yet Humphries is in absolute control. The process of translation, layering, scraping away, scribbling over with paint, is painstakingly performed. It is also centred in the body as she cuts long, unwieldy stencils, before engaging in the physically demanding plying of viscid paint. The result is unpredictable or, as Humphries herself describes it, 'incoherent'.[31] Codes, symbols, systems, and images are worked through and over before arriving on the canvas where they belong to an image from which the artist is shut out. She says, 'I feel I've finished a painting when it opens up and banishes me, puts me outside the process.'[32]

The painting, having eschewed its creator, awaits the presence of a viewer, or interpreter, to further 'reinvent the discourses'. Humphries removes herself so that we are confounded by our contemporary condition and consequently are moved to reinvent our technologically defined existence. To see what this looks like, let me turn to Humphries's use of emoticons and emojis and our resultant responses.

32. :) green 2017

Oil on linen
96.5 × 101.6 cm (38 × 40 in)

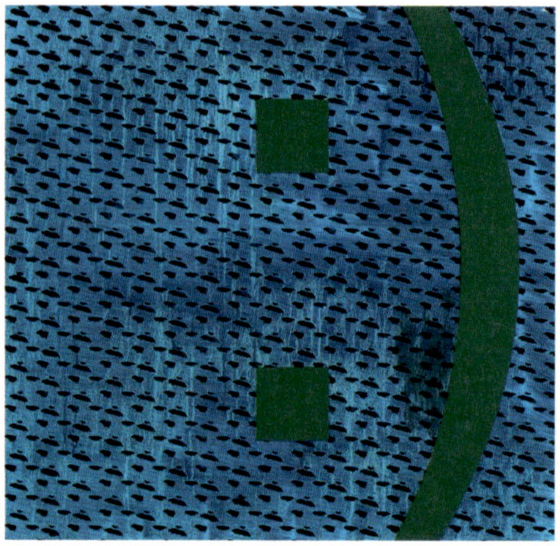

Emojis and emoticons

Usually, the emoticons and emojis are found floating on or just under the surface. Alternatively, they hover over the painting's edges, are repeated, and layered to the point where it becomes impossible to say whether they are figure or ground. Sometimes, in the case of a work such as *:) green*, 2017 (fig.32), one smiling emoticon playfully consumes the right half of the painting. Distinct from the use of the emoji button on *sysysy/:|*, it draws attention to the painting's illusory depth. When it is underneath the surface, the emoticon casts a veil of iconoclasm over the work, communicating that the rogue element is being used to reproduce the apparently outmoded medium of painting.

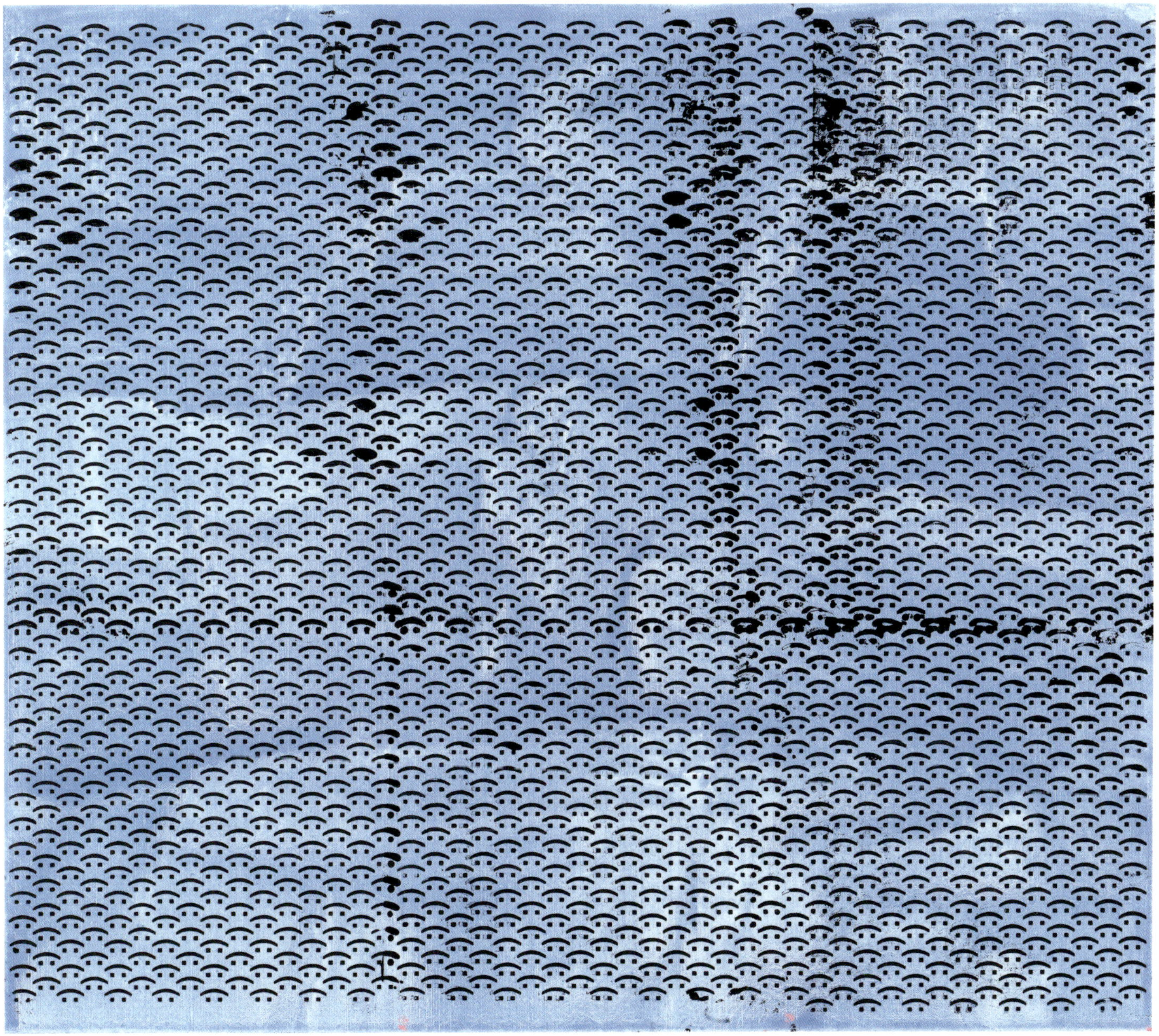

33. Untitled 2014

Oil on linen
66 × 76.2 cm (26 × 30 in)

In what sometimes appears as an afterthought, Humphries adds an emoticon to create a contemporary language that hovers between image and script. When the emoticon or emoji is added to the painting, we are confronted with a painting-as-screen that is emptied of concrete meaning. The emoticon seems to be added for effect as much as for communication. We smile, smirk, turn our heads, and contort our bodies to observe and converse with the cheeky symbol. If we stand, contemplating in disbelief the superficiality and illusion with which we are confronted, we may start to wonder: What do we do in front of the painting? Do we look at it? Read it? Decode it? Is it a script or an image? The painting as object becomes an impossible-to-read surface that leaves us guessing. Such is the purpose of much abstract painting, particularly in its modernist instantiations.

As Lloyd Wise says, Humphries adds the language of contemporary images and visual fields to the familiar forms and functions of modernist abstraction: 'By adding the emoticon to her painterly vocabulary, Humphries has yoked a wide swathe of painting's history to a contemporary argot, elegantly articulating the parallels between the self-negating tendencies of a certain strain of painting and our shared online vernacular.'[33] Following Wise's logic, the emoticons marry painting and screen, past and present, depth and illusion. However, something else happens in Humphries's process of distension and simultaneous coalescence. Namely, we are likely to have an emotional response before the painting, albeit one that is distinct from the expressions (as opposed to emotions) of the various emoticons and emojis.

In some early uses of the emoticon, Humphries repeatedly stencilled it over the whole canvas. This gives the painting an ostensibly formal structure. For example, in *Untitled*, 2014 (fig.33), upside-down emoticons cover the canvas, evenly spaced and predictable. That is, until the paint seeps underneath the stencil and the formal pattern and structure are smudged by paint that has coagulated where strips of stencil are joined (reminding us of the moving dots of *Out*, fig.20). The anti-gestural austerity of postwar American modernism disintegrates to reveal mistakes, flaws that are the site of creative inspiration for the viewer. In a work such as *:):):)*, 2016 (fig.34), the emoticon is having fun, upside down, cheekily smiling back at us as it floats around the painting. Large and small emoticons cover the canvas, creating a ground. But they are also negated. The next layer is an unruly splotch of paint, a patch of seemingly random colour, and an added white line resembling a technological blip. Or alternatively, the white blip may remind us of the trace of an oily finger left on a dirty screen. The pattern of emoticons, as figure and ground, is obliterated by a white glitch. Nevertheless, as a negation, it is always pleasing, bright, and fascinating. The blip encourages laughter at the imperfections of painting. Humphries does not actually cancel one language or layer by another. Rather, layering is achieved through a process in which paint is scraped away, or built up, like a sculpture. The surface of a Humphries painting makes layers of paint, languages, and effects into a democratic arena.

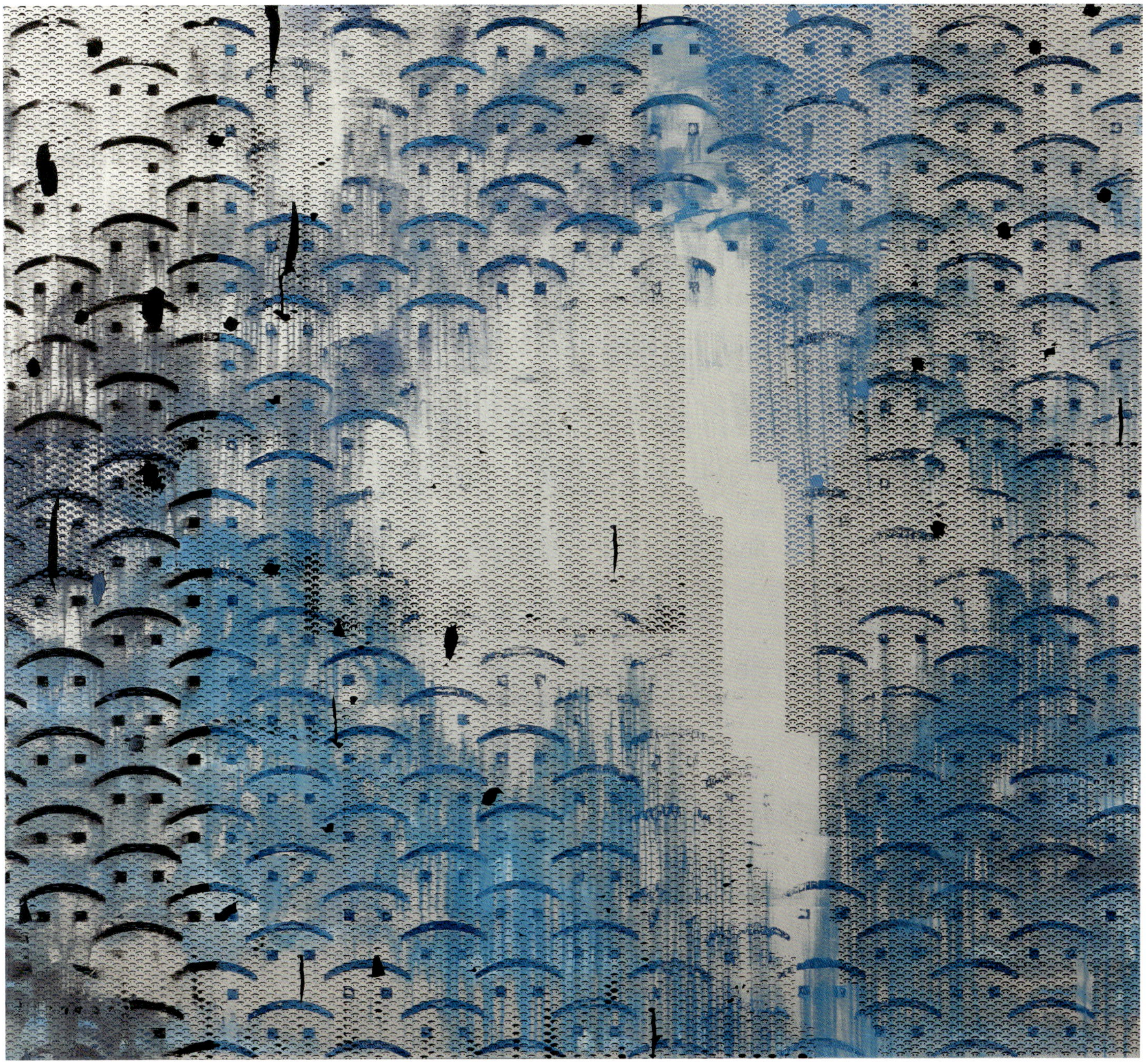

34. :) :) :) 2016

Oil on linen
254 × 281.9 cm (100 × 111 in)

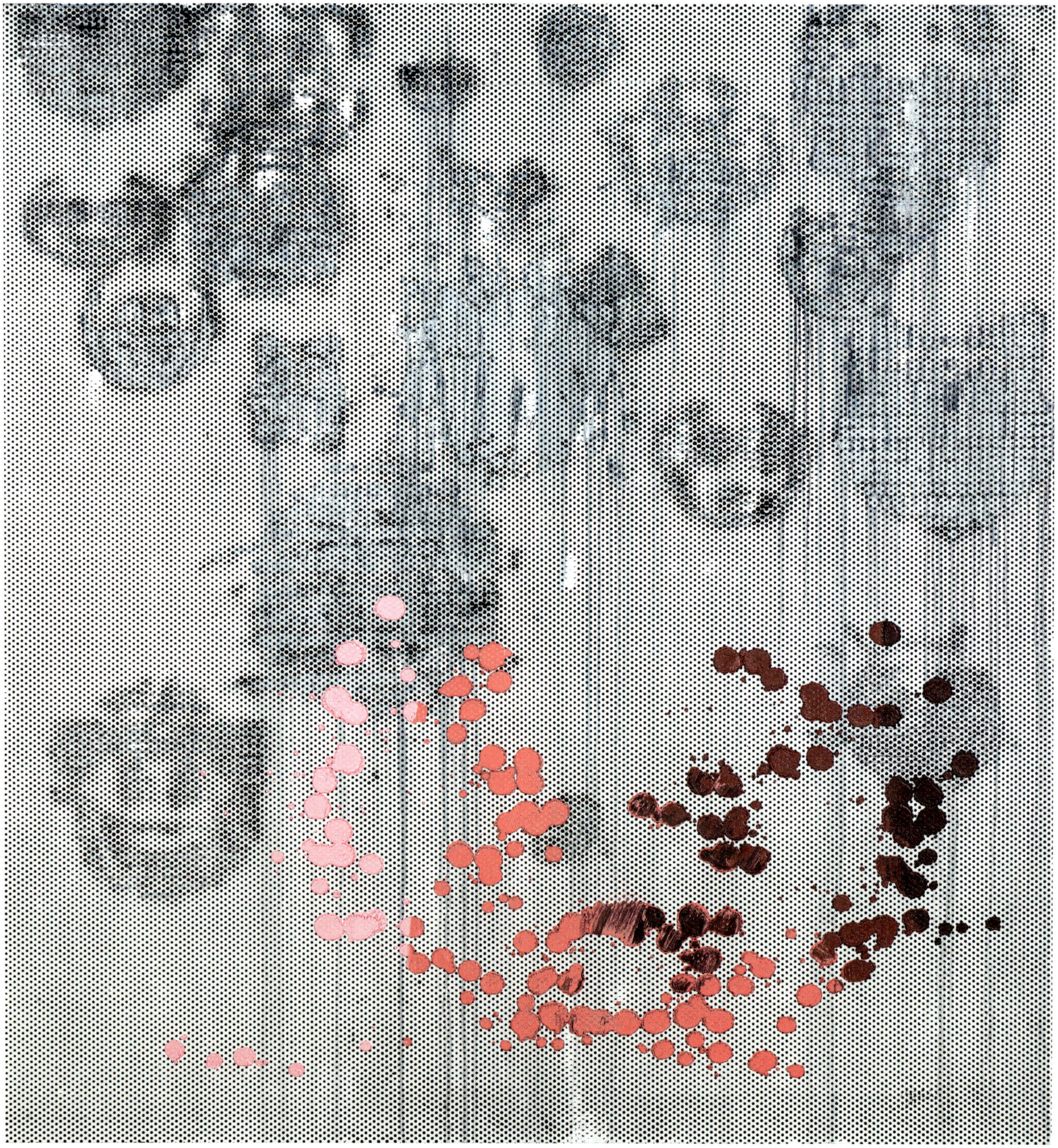

35. 🤠😣 2020

Oil on linen
152.4 × 144.8 cm (60 × 57 in)

Elements that do not belong together are integrated onto a single surface of equality, transforming depending on our temporal and spatial interaction. The surprise effect, thus uniqueness, of each canvas is generated by this dynamism. In addition, the transience of painted elements and the painting as a whole produce a response defined by an altogether different and unanticipated experience of the viewer before a painting. We enjoy an authentic response to an otherwise hackneyed symbol.

To elaborate: in a recent work such as 🤠😣, 2020 (fig.35), the black paint is thick and luscious in places, with pink and dark red splotches tracing the emoji expression. Up close, pink and red paint becomes reminiscent of drops of blood trailing across the bottom of the canvas. Simultaneously, we recognise Humphries's familiar technique of applying paint through a stencil. Standing at a distance, we see other emojis emerge, floating like ghouls around the painting. Seen from the side of the canvas, the faces disintegrate into dots, like pixellations. The painted surface takes on the illusion of a velvet cover enticing us to stroke it, to feel its pile under our fingertips. In the shift from emoticon to emoji – a shift ordinarily executed by the computer keyboard, but here realised across Humphries's oeuvre – comes a 'genuine' emotional reponse. From afar, the highly structured, messy drips are like tears, eliciting sadness. The bloody trails of an emoji might be understood as the cause or the effect – it is unclear which – of the tears. Thus, in time spent with this painting, the 'genuine' emotional response is not represented by the perseverance emoji, but stirred up by Humphries's painting as it manipulates its way into our sentient perception.

🤠😣 and other recent works see Humphries using a new technique: reproduction through a hand-held printer of an emoji which is then enlarged on a computer, printed out, and cut into a stencil. As in the ASCII paintings, Humphries pushes paint through the stencil onto a primed canvas and layers on more paint. When she pulls away the stencil, the overlayer catches on the physicality of the stenciled pattern underneath, allowing ghosted images beneath to re-emerge as texture. In a further layer of repetition, the hyperinflated, disintegrating emoji in pink and red that has been painted over the stencilled layer reappears on other canvases. It recurs in different colours, on different paintings, in different locations. When seeing the figure for the second and third times, the initial struggle to cognise an unrecognisable marking is transformed into a relaxed encounter with a familiar friend. Again, in distinction from modernist painters of earlier generations, Humphries's particular vein of repetition does not bring about a conceptual search for the ultimate solution to the questions asked of painting. Rather, the reappearance of a coded language transformed into unrecognisable marks on multiple paintings across geographical borders brings recognition and familarity to a knowing viewer. The joke, like the language in which it is told, or painted, is already in our vocabulary. Yet, the joke, like the emoji, tends to leave us wondering what it means.

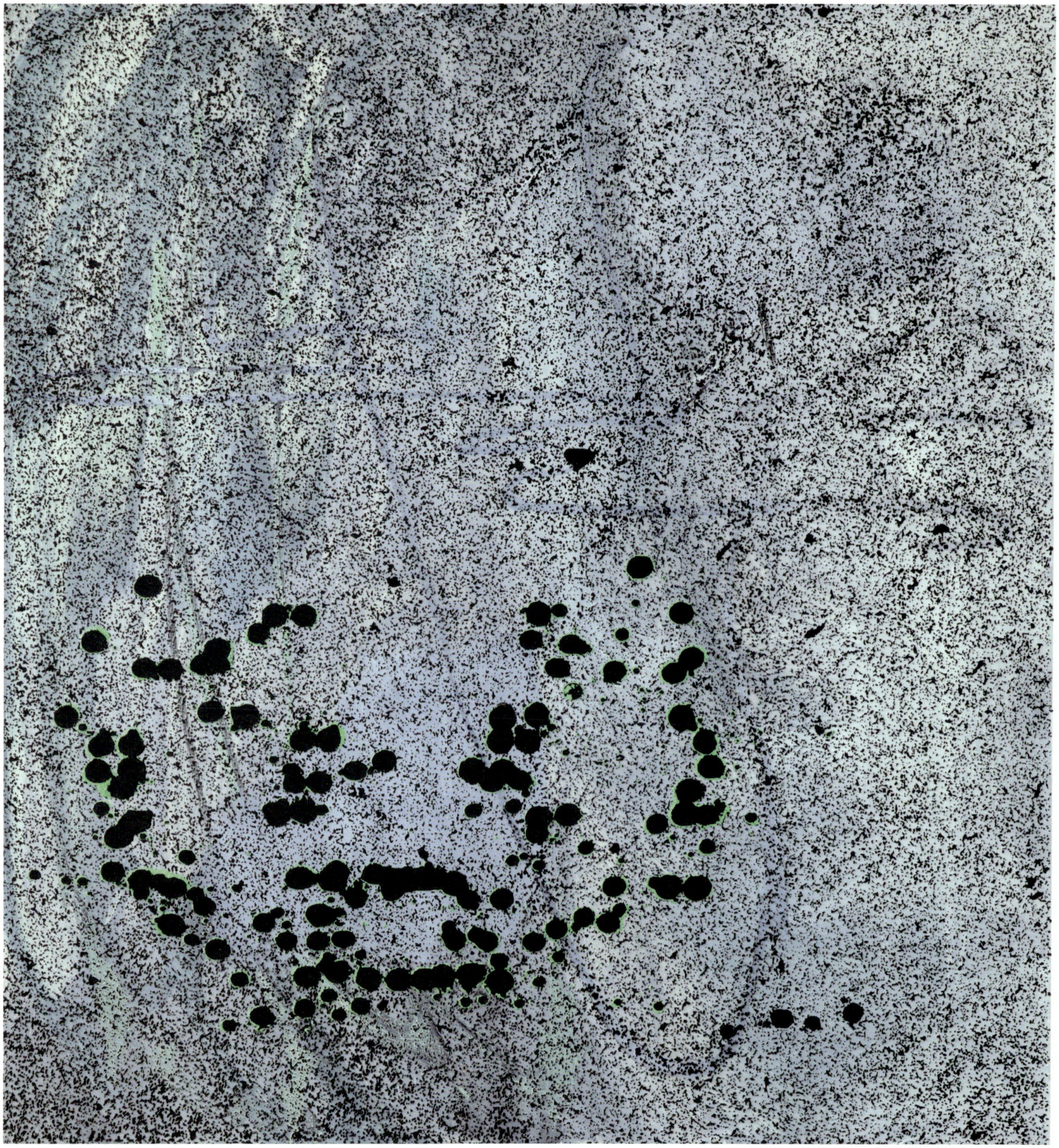

36. 😣 2020

Oil on linen
152.4 × 144.8 cm (60 × 57 in)

37. 😣 2020 (detail)

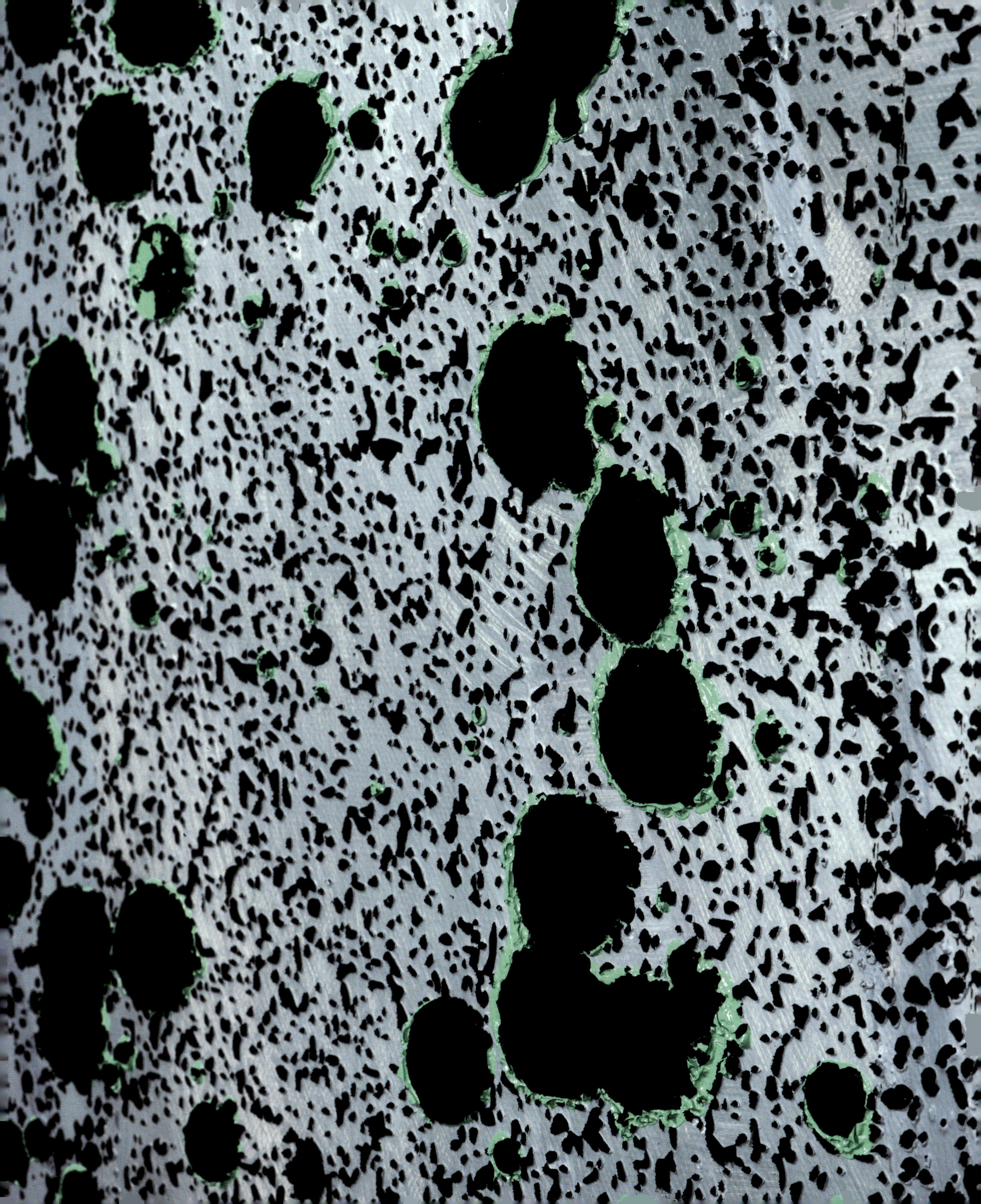

Cinematic painting

Asked of her intentions for painting, Humphries says, 'I have to keep people looking somehow.'[34] Surely this is what all painters want? Of course; however, Humphries is searching for a specific kind of viewer. Elsewhere she talks of her envy of filmmakers who use their medium to hold an audience over an extended period of time.[35] Humphries wants an audience to watch her paintings unfold like a movie. She wants the eyes of a mass public to be glued to her paintings for a protracted duration. What she gets is quite different but, nevertheless, related. Painting demands a viewer with a physical body, in motion, to engage with a material object, in the light of day. This is contrary to the film audience: sedentary, in darkness, before an illusion. In the 1990s, Humphries experimented with reproducing filmic effects through painting. She reduced the medium of cinema to light flickering across grey paint. In the 1990s, paintings such as *Black Sheep*, 1999 (fig.38), and the *Horizontal* works (see figs 10, 13, 39, 44, 65) used paint to create an illusionistic rendering of real space that exerts a magnetic pull. In the mid-2000s, Humphries progressed to evoke the cinema screen by using silver paint to achieve an effect rather than a representation. The silver paintings are vivid examples of Humphries's use of the language of painting to elicit the response previously triggered by another medium: the cinema.

Likewise, the silver paintings see Humphries reach for a democracy of images that coalesces into a new visual language. Here, the coexistence of signs – painting, film, stencilled and taped gestures – are reworked into painting as a screen, both filled with illusions and a material object in its own right.

In a series of paintings from 2008, Humphries took the motif of light dancing over wet pavement in the dark of the night. The glistening of wet streets and the clandestine events of film noir are invoked, hiding behind or in front of these surfaces. Yet, Humphries leaves the narrative of the film noir outside of the frame. As Paul Schrader notes in an essay of 1972, verticals and oblique lines connect *film noir* to German expressionist cinema, filling the frame with anxiety and uncertainty. As if taken directly from a 1940s Hollywood film noir, red wisps float around Humphries's *Dirty Mind*, 2008 (fig.41), like a cloud of blood merging with water under flickering lights. It is as if we are looking out onto the streets, from behind louvred blind slats, our view consumed by the blood of a murdered corpse. Such is the underworld. To quote Schrader, 'Light enters the dingy rooms of film noir in such odd shapes – jagged trapezoids, obtuse triangles, vertical slits – that one suspects the windows were cut out with a penknife. No character can speak authoritatively from a space that is being continually cut into ribbons of light.'[36]

Humphries does not simply replicate the aesthetic of film noir through her painterly process. She pushes at the boundaries of painting by giving her viewer a cinema-like experience. In an oscillation between perception through a window and in the reflective silver paint, we embark on a restless search within and of the image. In motion around

38. Black Sheep 1999

Oil on linen
157.5 × 198.1 cm (62 × 78 in)

39. Horizontal #18 1997

Oil on linen
228.6 × 257.8 cm (90 × 101½ in)

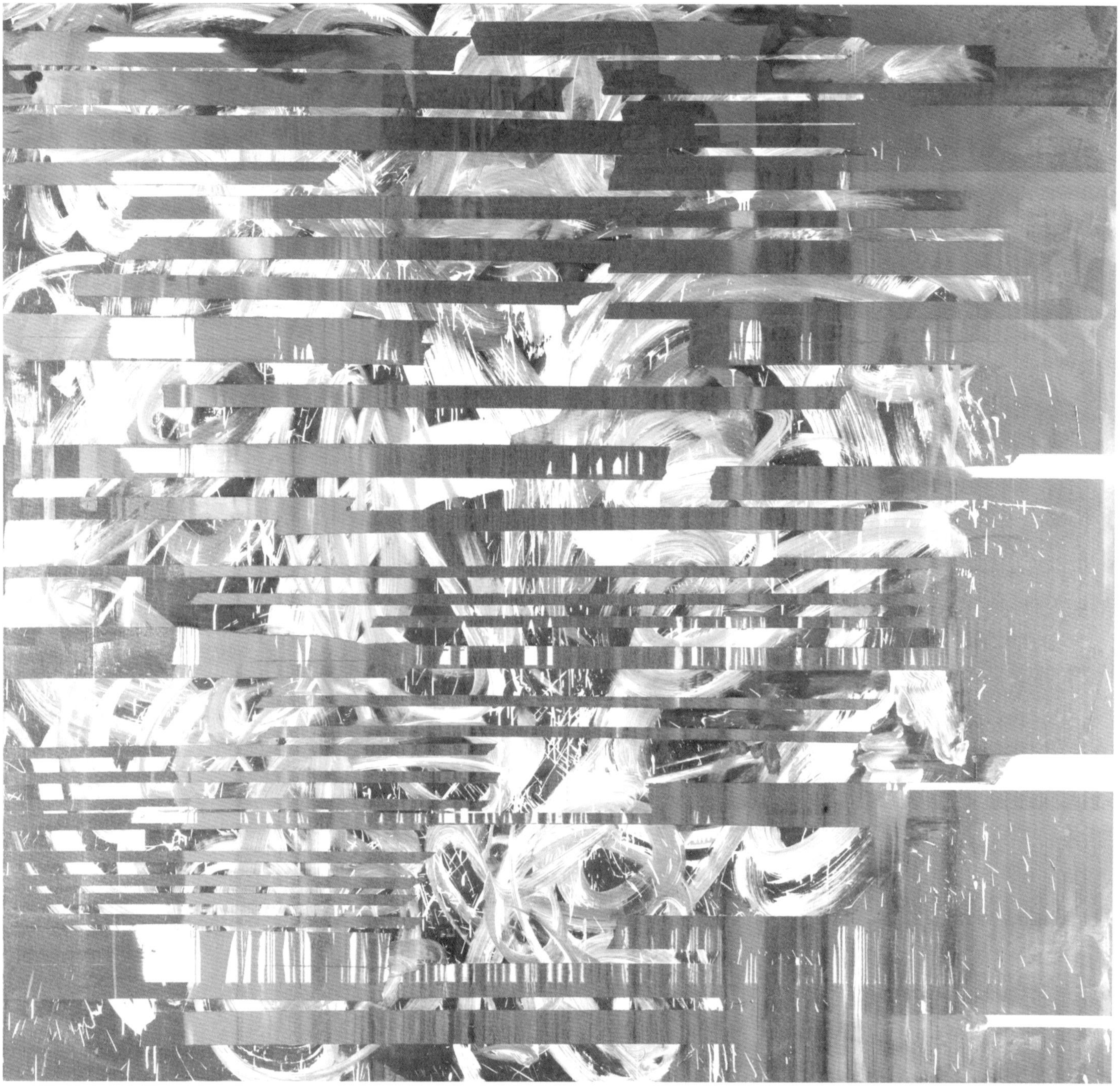

40. Blondnoir 2008

Oil and enamel on linen
228.6 × 243.8 cm (90 × 96 in)

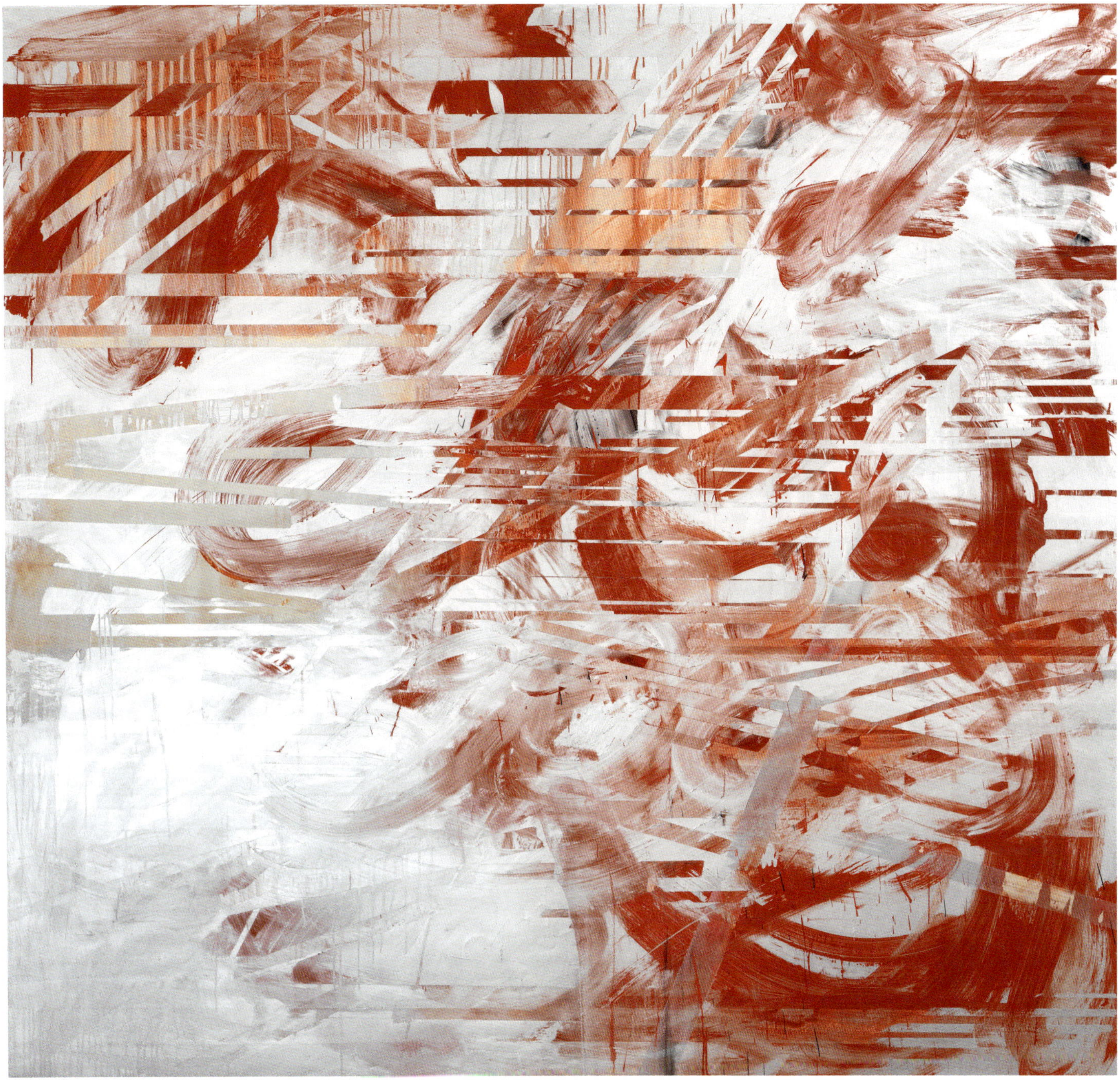

41. Dirty Mind 2008

Oil and enamel on linen
228.6 × 243.8 cm (90 × 96 in)
Zabludowicz Collection, London

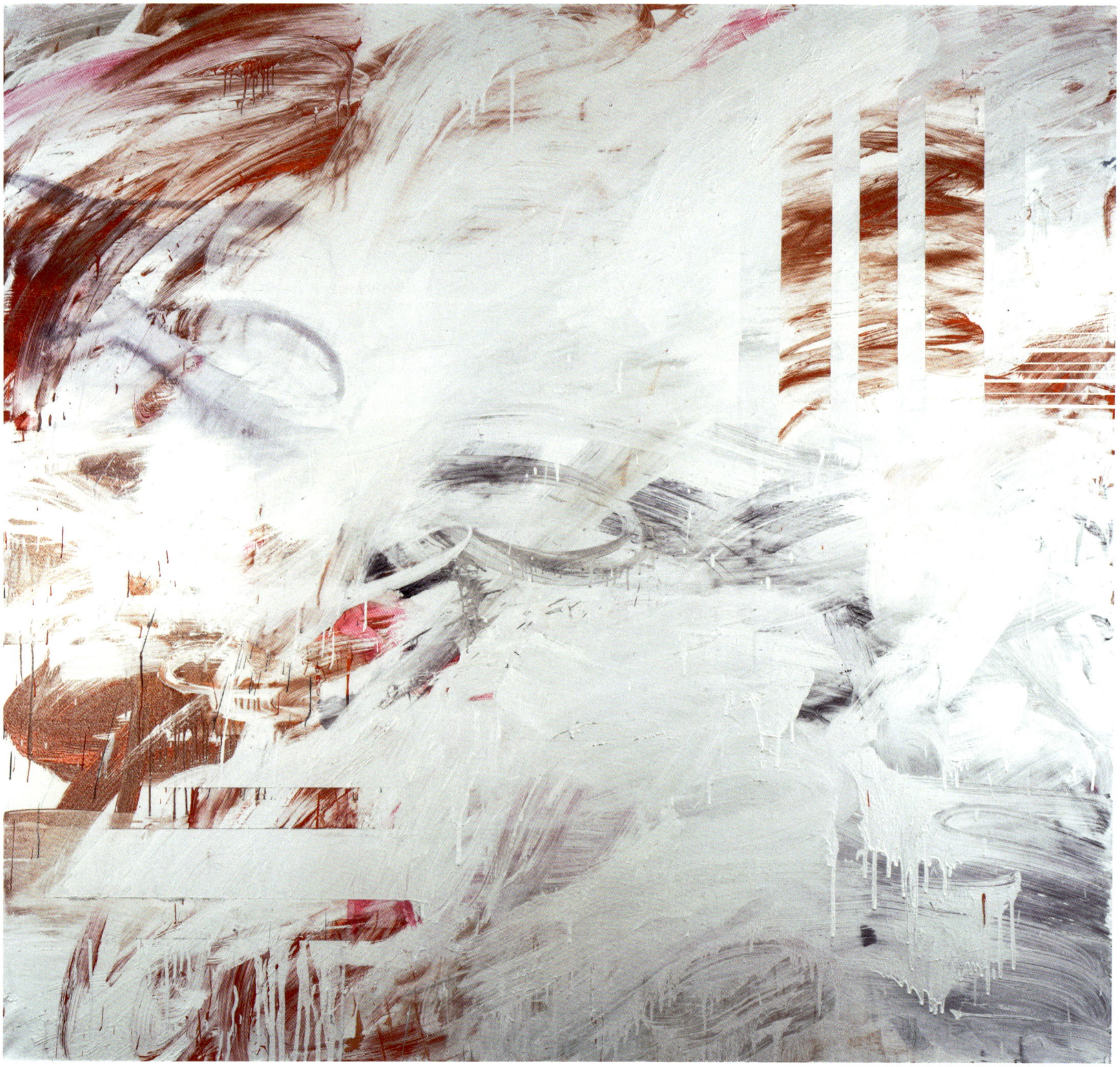

42. Brown Stare 2006

Oil on linen
182.9 × 198.1 cm (72 × 78 in)

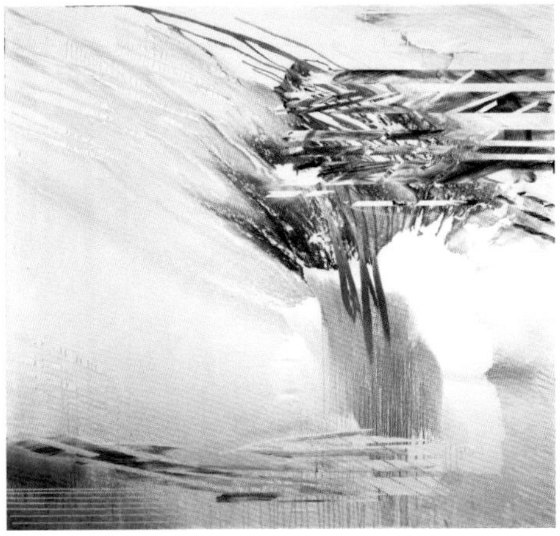

43. Untitled 2007

Oil on linen
228.6 × 243.8 cm (90 × 96 in)
Fondation Louis Vuitton

these images, the viewer is thrown into a conundrum amid the clouds of silver and coloured paint. We feel the agitation and anxiety of the surface of a work such as *Brown Stare*, 2006 (fig.42). Humphries's goal of holding the viewer's attention is achieved with the silver screens keeping the viewer looking, endlessly fascinated, as if watching fleeting images at the movies. And yet, unlike the cinematic audience, we continue to stretch and strain to see behind the silver slats. We are aware that we are looking at an object, even when it disappears into a flat surface. We remain conscious that we are looking at paintings.

Like the cinematic image, and distinct from the sculptural surface of Humphries's stencilled works, there is no dimensionality to these paintings. Humphries's process of layering and removing paint is meticulous. The black or colour is applied first, the silver over the top, before the surface is scraped away so that all pigment exists on the same surface. The works are, on the one hand, akin to the cinema image: a two-dimensional surface in which all elements are equal, and yet give the illusion of three-dimensionality. On the other hand, the two-dimensional surface entices the viewer into an experience of motion, thus encouraging us to recognise it as a three-dimensional object. The collapse of figure and ground created through Humphries's language of painting makes the experience recognisable and unrecognisable, like and unlike the cinema, like and unlike painting.

Nevertheless, the cinema offers multiple points of view or perspectives within a single frame through camera movement and editing. That is, in the cinema, multiple images within a fixed frame are put into motion for a passive viewer. Humphries appropriates this possibility of motion and translates it to painting. However, in painting, the viewer's body is put into motion, and while looking at a fixed frame, we are guided towards seeing ephemeral images. The viewer's body, not the camera, enables movement within a static frame. In another layer of complexity, Humphries's abstraction also has a history in painting. In the early twentieth century, the creation of movement and multiple perspectives on a static canvas was the intention of cubist painting, photocollage, and architectural transparency. In its twenty-first-century iteration on Humphries's canvases, fragmented modernism is the result of a peripatetic vision.

44. Horizontal #16 1998

Oil and enamel on linen
228.6 × 259.1 cm (90 × 102 in)

3 Beyond the Threshold

> 'I'm forced to accept this oblivion, of being outside painting's history, as a starting point perhaps for creating a new outside from within conditions as I see them.' – Jacqueline Humphries [37]

Humphries repeatedly paints limits, false edges, frames within frames, windows, and mirrors. She pushes the frame to the centre, leaving areas of colour to fall off the canvas. At times, the frame is thrown on as an afterthought, and at others – in works such as *[_]*, 2014 (fig.45), for example – frames appear to be both underneath and on top of gestural marks. Alternatively, what might be perceived from a distance as a frame placed over a layer of paint is in fact a smooth, even surface that has been achieved through scraping away the build-up of paint. Humphries's frames hover in the spaces between paint applied through the stencil: a shadow appears and disappears as we look at the frame within the painting. These ethereal and ephemeral frames shift depending on our distance from the paintings.

In Humphries's paintings of the 1990s, the frame within the frame resembles that of the cinema screens as seen in, for example, the *Horizontal* paintings. Works such as *Horizontal #18*, 1997 (fig.39), reproduce the standard aspect ratio of the cinema screen, and others such as *Horizontal #5*, 1997 (fig.65), have thick brushstrokes that recall the path of a film camera's horizontal pan. Ironically, the frames and edges, those places on and organizational structures of the canvas are also the places of most uncertainty in Humphries's paintings. The most resilient and traditionally reliable aspects of painting – frame and support – are the sites where everything we think that we know about painting is challenged. We end up in front of, for example, *Horizontal #18* asking: Where does this painting begin and end? Is it a panel within a panel? Is it half of a painting? Standing before *Horizontal #5*, we may ask: Why is the image split? Is it two separate canvases? Such questions born of confusion are often asked of modernist abstraction. The innovation, 'the outside' as Humphries would have it, comes in her pilfering of the age-old tropes of lines, structures, frames, and limits, to create spaces into which she introduces everything that is not meant to be in a painting. Ironically, this is how she keeps painting alive.

Historically, the frame of a painting has functioned as everything from a cultural marker – size, material, ornateness – to a material and conceptual boundary between reality and representation. The frame has been used by the art market to stamp the work, carrying the signatures of dealers and collectors. Frames define the painting as an object. Frames have also been used to define painting as a window onto the

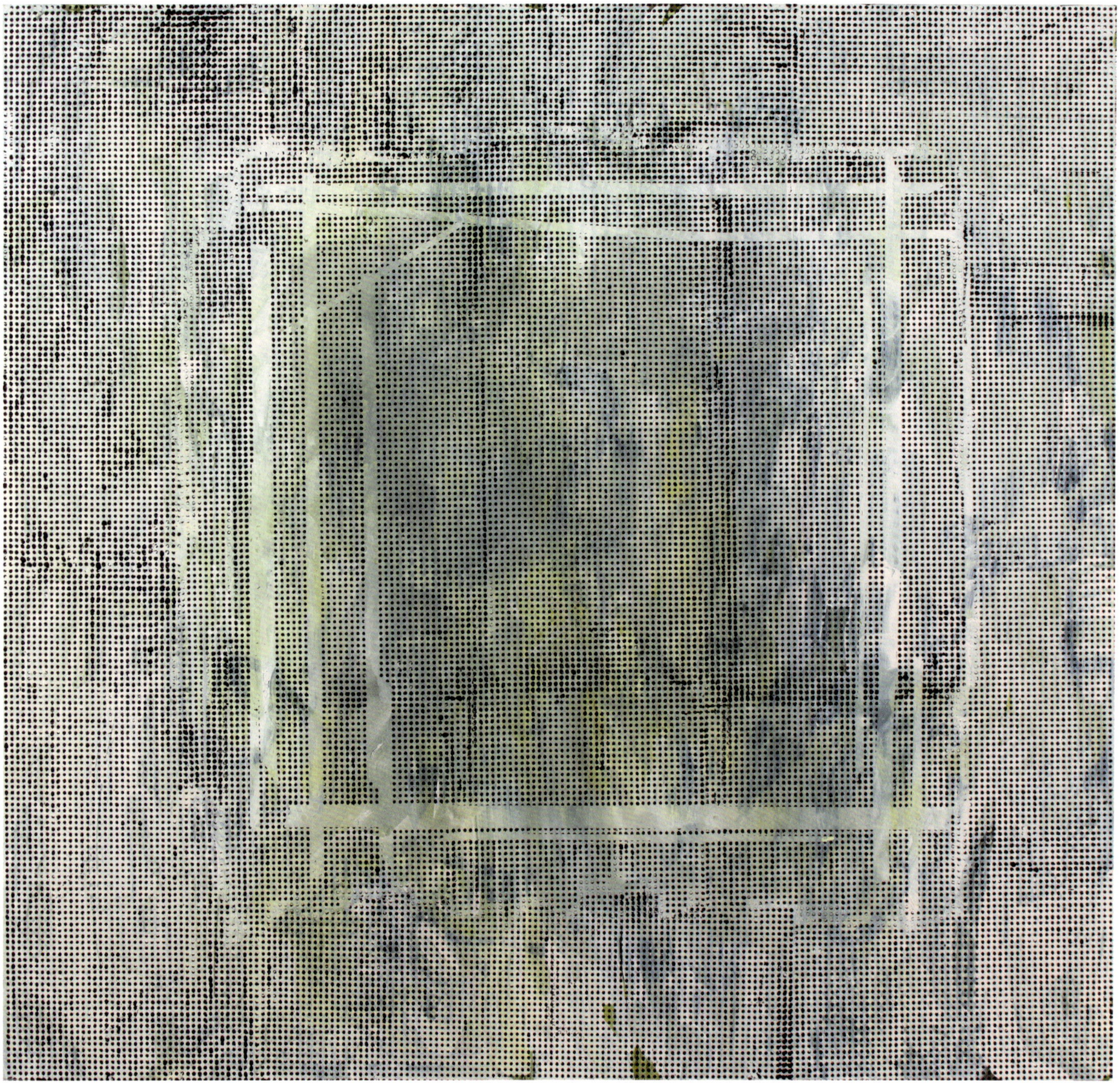

45. [_] 2014

Oil on linen
228.6 × 243.8 cm (90 × 96 in)

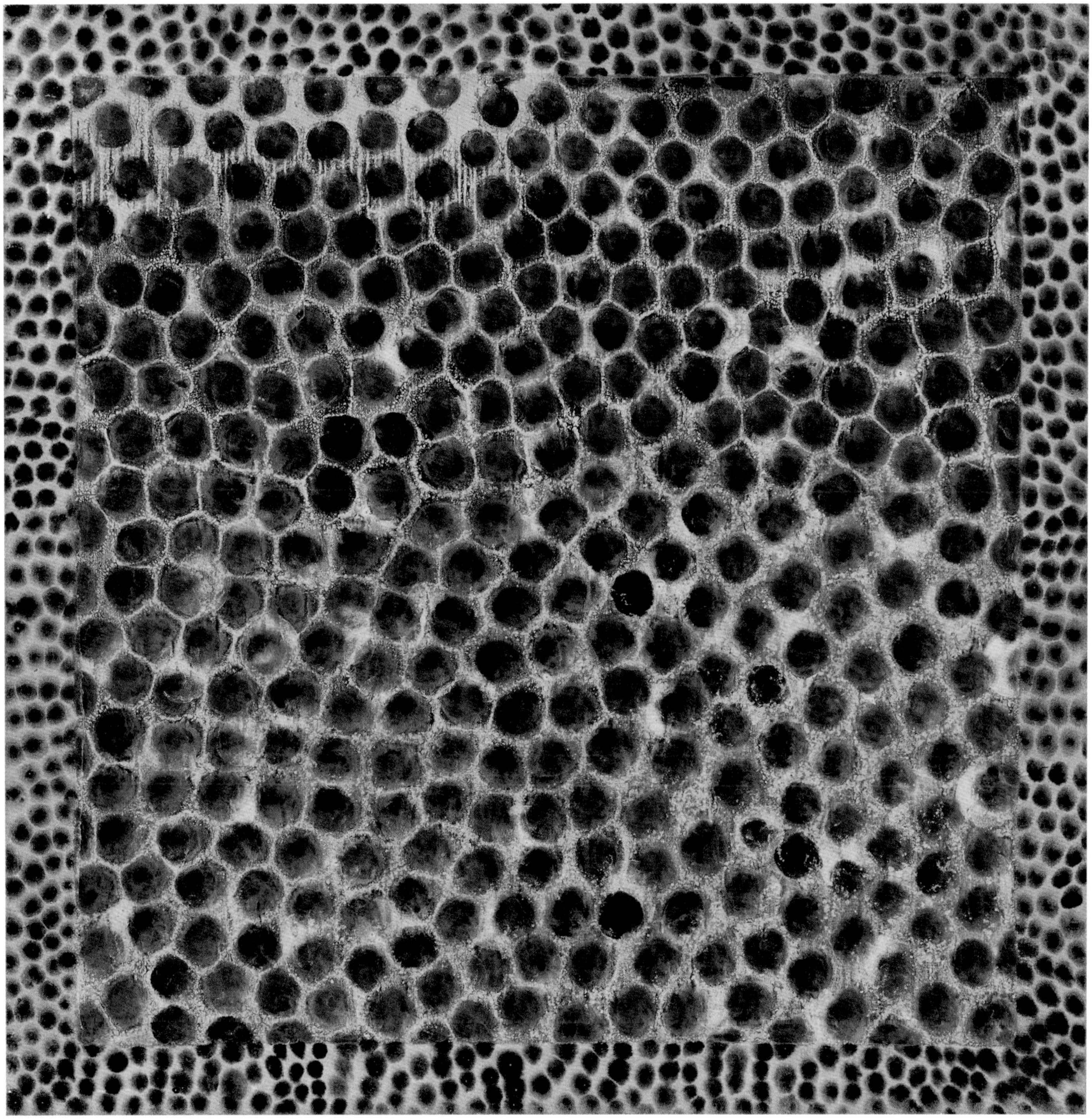

46. Untitled 1988

Oil on linen
116.8 × 116.8 cm (46 × 46 in)

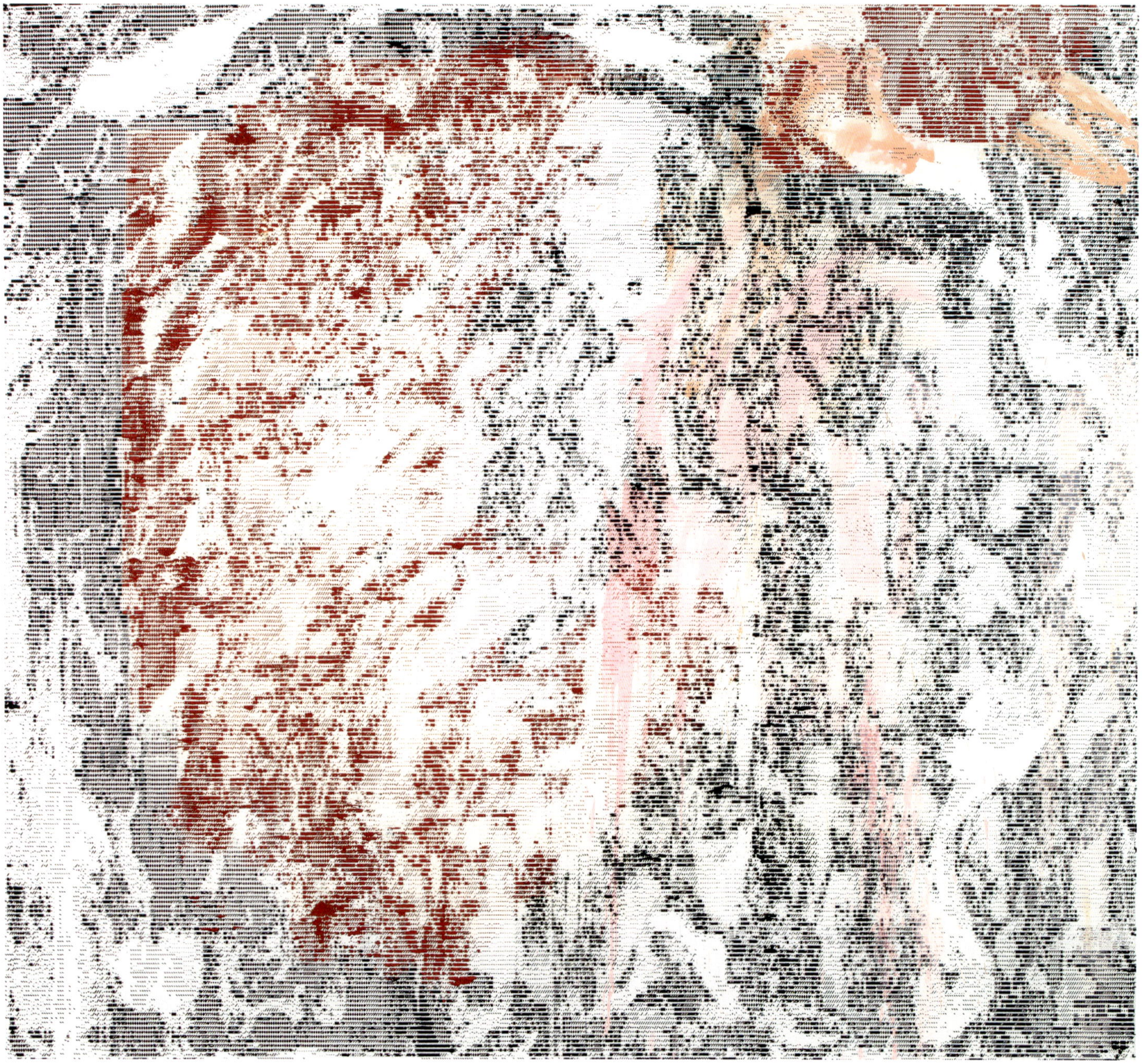

47. YHY/// 2020

Oil on linen
254 x 281.9 cm (100 x 111 in)

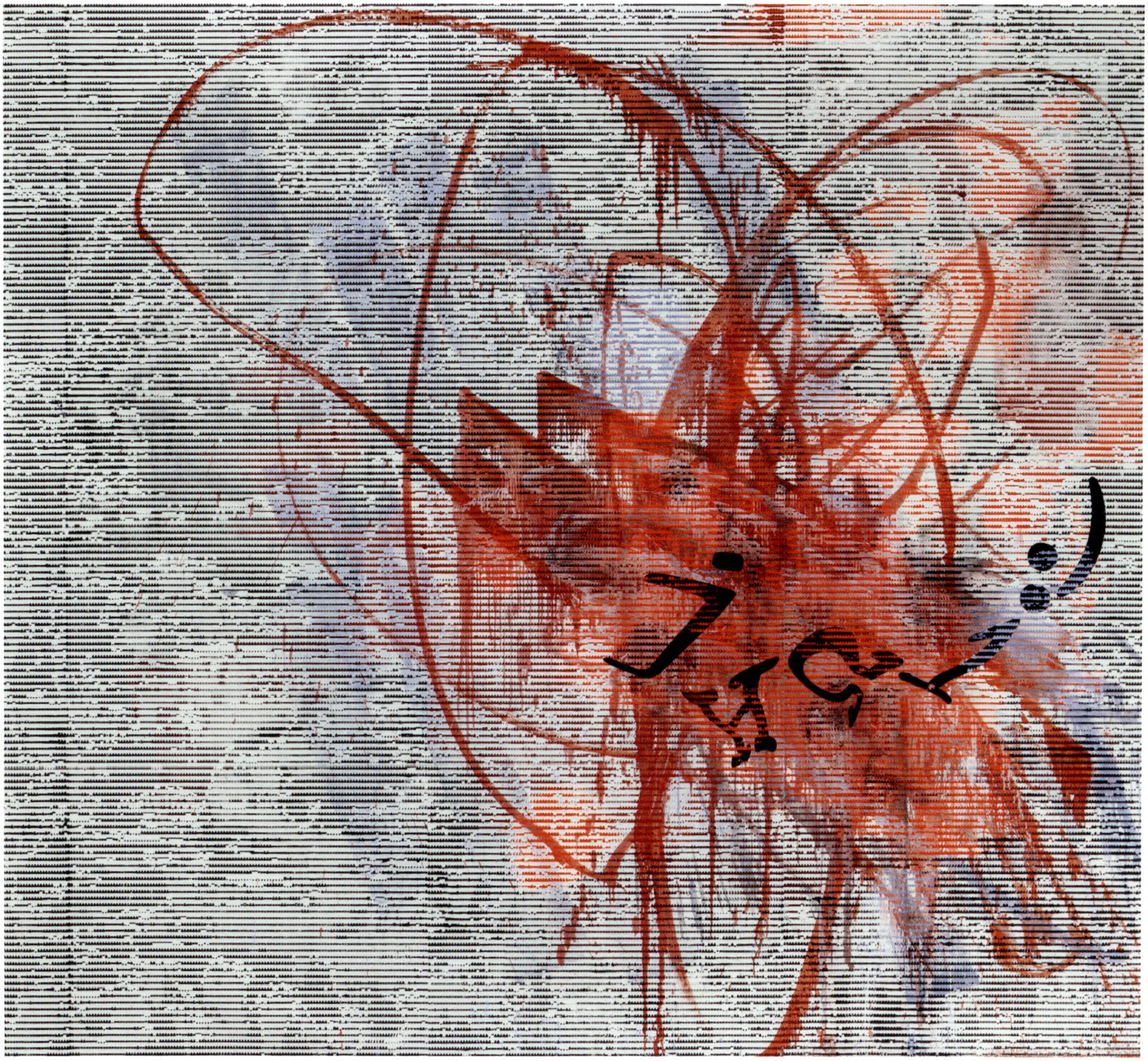

48. jHΩ1:) 2018

Oil on linen
289.6 x 322.6 cm (114 x 127 in)

world. From the late nineteenth century, the frame confirmed the painting as a discrete illusory world.[38] As the twentieth century progressed, painters frequently discarded the frame. Abstract painting did away with the physical frame and questioned the invisible frame given it by the concerns of the artist, the historical and cultural conditions of production, the ideology of consumption. For early twentieth-century abstract painting, the removal of the frame exposed the otherwise invisible institutional and economic frames.[39] Its removal drew attention to the frames, edges, and boundaries that determined a painting in the first place.[40] Likewise, mid-century American artists such as Frank Stella used the frame as the place of innovation. His unconventionally shaped stretchers announced that rectangular frames were over. If painting was to develop, the frame had to be reshaped. Humphries does something different again. Frames, limits, grids proliferate on and across her paintings, only to be transgressed. Humphries does not literally reject the frame, but rather insults it by allowing an array of otherwise excluded forms inside the painting's limits. Thus, when seen through the figure of the frame, we find Humphries's 'oblivion', to use her word, as a place and conceptual space within.

Humphries has always painted gridded structures, frames within frames, motifs denoting limits repeated within single paintings and from work to work. She also includes elements emphasising the formal dimensions and shape of the canvas: geometrical form, limits, and edges are often the centre of attention, though not the centre of painting.[41] Subsequently, she introduces rogue elements that do not, strictly speaking, belong on a painting, such as emojis and CAPTCHA symbols. Furthermore, as we have seen in a work such as *:cat:* (fig.23), no layer, icon, or image is reliably self-contained. Depending upon our viewing position, it might become the background. Alternatively, the object or figure can be on the edge, denoting the limit. Painting thus expands into unexplored possibilities. Humphries uses structural figures and frames to create further democracy on the canvas. Frames open painting up to embrace the invisible frames that condition our viewing processes. For Humphries, these happen to be the screens of video games, movies, computers, smartphones, and other elements of the contemporary visual landscape. The spaces of Humphries's screens are characterised by overlapping layers, frontality, and a simultaneity of above, below, in front of, and behind. The networked screens on which our constantly-updating-and-refreshed world is created in its own image are the cultural context within which her painting functions.[42] In this way, Humphries liberally introduces images and effects that sit uncomfortably inside the limits of painting as we know it.

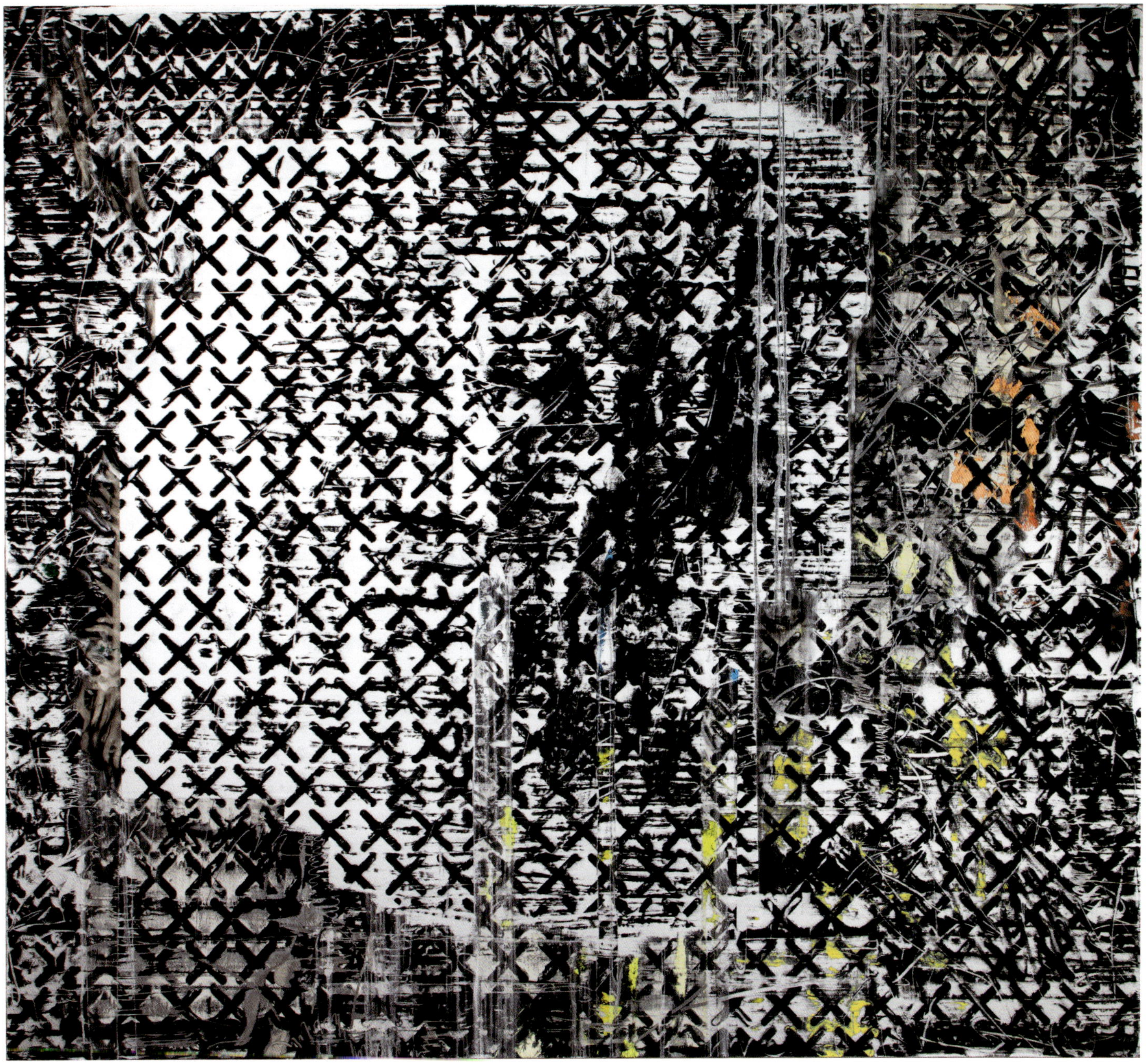

49. Untitled 2015

Oil on linen
254 × 281.9 cm (100 × 111 in)
Glenstone Museum, Potomac, Maryland

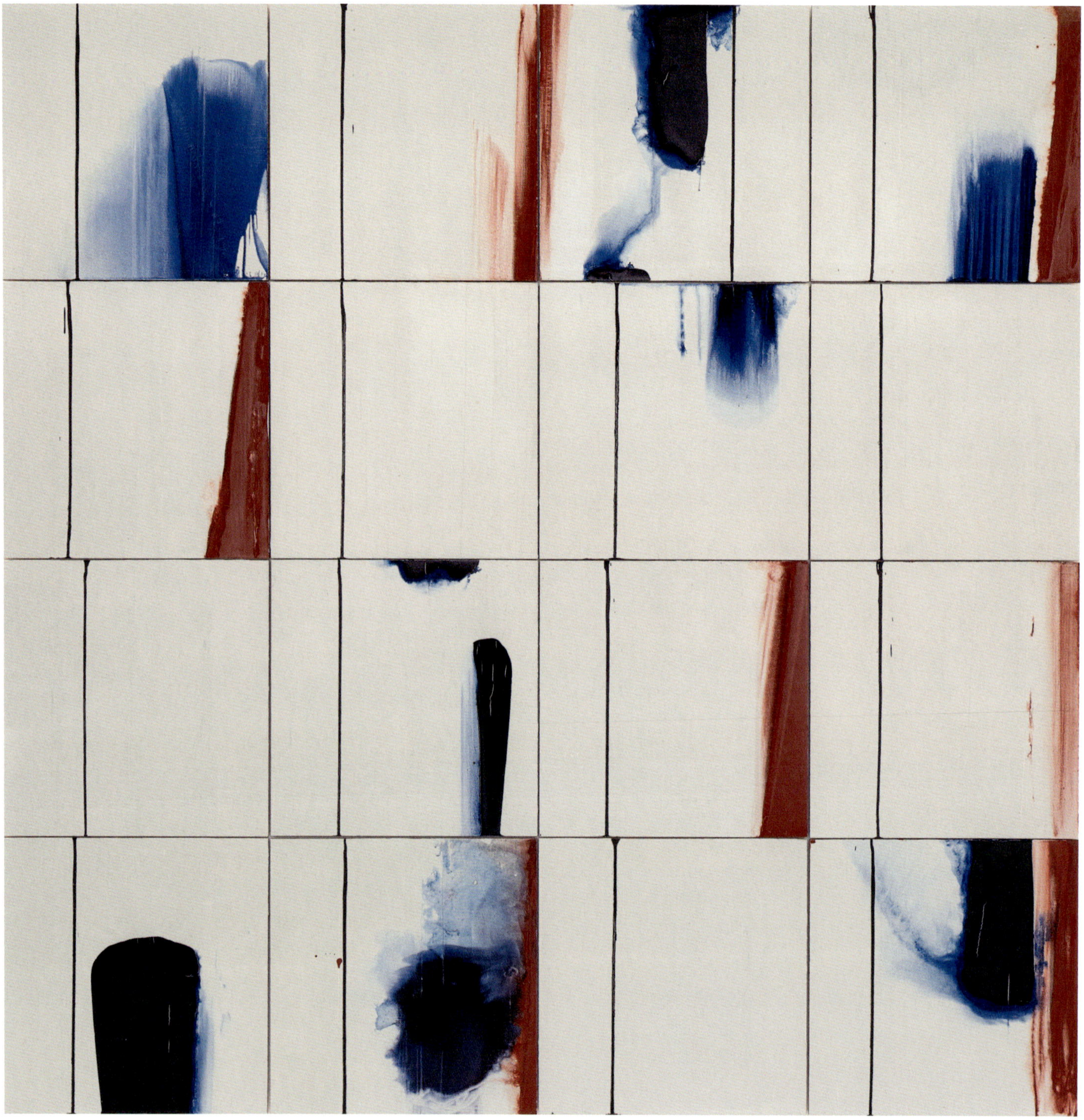

50. Untitled 1994

Oil on wood
225.4 × 225.4 cm (88¾ × 88¾ in)
Zabludowicz Collection, London

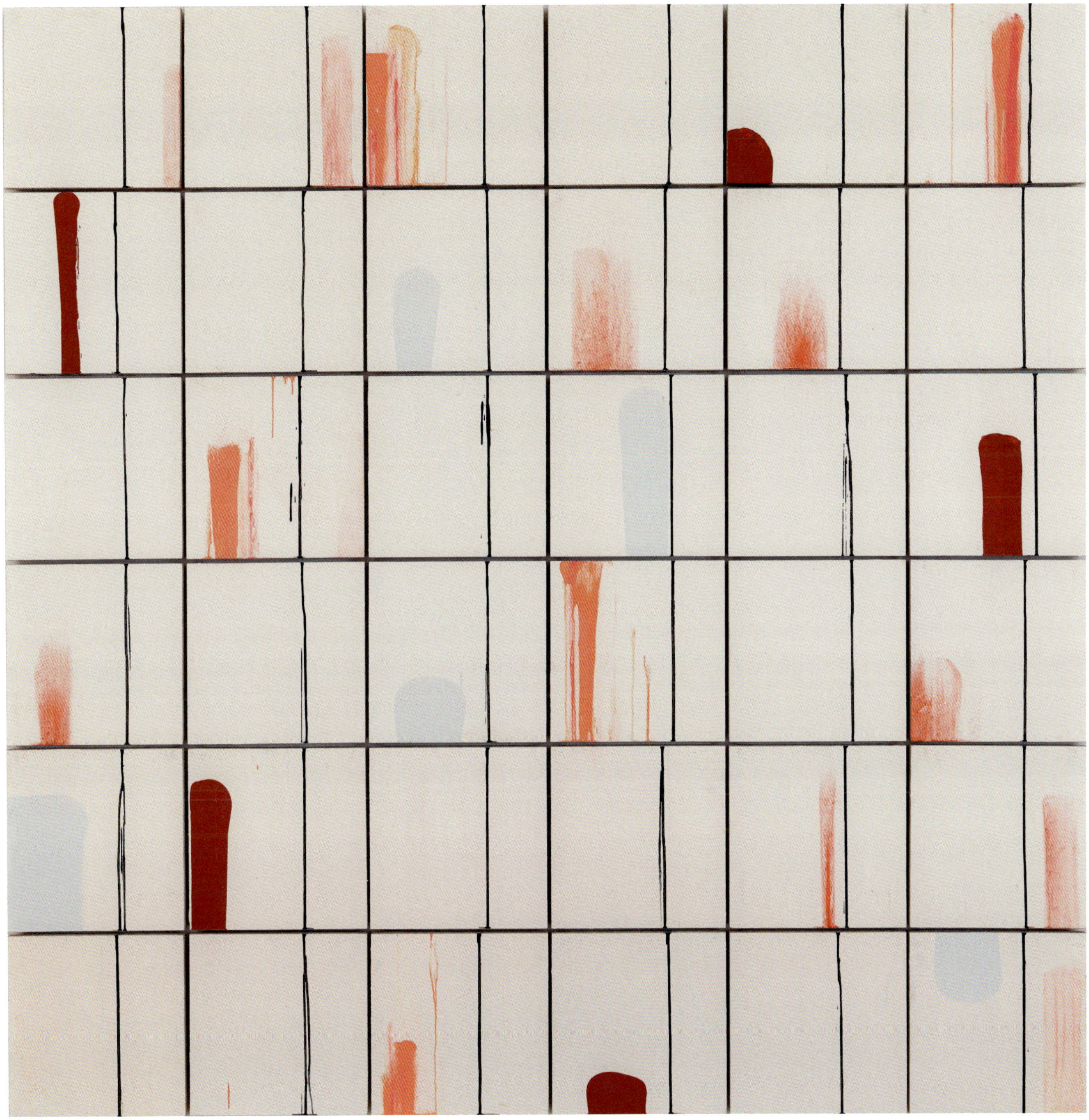

51. Untitled 1995

Oil on wood
213.4 × 213.4 cm (84 × 84 in)

The artist as outsider

Returning to her self-declared identity as an artist working beyond art history's temporal limits, it is unclear what Humphries means, particularly today, at a moment when she enjoys a reputation as an important American painter. It is difficult to see her as literally excluded given that her paintings are housed within the world's great museum collections and regularly enjoy high-profile exhibitions. However, her use of painted framing devices suggests that her outsider status may be conceptually motivated. The proliferation of frames, the pushing of painting off the edge, past the limit as it is represented on the canvases, might be translated as an insistent disrespect for art history. In turn, 'beyond art history' might be translated as a stance or performance, not a reality. She invokes and refers to art history, but only to insult it by saying, 'I'm refusing to adhere to convention, and I don't care if you throw me out of the club. I operate within a new landscape.' She flouts the rules (frames) to create a 'new outside seen from within', a new set of references taken from the contemporary image environment. Thus, when the recurrence of the relationship between abstract painter and history is transposed to the visual centre, or frame, of paintings such as *[_]* (fig.45), it makes sense within a world of images not simply populated by screens and emojis, but formed in their image.

In the ultimate eschewal of past preoccupations, Humphries combines the modernist visual vocabulary with unorthodox partners: emojis, CAPTCHA symbols, white noise translated into stencils. Thus, the oblivion of which she speaks might be understood as the void of addiction to gaming, for example, or the daze of too much time spent on a technological device. Oblivion is the shallow (unsatisfying) slumber surrounded by white noise of late-night television. These media screens have altered our space-time relations as the cinema did at the turn of the previous century. Ultimately, the proliferation within today's image environment has created confusion, especially between reality and illusion as they are explored in images.

To explain this through reference to another example: in *Four Cat,* 2017 (fig.53), multiple visual signs – 'meh' emoticons, dots, drips, blobs – cohabit the surface with stencils of variously sized cat emojis. These laser-cut stencils are used alongside hand-cut ones that generate the drips, derived from an earlier painting. Together, the cat stencils produce multiple frames vying for attention with this spill of lemon-yellow paint on the left-hand side of the canvas. From a distance, the spread of black dots appears as a screen. Moving towards the painting, more is revealed, and we discover not only the physicality of the image – the texture of paint – but that, up close, the dots reveal themselves as a thick, three-dimensional carpet of cat emojis. Paint of different intensities, viscosities, and modes of application coexists in an experience that reinstates the presentness of painting and simultaneously causes us to question what we are seeing. Artist, painting, viewer come together to complete the narrative of *Four Cat*. When the initial moment passes, and the viewer is no longer confused by its ambiguity, the painting reasserts its existence as a painting.

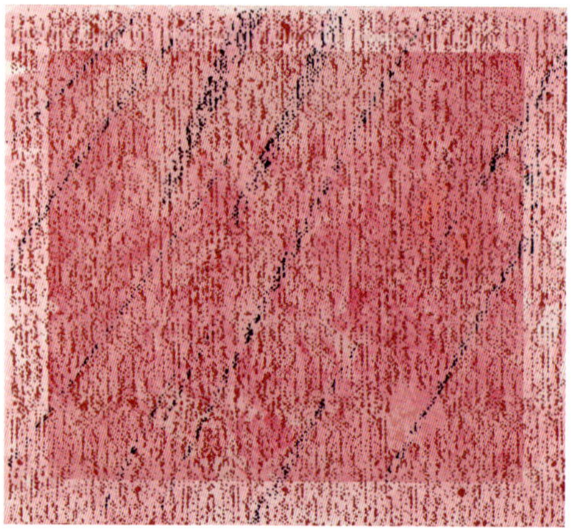

52. ☐ 2015

Oil and enamel on linen
254 × 281.9 cm (100 × 111 in)

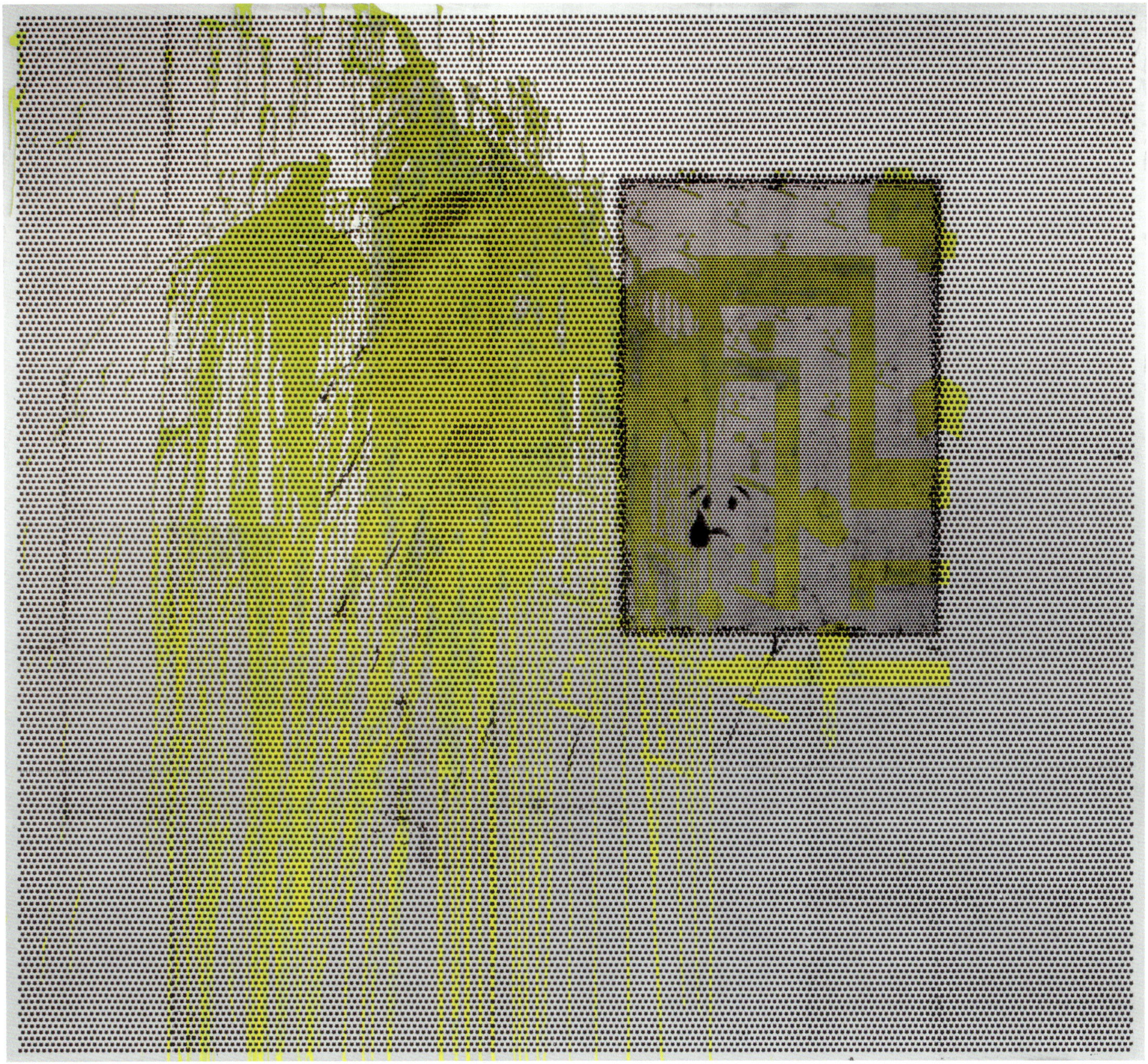

53. Four Cat 2017

Oil on linen
254 × 281.9 cm (100 × 111 in)

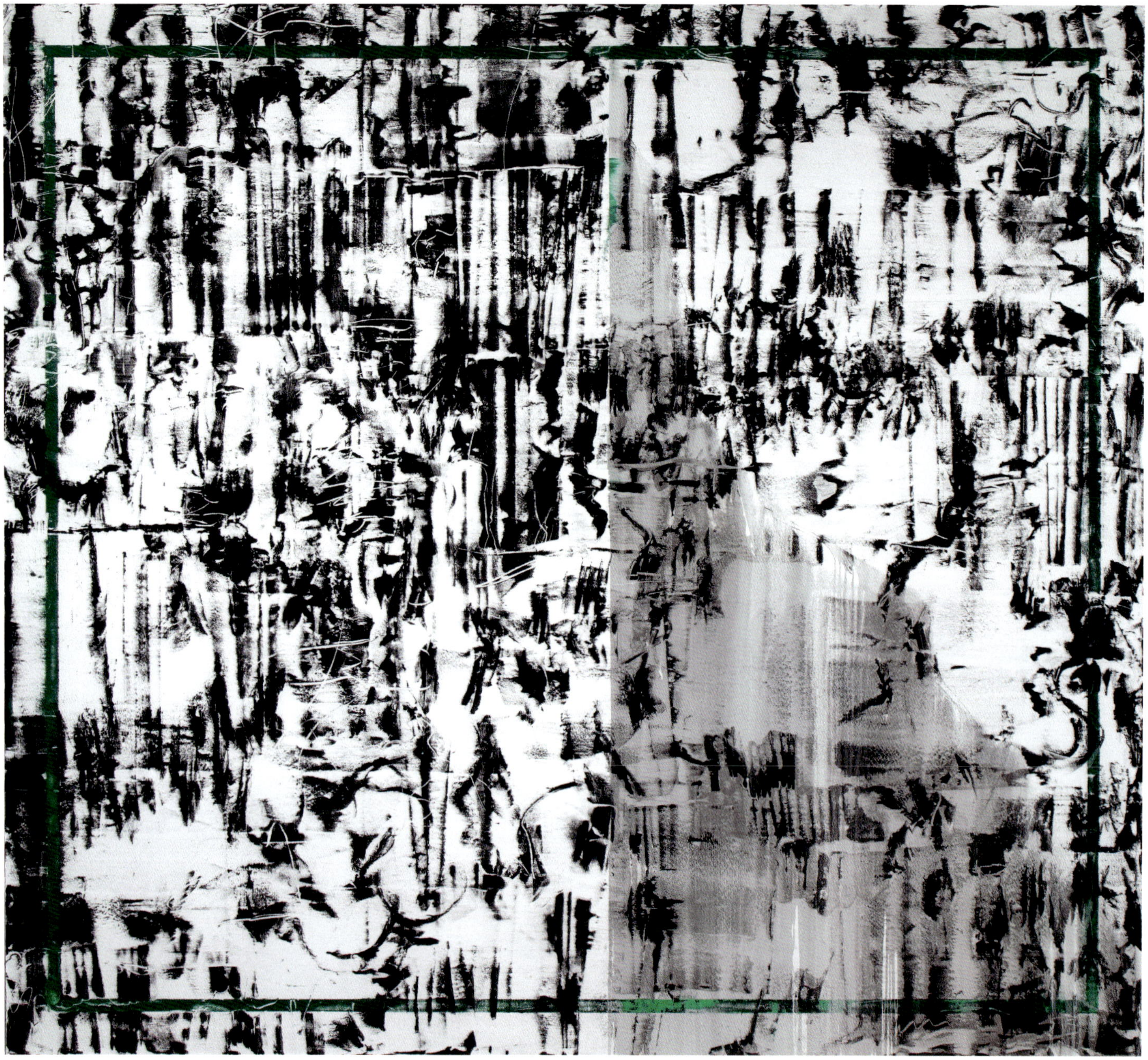

54. 41/14 2014

Oil on linen
289.6 × 322.6 cm (114 × 127 in)

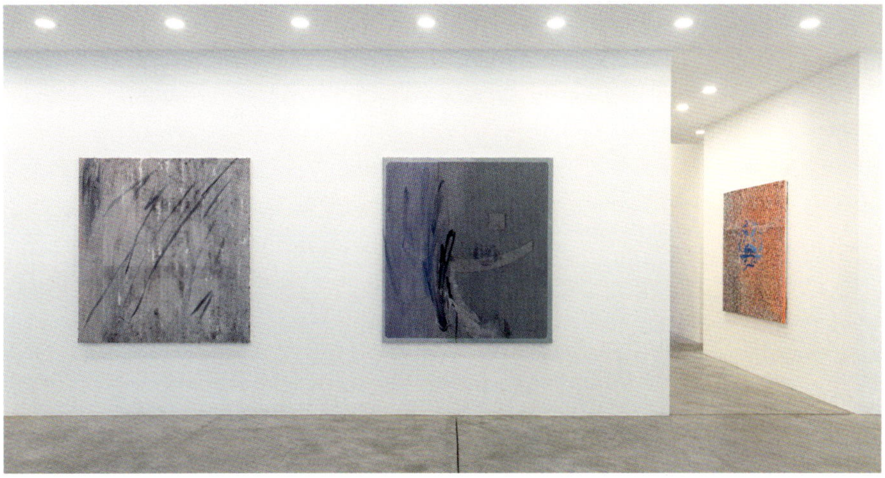

55. Installation view
Galerie Gisela Capitain, Cologne, 2020

The presentness of modernist abstraction, as Fried defined it, is alive and well in Humphries's work. The extraordinariness of Humphries's paintings presents itself, as Fried would say, in a claim made upon the beholder to 'compel our conviction'.[43] However, the 'beyond', or the innovation, of Humphries's paintings comes in their embrace of computer and technological imaging, video games, the movies, and emojis inside a painted frame. This, in turn, introduces a presentness that verges into a pleasure or recognition of the immersion that might be had with a screen image. Humphries stands within the modernist frame and welcomes all that was excluded from Fried's characterisation of modern art. Commercial culture and its alienation, popular imagery, and its deleterious effects are not simply included in this new presentness, they are generously stirred into the mix and given value. They continually inform the viewing experience, even if they are not replicated by the painting. Consequently, the unique presentness of Humphries's paintings invites the viewer inside their performance while simultaneously being observer to it.

The beyond of painting's history – emerging from within its frames – can only be recognised within the context of another relationship: namely, that between painting and viewer. The pulsation of the painted surface of a work such as *Untitled*, 2014 (fig.12), seen at a distance or in reproduction are reminiscent of the distortions of a defective LCD screen. Lines and colours appear in the wrong places, like unpredictable patterns of static buzz. A frame within the frame that could also be one of many nested windows open on a computer screen convinces the viewer that they are looking at an image within an image. Viewing the painting in person from a midway point, the surface gleams thanks to the silver. It teases the viewer, reminding them of the glare from a desensitised touch screen imploring a stroke or a swipe. How we look at the painting is informed by computerised and technological screens. It is, by contrast, art on a gallery wall that we cannot touch. In addition, the paint invades the stencilled frame within the frame: the static and swirls of an image 'on the blink' proliferate within the window. Like the screens that determine our visual relationships, nothing is contained or limited by Humphries's frames within frames. Here, the singular frame of a perspectival painting has given way to a multiplicity of windows, nested frames on a screen.[44] However, the viewer's experience is still anchored to the existence of the painting as object, even if it is reproduced in a book or represented on a screen. Our knowledge of painting gives access to the picture's departure from the history of its medium. Lastly, the physicality of the viewer's body in relation to the object also defines the work's specific ephemerality. Painting gives us an experience that draws on what we know through our relationship to technology, but that could only be had with a painting.

Unlike Barnett Newman's zip, for example, the multiple frames of Humphries's paintings do not obstruct the viewer's fall into their depths. Rather, the frames create a new relationship between two physical bodies – the painting's and the viewer's. What started as the work's structure – the stencil – begins to expose our shifting, uncertain relationship to painting, transforming it into something beyond painting as we once knew it. If we use Slavoj Žižek's discussion of the political parallax of art as an interpretive frame, Humphries creates multiple gaps: between artist and painting, painting and history, painting and viewer, viewer and the historico-cultural moment of interaction. The 'beyond' on the inside is the parallax internal to these gaps or interstices created through reference to the technological imagescape.

Humphries's exploitation of frames and limits to create innovative paintings spills over into her use of sequences. She says, 'I think of my work in sequence more than in series, because as I work on many canvases at once, the ideas are flowing through all of them, until eventually, like in musical chairs, the ideas find their place in certain objects.'[45] No work is a self-contained site of possibility. Rather, meaning emerges across the decades-long development of her paintings. Humphries repeats this trope of breaching frames – differently – over and across multiple works and decades. A bird's-eye view of her career also reveals stops, turns, and new approaches to painting. She segues to new forms, marks, and tools of application. Yet she always comes back to her habit of pilfering the vocabulary and expression of paintings from the past, both her own and those of other artists. Repetition is another modernist trope (or frame) to be pilfered. Moreover, temporality moves paradigmatically as well as historically within a painting. That is, everything makes sense within the context of contemporary visual culture. Despite Humphries's understanding of her works as belonging to a sequence rather than a series, the mode of seeing a multiplicity of discrete images in adjacent organisation – whether through split screens, multiple screens, or overlapping windows – follows the logic of the series. The ideas might 'find their place in certain objects', but they are taken up again at a later date to restart the process of searching. There is no definitive endpoint for these iterations.

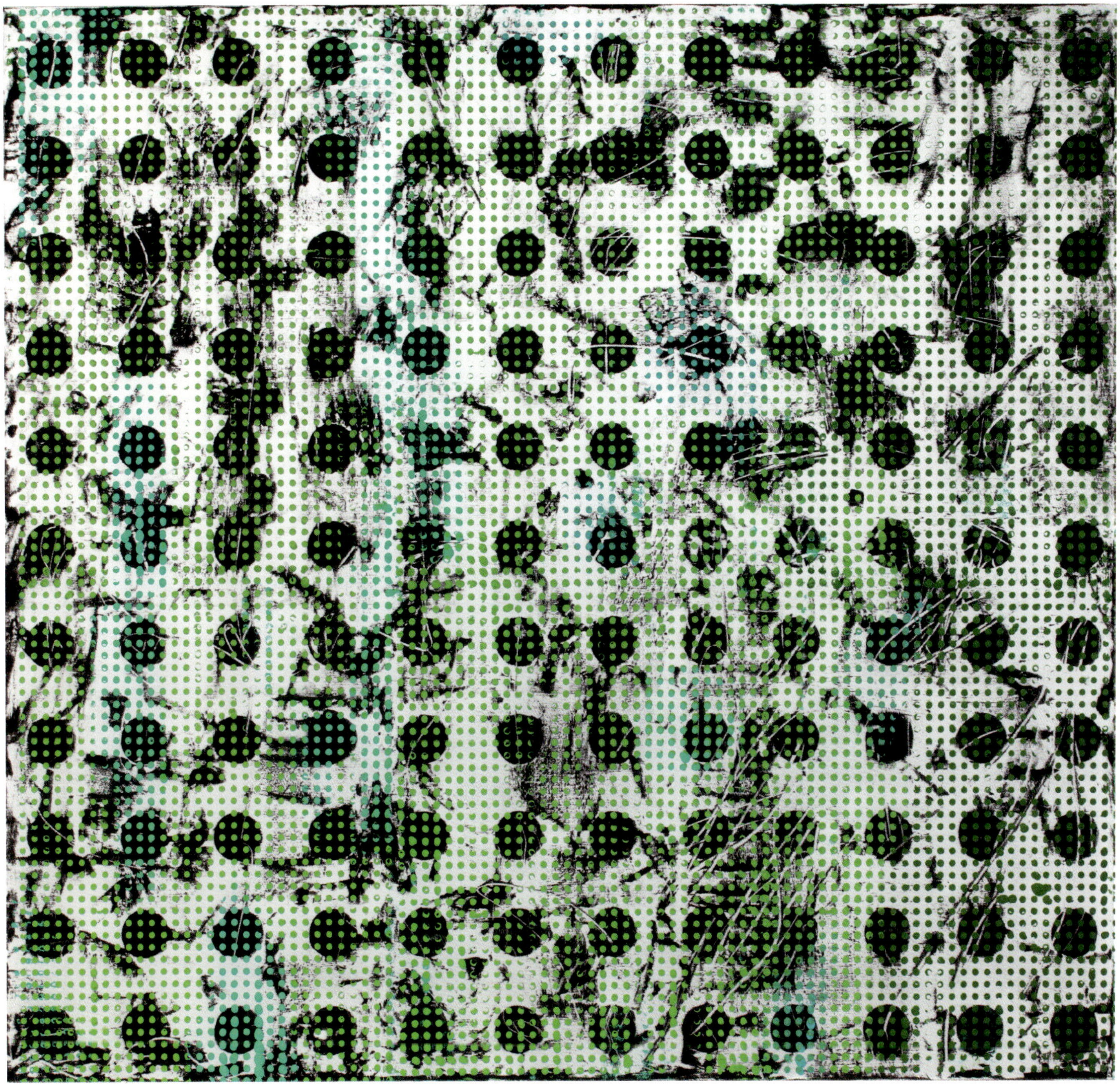

56. Alpha3 2014

Oil on linen
228.6 × 254 cm (90 × 100 in)

57. Nobody's Fool 2013

Oil on linen
228.6 × 243.8 cm (90 × 96 in)
Collection SFMOMA; Purchase, by exchange, through fractional gifts of Elaine McKeon and Shirley Ross Davis

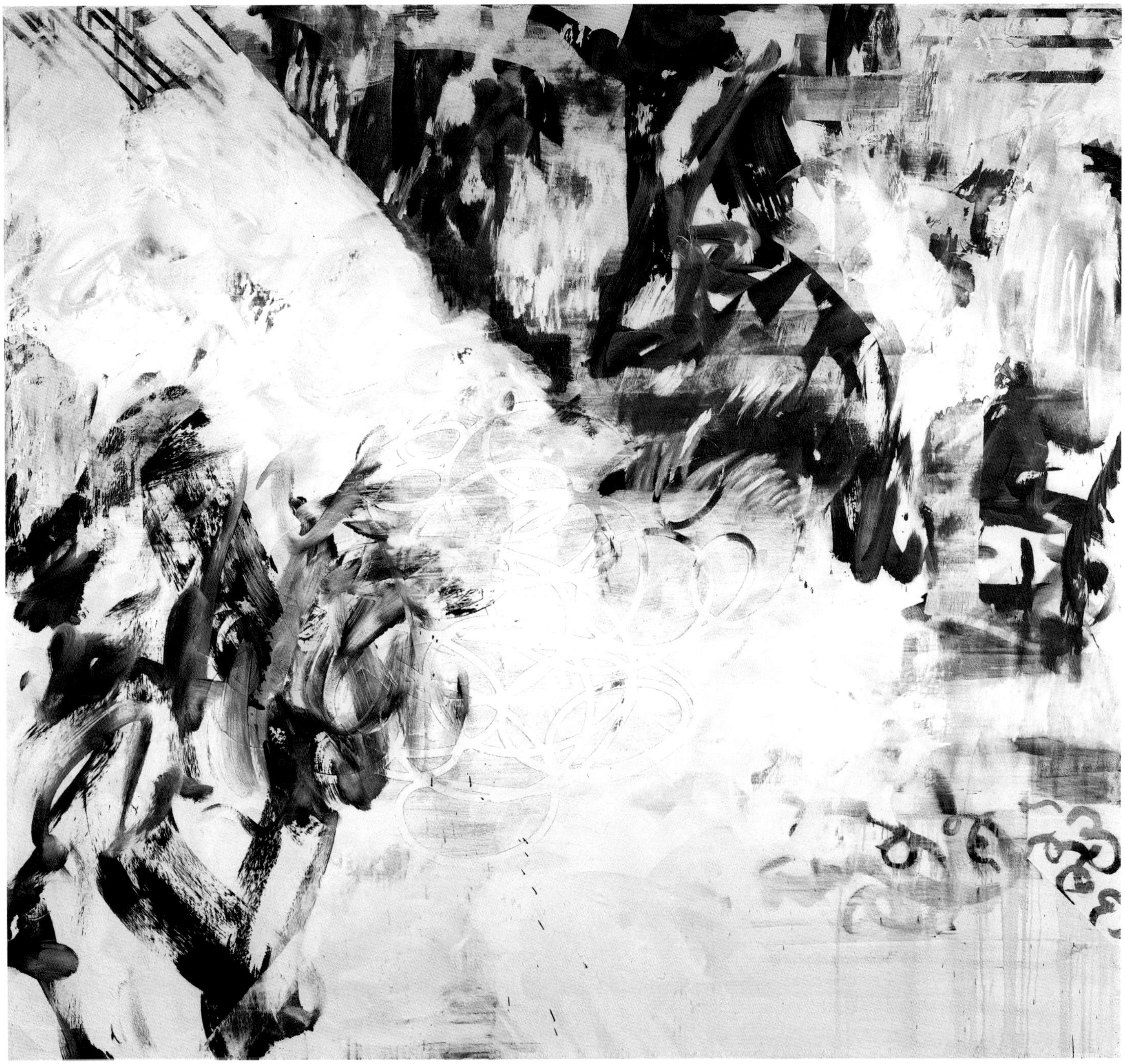

58. Narcissus 2010

Oil on linen
203.2 × 221 cm (80 × 87 in)

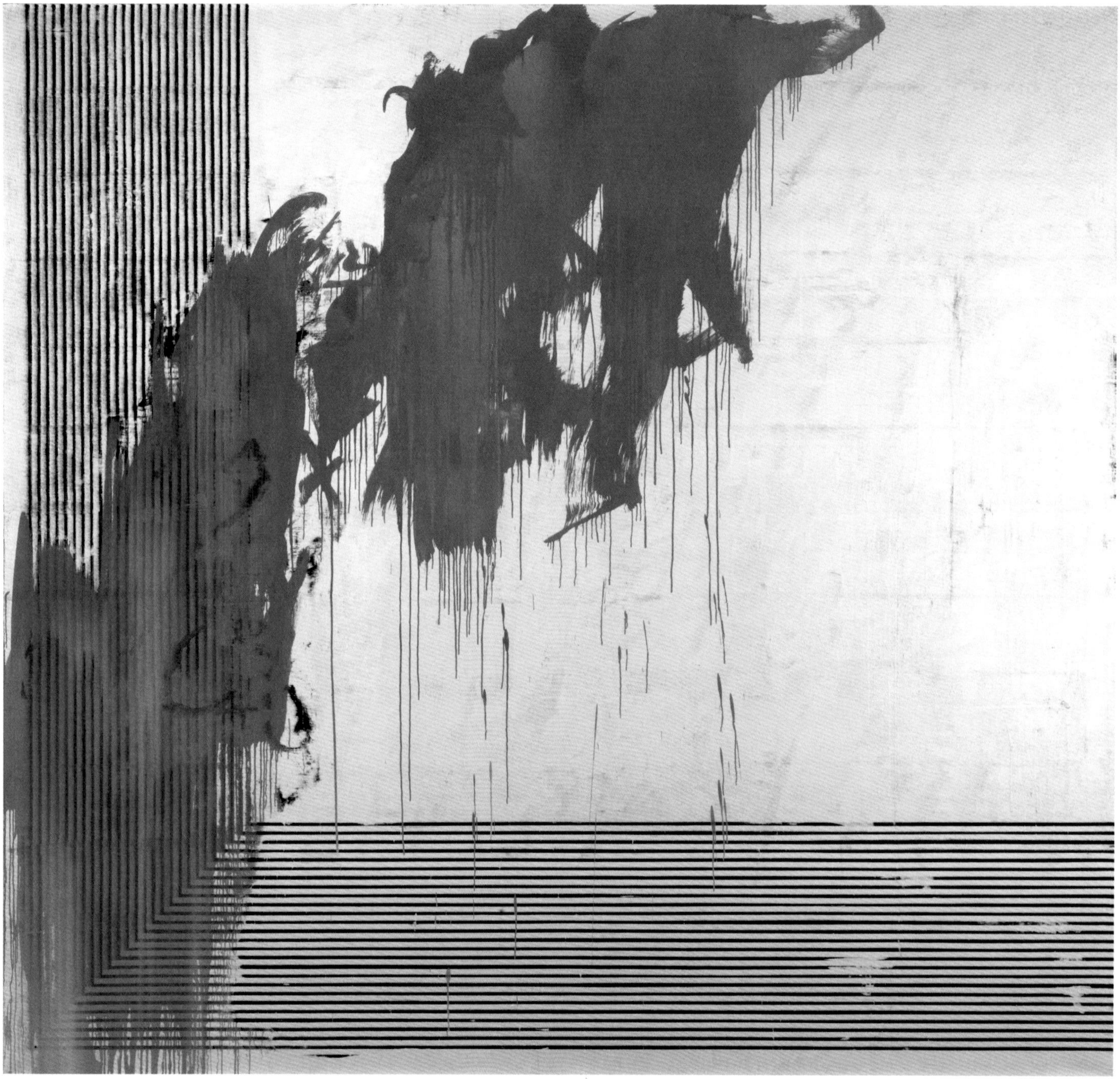

59. Untitled 2012

Oil on linen
228.6 × 243.8 cm (90 × 96 in)

A proliferation of frames

In the early 2010s, Humphries's frames and edges directly referenced computer screens. Paintings such as *Untitled*, 2012 (fig.59), use the motif of multiple stacked edges of open windows on a computer screen. In other works, such as *Narcissus*, 2010 (fig.58), parallel lines in the top right-hand corner and falling from the top-left along the diagonal become occluded; a heterogeneity of windows is thus transformed and transposed onto painting. The infinity of open windows on the computer screen unwittingly reveals the abstraction of the interface. When windows are referenced on Humphries's paintings, they simultaneously become the point at which proliferation continues to infinity. This is the beyond (both computer screen and painting) that reveals itself on the painted canvas thanks to the possibility enabled by texture, imperfection, and interventions by the painter's hand. It is, in turn, thanks to these imperfections that our eyes search and move around the canvas. In another characteristic Humphries gesture, the frame within the painting pulls our eye towards it or deflects our attention elsewhere. In *Untitled*, 2007 (fig.43), the frame points to the area of green, gestures that are both inside and outside its limits. On inspection, green begins to appear across the canvas, lurking beneath the silver, pushing against the flow. The movement of silver and green becomes frenetic when they meet black in the top right-hand corner, creating a sense of being churned up. The paint is applied with sponges and brushes, testifying to the hand of the painter, in contrast to the frames that are realised through applying tape.

The multiple frames within frames, like open windows on a computer screen, are cold and flat. Abstract frames and edges pull towards what they are not: tactile areas of colour. Inside and outside, frame and centre discourse in visual languages that come alive on these canvases. True to the proliferation of images and digital dimensionalities promised by a computer screen's nested windows, in Humphries's paintings one image jostles with another inside the space denoted by the frame. Traditionally, the frame and the painted space within it are fixed; on the screen, the relationship is fluid. In turn, abstraction enables Humphries to demonstrate that frames are ephemeral, like images in the contemporary visual landscape. Frames appear and disappear, fall in and out of view. They are always on the verge of being replaced by another frame, overlaid with another image. Thus, Humphries's aesthetic gestures towards the immersive spaces of technological images. And yet nothing could be more painterly: the works beckon us to look at the marks on the canvas, to notice the inconsistencies of the surface, to search for evidence of the artist.

In the silver works from the 2000s, Humphries often composes one or more elements on the diagonal. In *Dark Star*, 2006 (fig.60), sumptuous purple flourishes and silver swishes are cut through with layers of silver revealed through now absent tape. The vibrant silver and purples dance around the top left of the canvas and along a diagonal stretching from bottom left to top right. A sense of folding in the lower

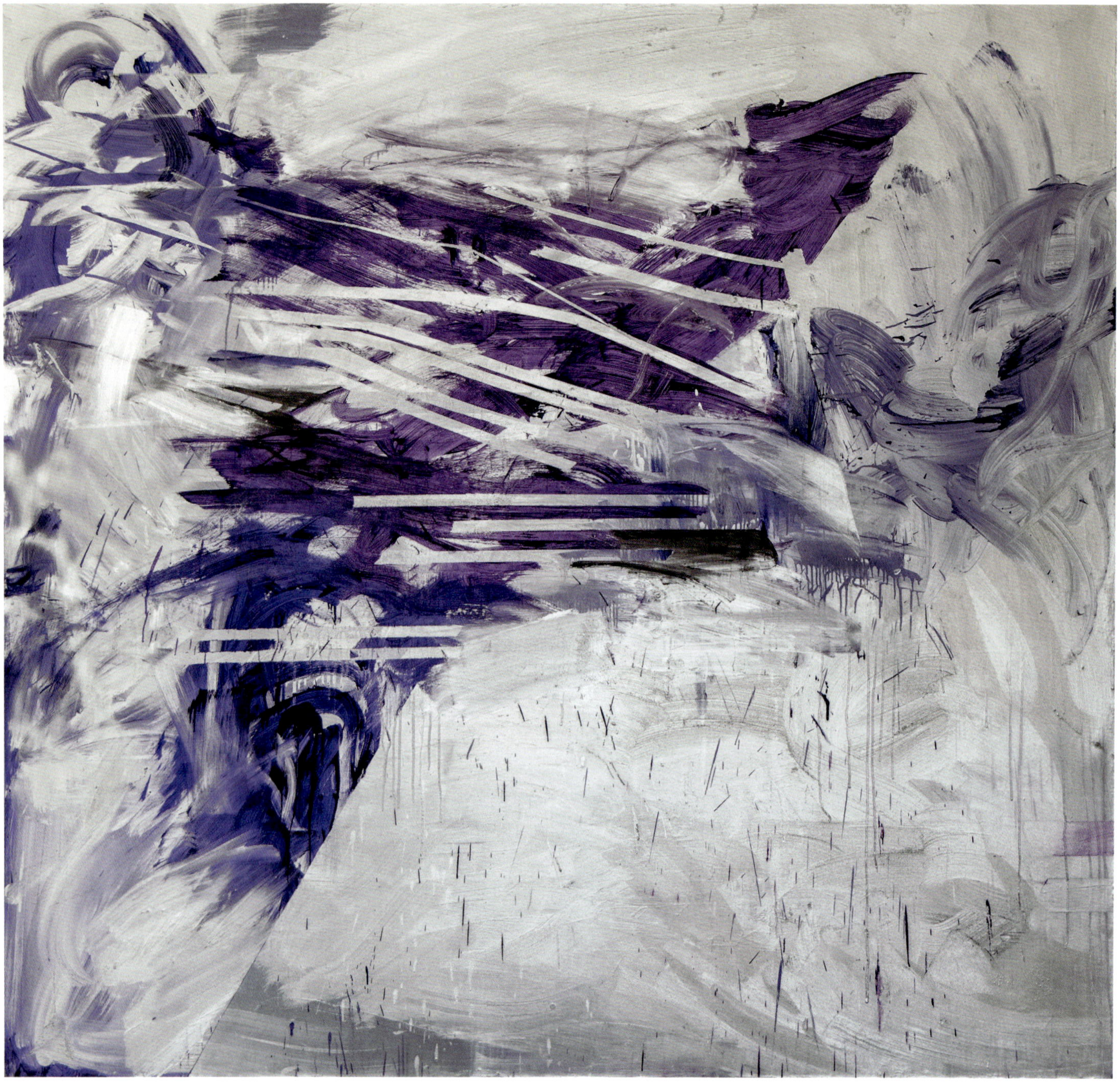

60. Dark Star 2006

Oil and enamel on linen
228.6 × 243.8 cm (90 × 96 in)

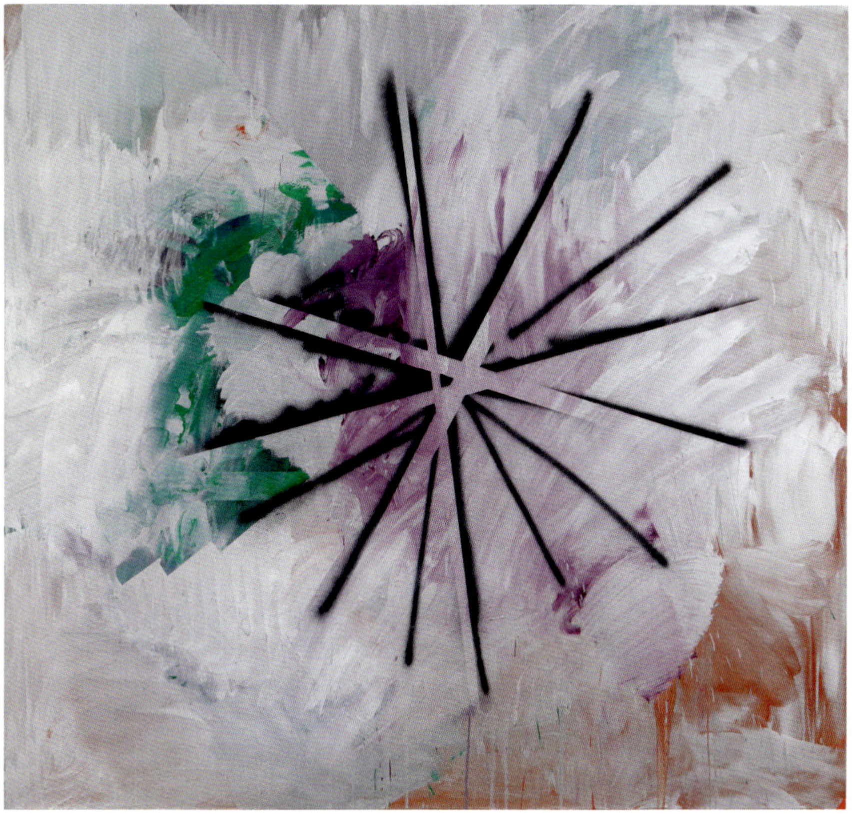

61. Untitled 2010

Oil on canvas
203.2 × 221 cm (80 × 87 in)

left pushes clouds of silver to billow over the base of the diagonal. The painting is arresting for its fullness of colour, confident strokes, and dynamic silver striated with deep purple drips. *Dark Star* is also a conventionally structured composition.

Composition on the diagonal was a trope of cinematic abstraction developed in the 1920s in Germany in particular. Directors such as Robert Wiene, with set designers such as Hermann Warm, Walter Reimann, and Walter Röhrig, composed on the diagonal to represent the characters' inner turmoil. Before them, painters such as Ernst Ludwig Kirchner and Lyonel Feininger used the diagonal to represent the First World War's consequent fragmentation and rendering askew of life in its midst.[46] Humphries does something more than these earlier uses of the diagonal. She teasingly appropriates the diagonal as one half of the diminishing perspective of classical painting before flattening it out on a field of opaque silver. Whether gleaned from early twentieth-century cinematic and painted abstraction or classical perspective, the diagonal is a familiar structuring device recast by Humphries.

The billowing silver clouds, and swathes and splatters of purple, over the lower half of the canvas are also key. They are bound together with the strips of more layers: purple and blue washes underneath the silver. For the viewer, the work's expression is complicated by multiple visual languages, use of different tools of application, and the blurring of figure and ground. What we think is on the surface, painted over the black, is in fact underneath. Once again, the painting morphs, the shapes and forms mutate, depending on where we stand. The painting deceives our vision and simultaneously can be seen to 'update' German art's expression of a chaotic world through the violation of classical perspective. *Dark Star* also plays a game of concealing from and revealing to a viewer who finds temporary stability in the illusion of mastery given by a single perspective. The illusory vanishing point of classical perspective has been removed altogether. In turn, like the frames and edges, Humphries's use of the diagonal as a structuring device comes undone over time. And with it, our comfort evaporates.

The drip as structure

> 'A drip, formerly a symbol of feckless artistic abandon, becomes for me a primary structuring agent . . . To enact a gestural mark, I must locate myself in the gap between its form and its received meaning.' – Jacqueline Humphries [47]

Humphries's merging of control and unpredictability in her use of drips as structure further distinguishes her work from that of abstract expressionism and classical modernism. It also gives insight into another element of the beyond into which her paintings pull their viewers. As mentioned earlier, Humphries's drips are not explicable through reference to Pollock's. Despite the tendency to return to Pollock when talking about drips, Humphries's execution of the drip in her painterly vocabulary has little relationship to his.[48] While drips were fashionable after Pollock, he did not invent them.[49] In their earlier twentieth-century iterations – for example, in the work of Francis Picabia, Max Ernst, or André Masson – drips resulted from carefully controlled techniques.[50] Even for Picabia, who allowed partially dried paint to sag under the skin of the surface, the drip was managed and manipulated. For Humphries, in works such as *Hit or Miss*, 1993 (fig.62), and *Hover*, 1994 (fig.63), both filled with structured, graphic drips, the paint has been applied to a canvas on a wall.[51] In both cases, the paint is applied in a single dab or touch and allowed to drip of its own accord. The paint is mixed with varying degrees of solvent to create greater or lesser intensity of colour, greater or lesser movement down the canvas. The result is both structured and unpredictable. The drips are traces or testimonies of the ongoing temporal journey of paint down the canvas. As the title of the first work suggests, the process is hit and miss. Aesthetically, the paint has an unfolding visual narrative independent of Humphries as painter and other external forces. However, this aesthetic is also inauthentic.

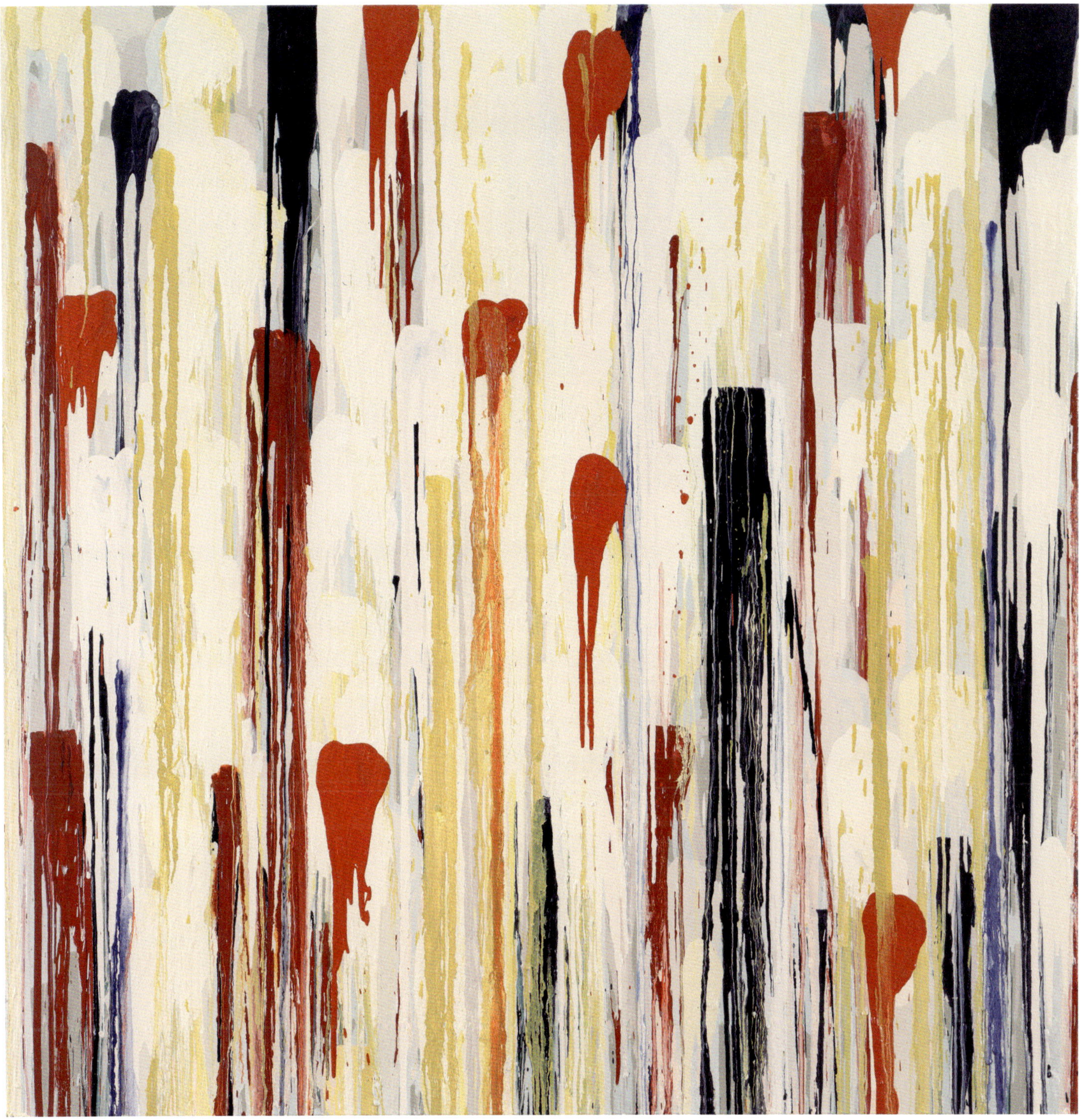

62. Hit or Miss 1993

Oil on linen
81.3 × 111.8 cm (32 × 44 in)
Albright-Knox Art Gallery, Buffalo, New York;
James G. Forsyth Fund, 1994

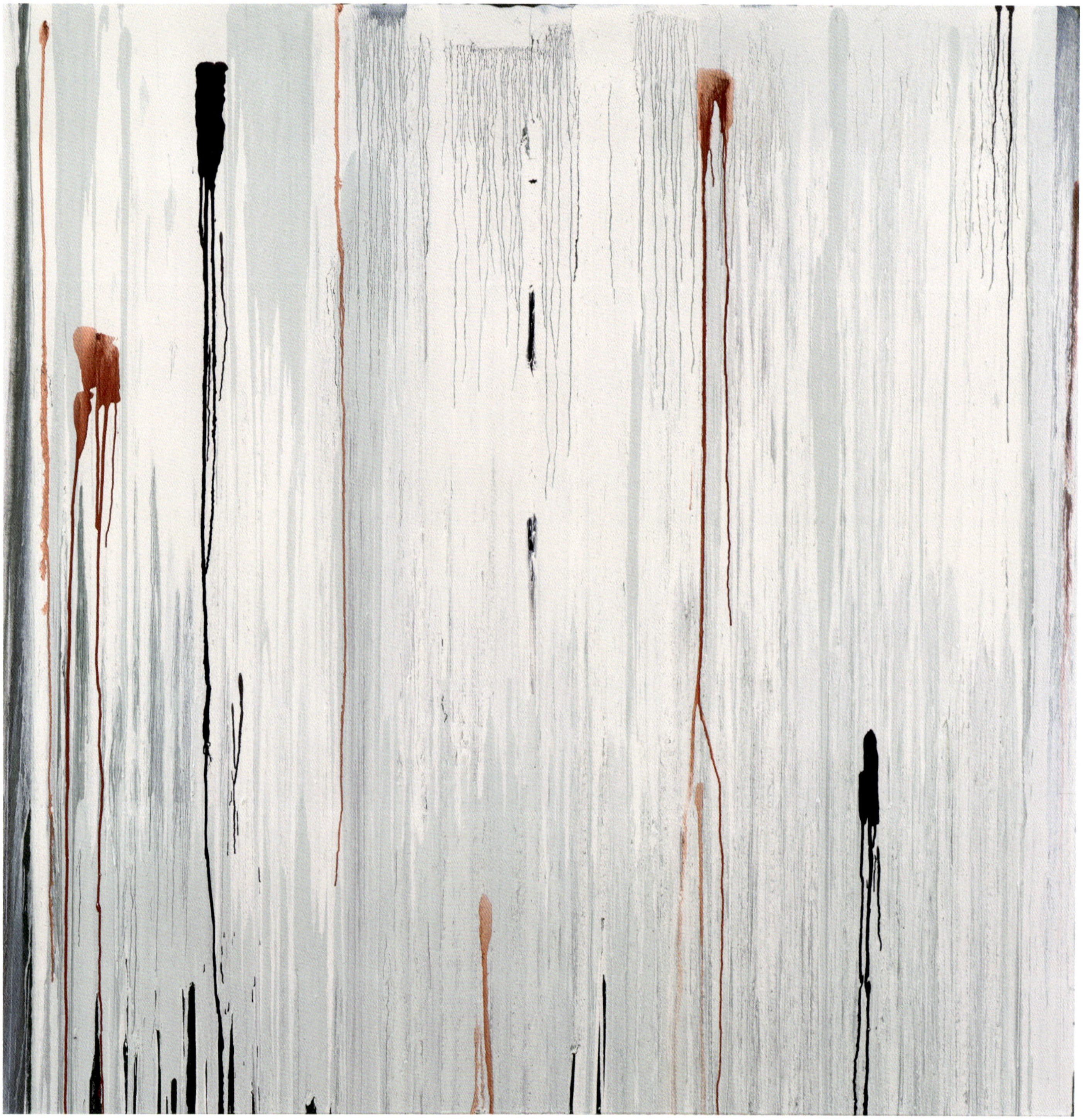

63. Hover 1994

Oil on linen
172.7 × 172.7 cm (68 × 68 in)

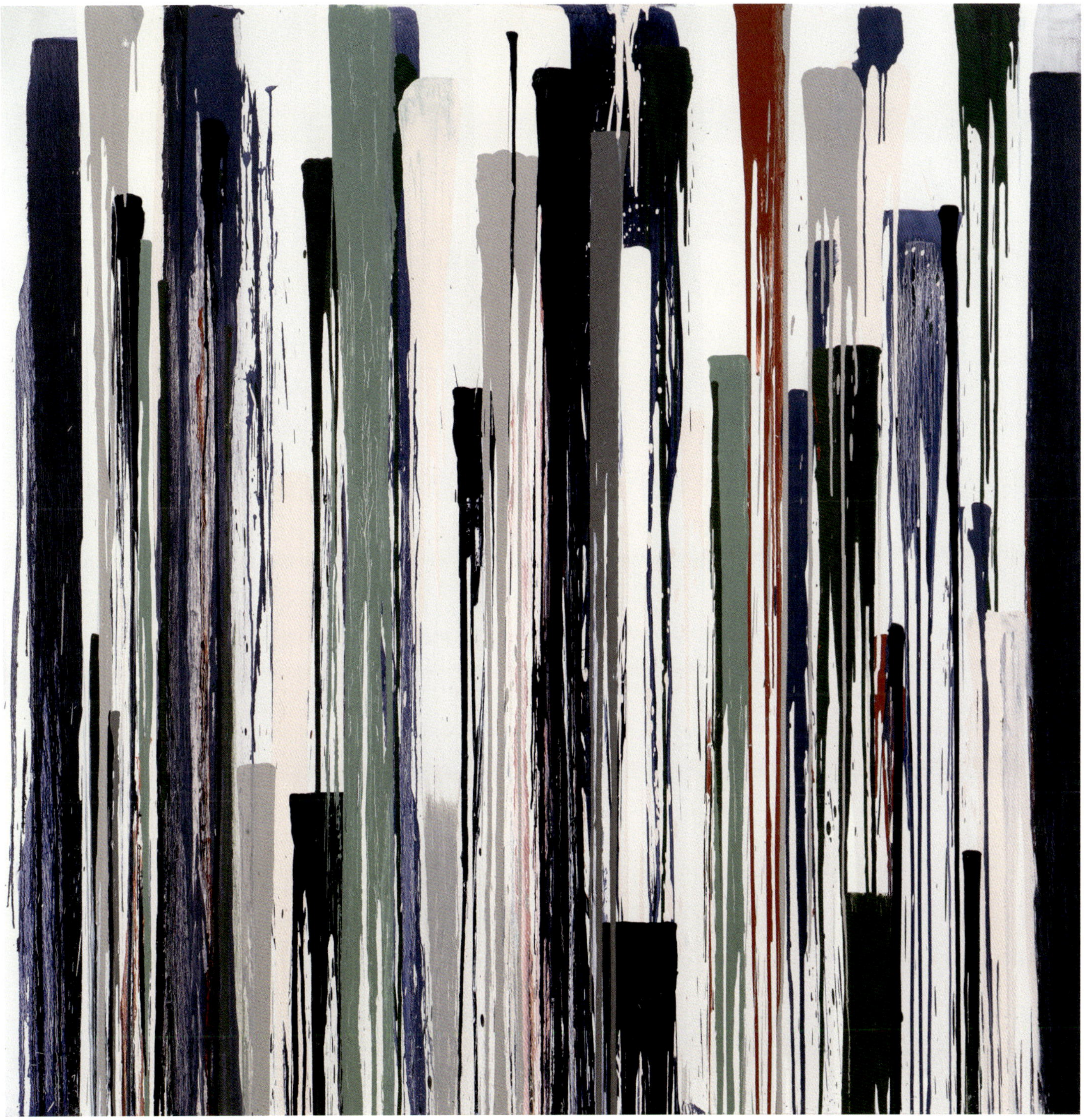

64. Antic 1994

Oil on linen
228.6 × 228.6 cm (90 × 90 in)
Museum of Fine Arts Boston; Gift of Robert W. Bingham, 1994

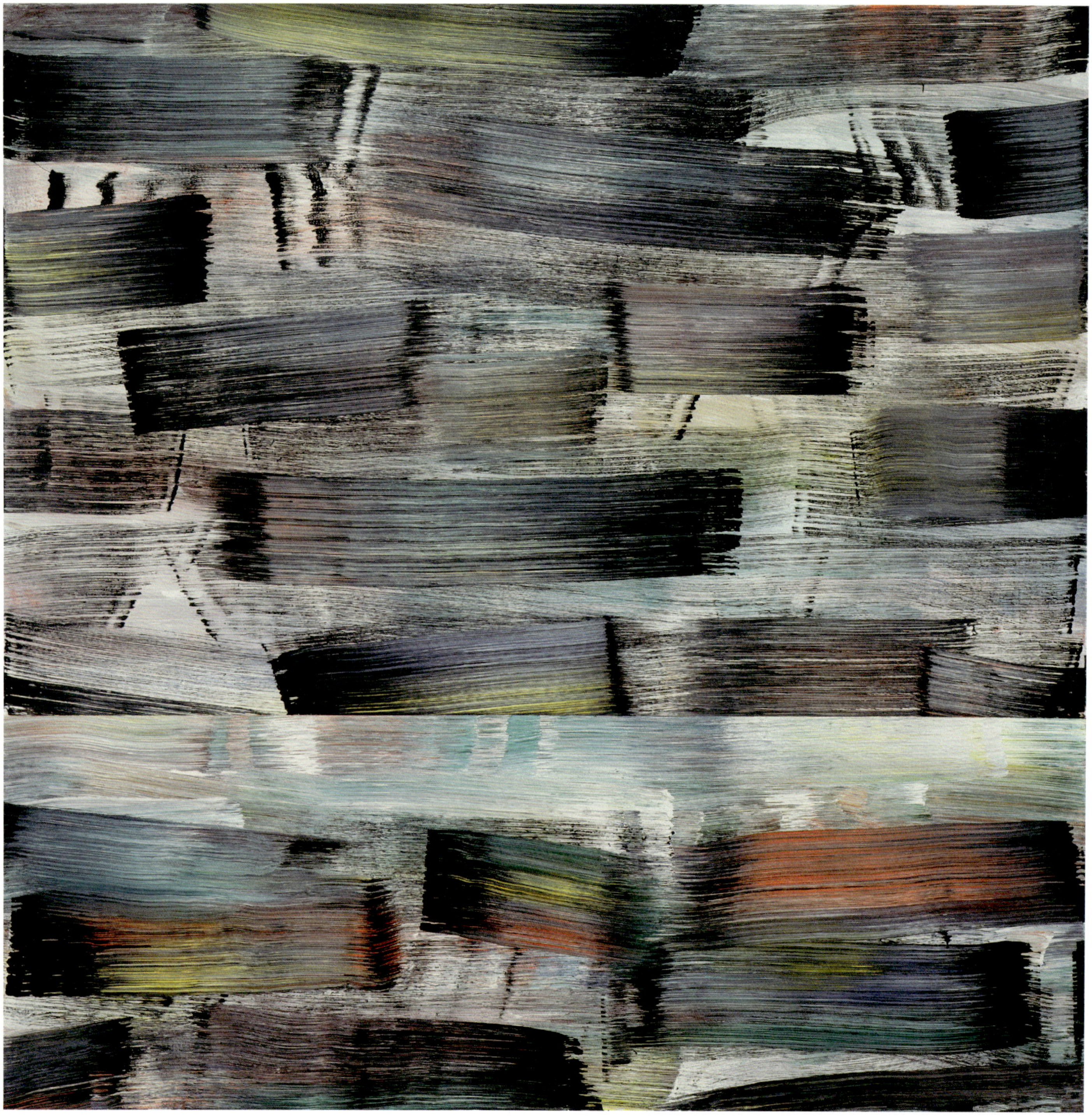

65. Horizontal #5 1997

Oil on linen
228.6 × 228.6 cm (90 × 90 in)

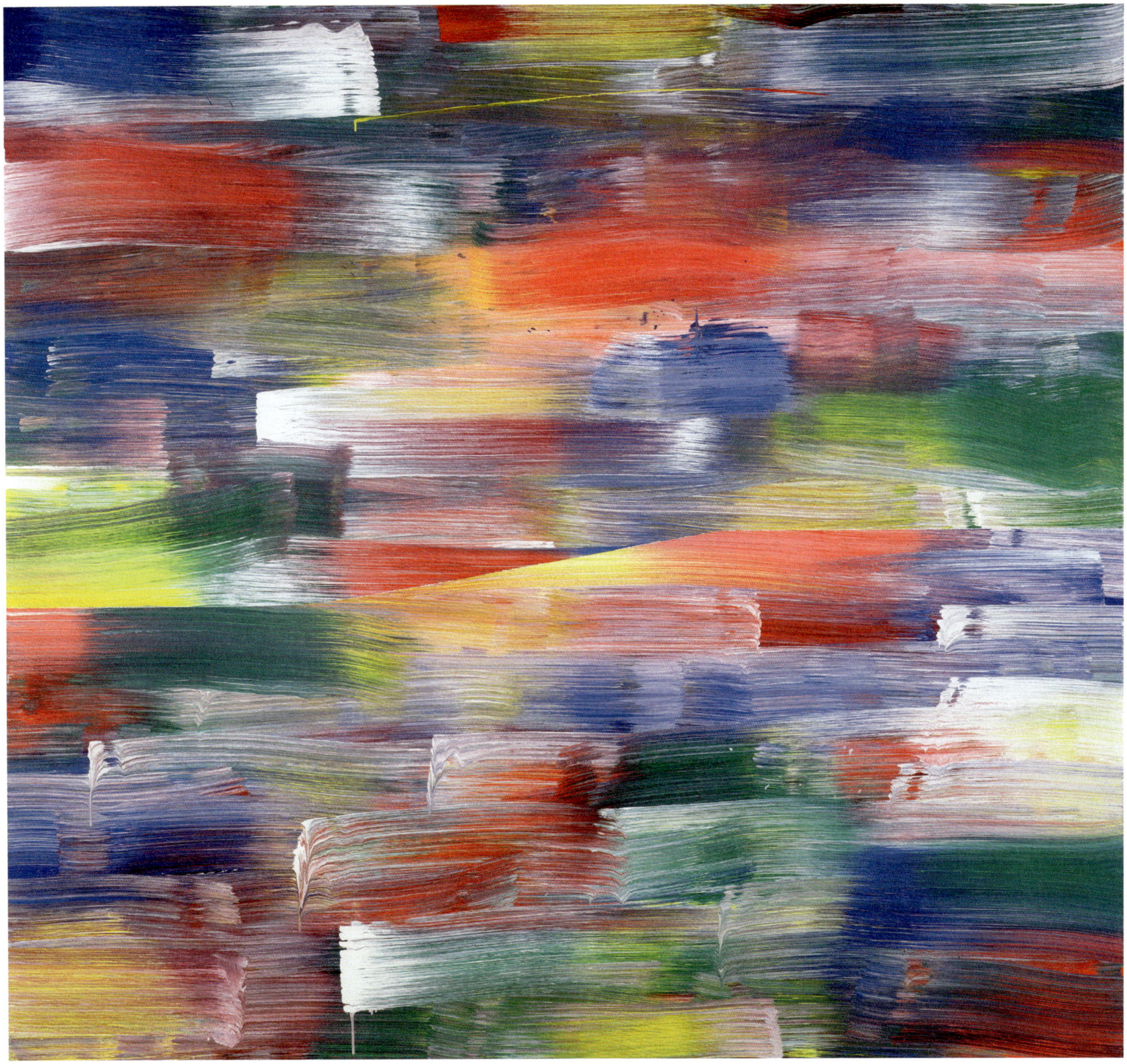

66. Untitled 1999

Oil on linen
203.2 × 223.5 cm (80 × 88 in)

Humphries's drips are sometimes stopped. The movement is abruptly curtailed by tape before paint is applied. Alternatively, the canvas edge forms a limit. Thus, the drip's end point (or its beginning) is not a random – albeit carefully chosen – place on the canvas, but a perfectly straight line. This creation of a threshold, truncating the flow of paint, visibly reinstates the intervention of the artist. Ironically, the tape, not the artist's hand, determines the straight line. Moreover, in these works, the paint is poured, not applied with a brush. The artist's hand is even further removed concurrently with it being made more visible. More curiously, this technique confuses the languages of painting: the purpose of a drip is for paint to run its course without interference. Thus, the drips use the properties of one visual system to present a different visual form. Paint controlled by the brush or another tool of intervention (in this case, tape) is a line. It cannot be both a drip and a line. But for Humphries, painting reaches the impossible when drip and line become merged so that viewers find themselves questioning which they are looking at. Hence the distinction between Humphries's process and aesthetic from Pollock's random drips and Ernst's contrived markings.

For Humphries, drips tell of the drying as well as the trickle of paint over time. Drips trace unpredictable paths, and yet are distinct from arbitrary patterns left by paint thrown over a canvas lying flat on the ground. Perceptually and conceptually, Humphries's drips are calculated. Yet they resemble the irregular drips of Cy Twombly's late paintings for which he squeezed scrunched-up pieces of paper soaked in paint onto the canvas. Simultaneously, Humphries's drips are lines that structure, divide, expand, and draw attention to and divert from themselves in the manner of Newman's zips. Even if there is a visual resonance with Twombly's and Newman's images, the connection to their execution and aesthetic is tenuous. In a departure from both Newman and Twombly, Humphries introduces the struggle between control and the chance movement of paint, the artist and paint, to produce works that have minds of their own. In a unique use of the drip as line, it is both and neither.

In other paintings from the 1990s, the drip is a structural element, carefully designed and worked over, integrated into disciplined lines of intense and brightly coloured paint. In *Untitled*, 1996 (fig.67), blood-red paint has been poured down the length of the canvas. At times, it stops or turns short of the edges. However much the lines look like blood, they are not blood: on closer inspection, their manipulated, structured quality and their variant colours convince that they are paint. In particular, the framing device of each line or section of paint repeats the verticality of the frame. Thus, the structural limitations of paint and painting, both on a flat surface – another limitation – create a rational depiction in *Untitled*. In characteristic Humphries style, the logic is undercut by ambiguity. While we think we are looking at drips, we move up close and discover that they are not in fact drips, but paint that has been poured into a line. The dissonance between what we know is a line, but see as a drip, turns this sequence of brightly coloured works into representations resembling oil slicks.

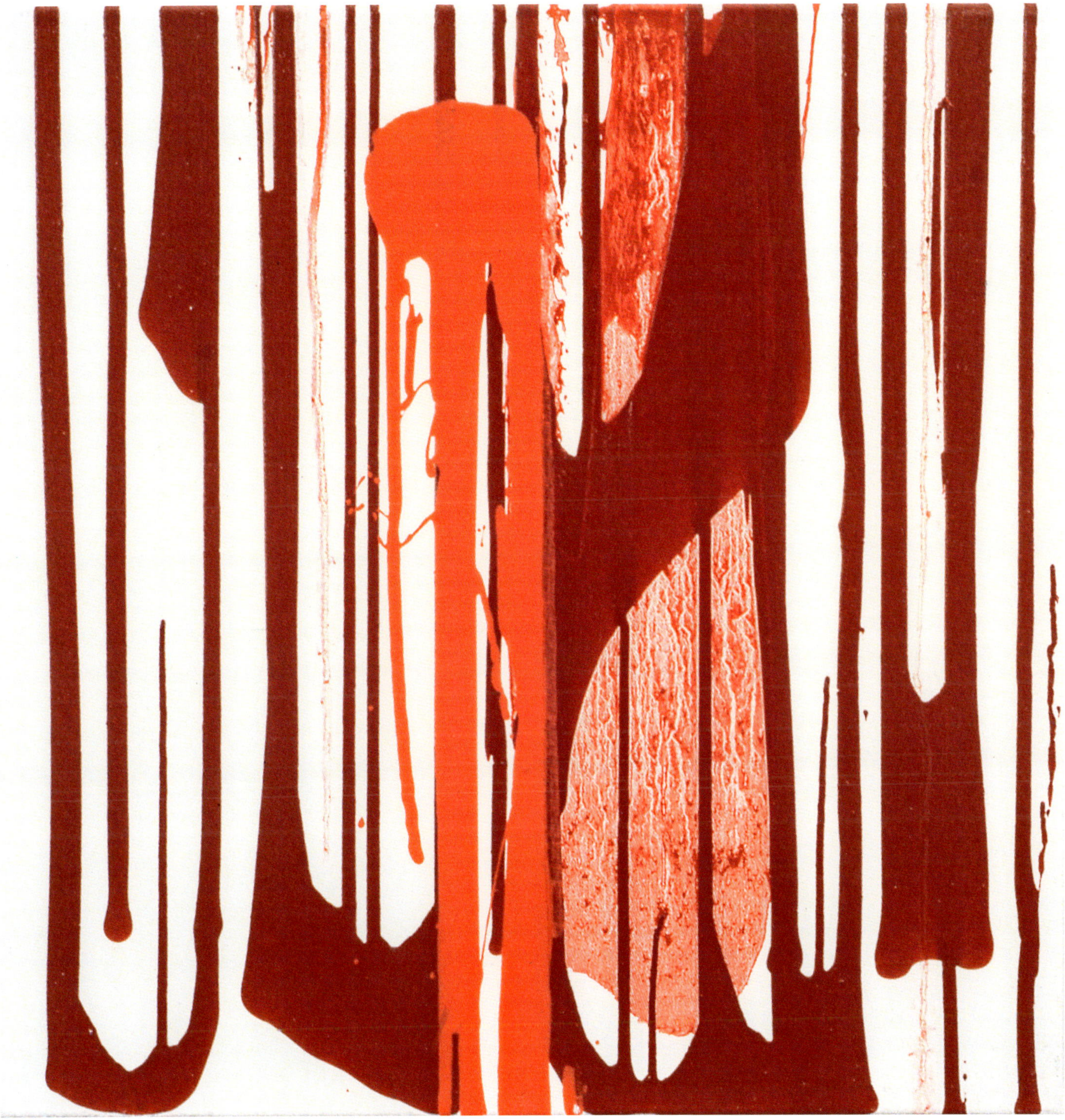

67. Untitled 1996

Oil and enamel on linen
45.7 × 45.7 cm (18 × 18 in)

The substance (of paint or oil) is separated over a surface of water, held by its own unique density and viscosity. Given these oscillations, as we look the meanings move beyond the material appearance of the painting.

The works bring up associations but never definitive claims. We are reminded of blood, but this interpretation does not settle for long in the viewer's mind. It looks like oil over water but is, in fact, oil or enamel over paint. Thus, it is not simply the question of drip or line, form or substance, but beyond painting in these drips is a tension between what we perceive at first glance and the actual painting. Physically moving around the painting reveals more tensions between drip and line, aleatory and controlled. Functioning inside these interstices, Humphries's paintings are ambiguous. The paintings keep the viewer looking, guessing, resituating. In front of works that represent drips but turn out to be something else, we enter into a physical and conceptual game.

In the 2000s, Humphries painted drips onto a vertical canvas on the wall. In *Blue Screen*, 2000 (fig.68), Humphries worked perpendicular to the picture plane to create white lines, dabs, spots, and curves across an Egyptian-blue ground. The white marks appear to bleed, drip, and trail on the blue, graded ground applied with a brush. However, this cannot explain that the white does not sit *on* the surface of blue; it is part *of* the surface, like a screen. Humphries achieves this ambiguity through applying white paint from a squeeze bottle onto a wet blue ground. We are not looking at drips created by paint running off, but a picturing of drips. This is another form of inauthenticity as it is so often discovered – over time – in Humphries's canvases.[52] It is a different painterly language from that which sees drips fall from lines that themselves could be drips. Often, we think we are looking at drips, but in fact they are painted lines. The deception causes uncertainty and unknowability, pushing the viewer to continue looking. As the eye follows the lines, looking for beginnings and endings, the mode of application, anything to make sense of the painting, we become lost. Further frustrating the experience of the drips is their diminishing occurrence towards the bottom, the place on the canvas where we would expect drips to collect. Here, their relative paucity draws our focus to the horizontal white brush strokes on the bottom edge. It is as if something has been wiped away, or is in the process of appearing.

The drips and lines in *Sunset (Rose)*, 2000 (fig.69) lose their identity altogether when they are broken across the division created by the paler pink band at the bottom. Viewers trace colours and lines across and around the surface, looking for logic, patterns, continuity, explanation. However, in *Sunset (Rose)* the line as structure is deliberately untethered, forcing the viewer to examine the most troubling element: where the pink band meets the upper four-fifths of the canvas. Here, the rough-hewn horizontal strokes made with a thick brush hold a fascination inconsistent with their significance, until they are recognised to repeat or mirror the red slither across the top of the frame – another interstitial, ill-defined site on the painting. Then, we start to see the setting sun. The familiar play between reality and the imagination begins again.

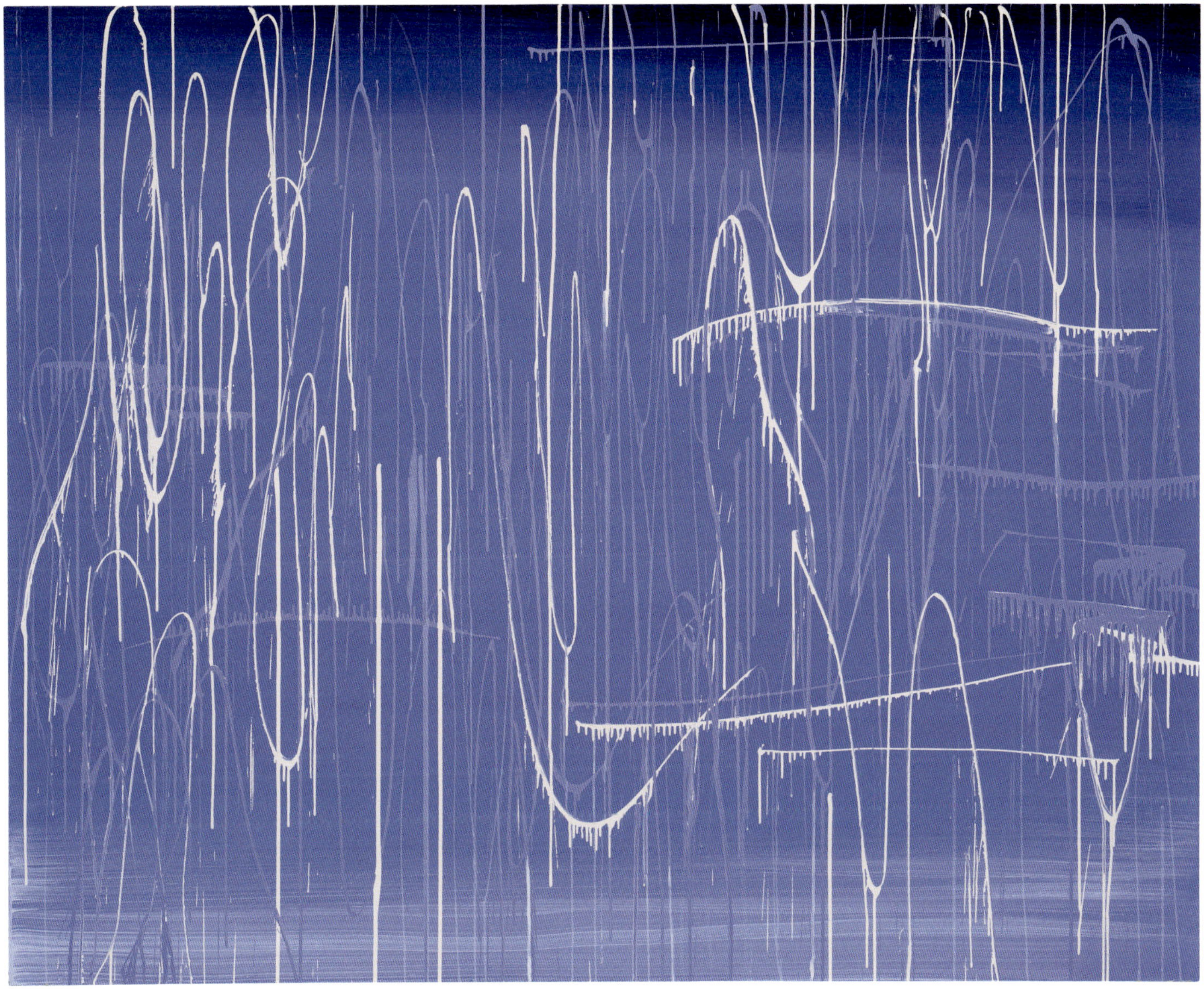

68. Blue Screen 2002

Oil on linen
157.5 × 198.1 cm (62 × 78 in)

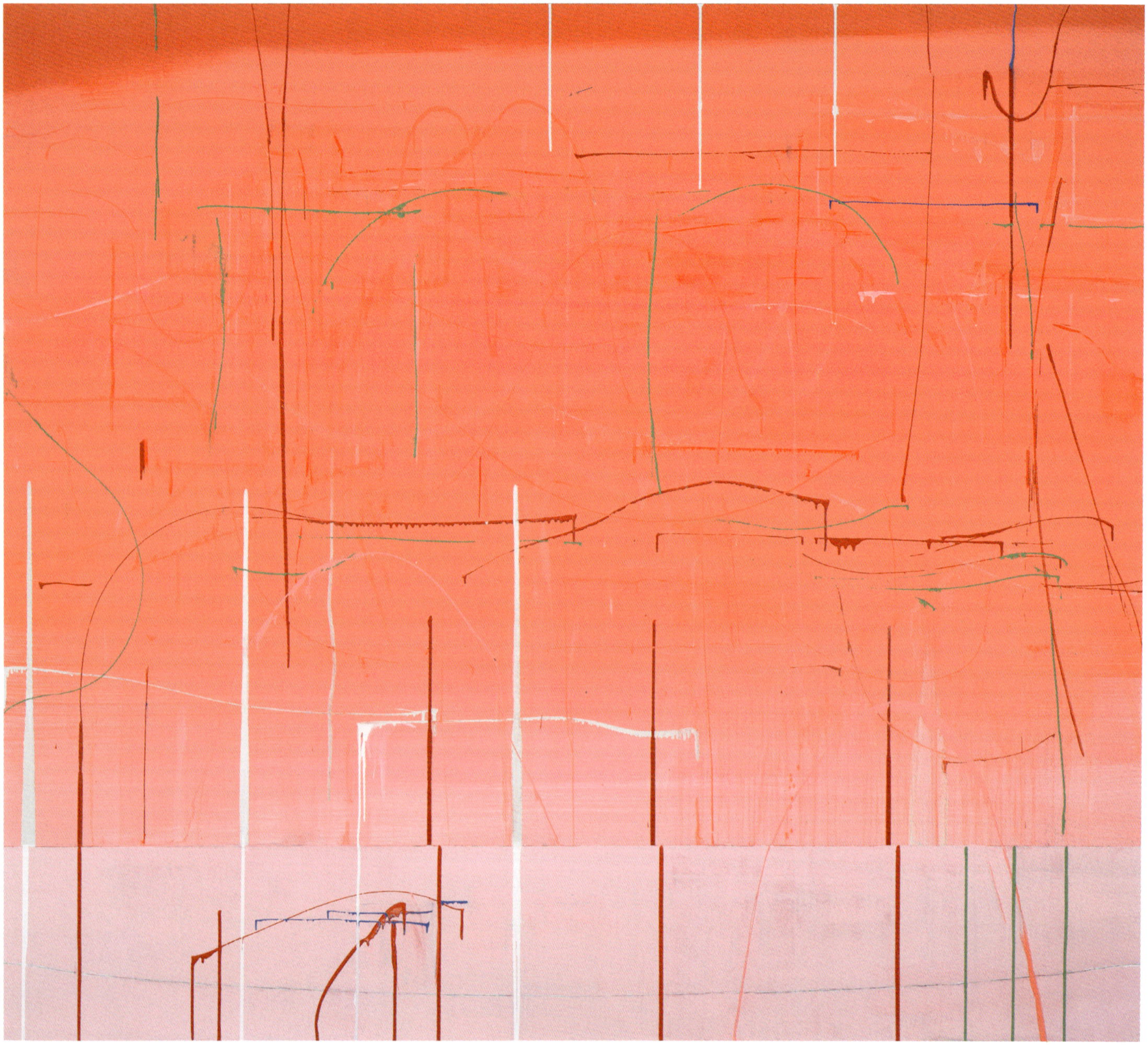

69. Sunset (Rose) 2000

Oil on linen
228.6 × 259.1 cm (90 × 102 in)
Ogden Museum of Southern Art, New Orleans; Gift of the American Academy of Arts and Letters, New York: Hassam, Speicher, Betts and Symons Fund, 2001.4

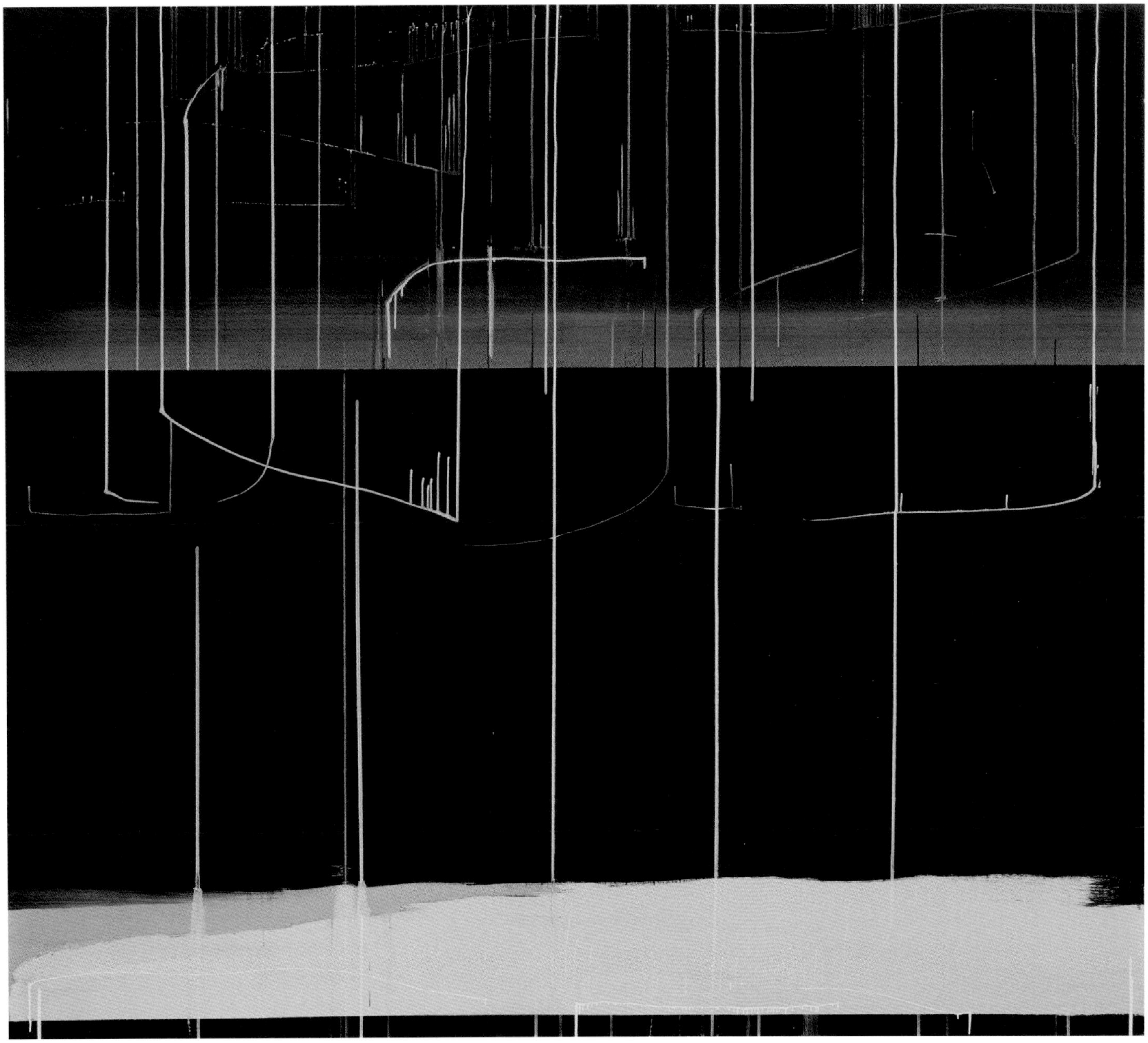

70. Black Monday 1999

Oil on linen
228.6 × 259.1 cm (90 × 102 in)
Cincinnati Art Museum, Cincinnati, Ohio; purchased with funds provided by the Contemporary Collectors Circle

Elsewhere, dripped passages are transformed into ASCII code, and subsequently made into stencils for later paintings. These early examples of drip as structure are a visual language that becomes reconceived and re-executed in the ASCII paintings. Once drips are developed into ASCII code stencils, drip and line, structure and mess, figure and ground are not simply in tension or conversation in Humphries's paintings. Rather, they become collaborators in the creation of a foundational language of a new kind of painting. They are, as described, photographed, transformed into computer-generated code, made into a stencil, itself turned into the structural form of painting characterised by vivid and kinetic vibrations. Seen in this way, across the oeuvre, Humphries's drips – not Pollock's or abstract expressionism's – invite exploration of new ways of seeing and looking at contemporary visual culture.

Spaces on and beyond painting

Humphries has referred to her paintings as landscapes of a particular kind. 'Landscape is anything, like a parking lot, highway, blank piece of paper or cinema screen. It's the stage for stuff happening, the world. I want to welcome the viewer to wander in this space.'[53] Landscape is a space, a site, a canvas onto which Humphries introduces layers of paint in multiple languages, demanding interpretation by an engaged viewer. In a characteristically ironic move, Humphries appropriates computer images, digital networks, languages of new technologies in the digital sphere and makes them into two-dimensional, tactile spaces. In turn, two dimensions become three dimensions when the viewer experiences the works in situ, moving around the gallery, discovering the paintings as objects.

When thinking about painting as 'landscape', I am reminded again of Newman. Kenneth Allan extends Yve-Alain Bois's observations regarding the relationship between Newman's zips and the adjacent colour fields. Bois shows how certain Newman works organise space by putting, like a form of light art, paintings in dialogue with the space (volume) around them.[54] Newman's engagement of a viewer in space is designated through the colour fields on either side of the birfurcation. The process of perception is different from the bodily experience of a Humphries work, but the initial impetus is related. For Bois and later Allan, Newman's zip transcends the formal dimensions of painting as it creates a spatial assignation for the viewer. Thus, Newman forces an embodied perception in a space determined by the viewer's gaze in relationship to a flat, abstract painting. However, for Humphries, there is no transcendence. The painting – its colours, material, and structural elements – maintains a physicality that facilitates the viewer's exploration of a reorganised space.[55] Humphries's paintings offer a dynamic and evolving experience of the artwork and the surrounding space. Moreover, the viewer's response is culturally defined: what is seen makes sense

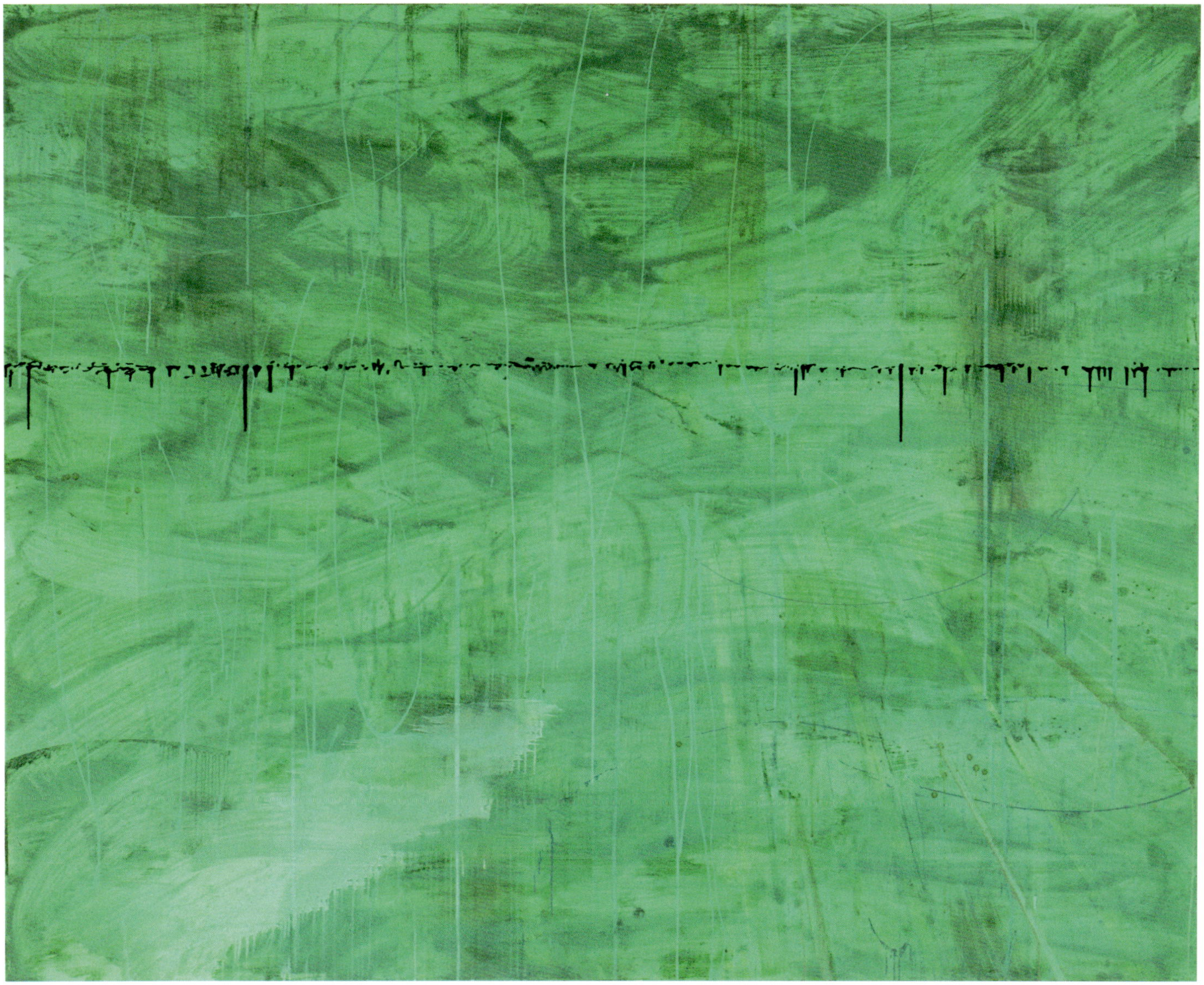

71. Untitled 2002

Oil on linen
157.5 × 198.1 cm (62 × 78 in)

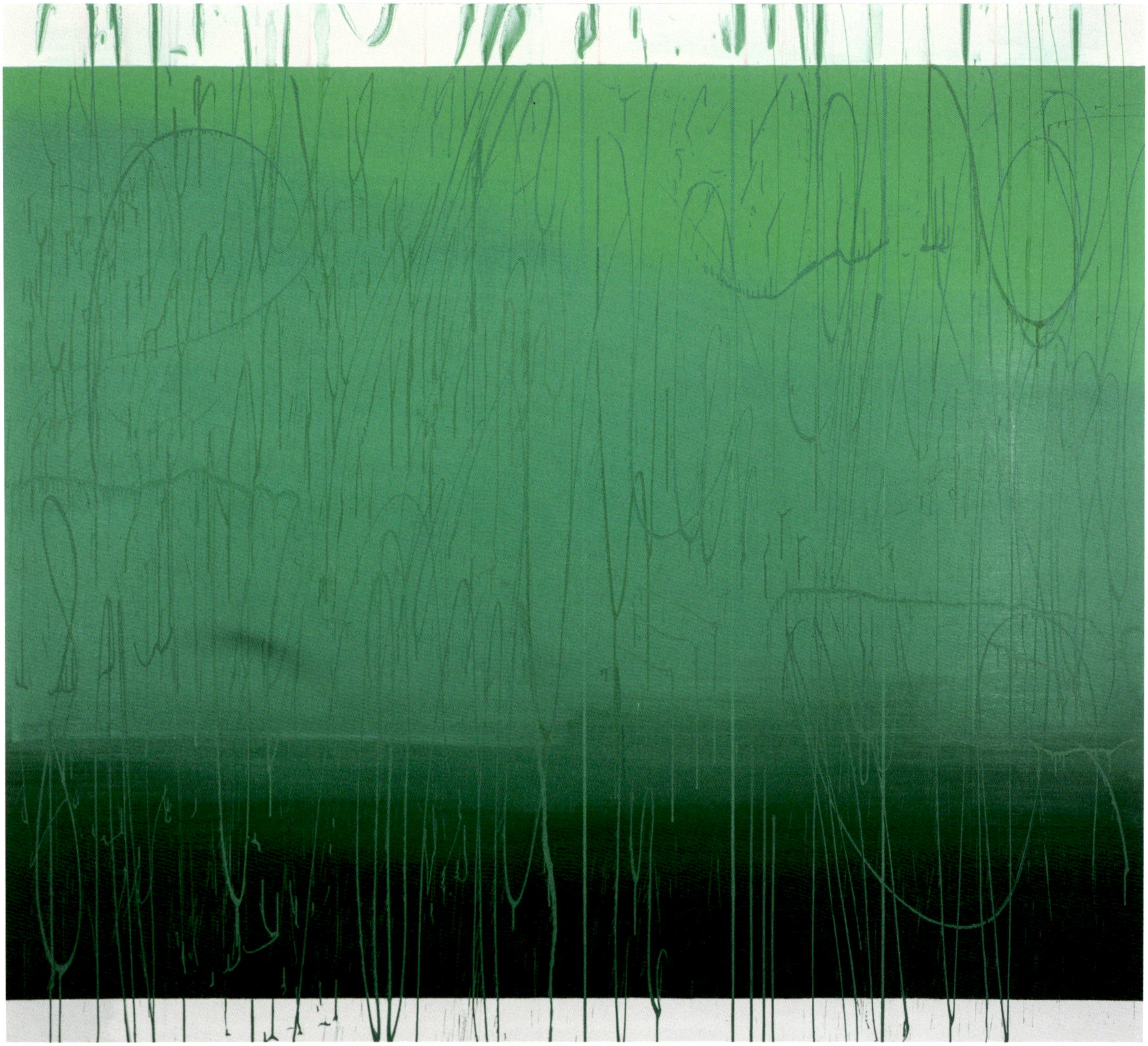

72. Materiel 2001

Oil on linen
233.7 × 259.1 cm (92 × 102 in)

within the context of patterns and practices of viewing screens. As the painting transforms before our eyes as we move around it, we recognise the images and effects of looking at contemporary screens, even though we are aware that we are looking at a painting.

All painting is, in one way or another, a landscape. By definition, landscape and painting both define and depict space. However, Humphries moves beyond an engagement with the discourses of painting and the representation of space as a landscape. Somewhere beyond painting, she reaches for the screens, monitors, and translucent casings of digital devices. Thus, space – or landscape – in and on Humphries's canvases does not symbolise national interests, the political play of war, or a physical site of power and ideology.[56] Landscape for Humphries belongs to the screen interfaces of her contemporary world. Popular culture and the willing absorption in technological worlds become the discursive sites of representation. Electronic light, the filament buzz, the reflecting face of the device are the landscapes we live by and in which we willingly immerse ourselves. From *Materiel*, 2001 (fig.72) to recent abstractions resembling a vast blue sea or a rainbow of plastic colours, the paintings are expanses illuminated by the abstract light of a computer screen.

Materiel also looks like an inverted landscape, or perhaps one that is the right way up. It is an abstract articulation of a Romantic landscape. Predictably, Humphries does not stop there. The image as interface is transposed from Romantic landscape to tactile painting with drips and other markings to create flatness and signal the illusion of the green colour field. As always with Humphries, there is a negation or destruction of the classical landscape. In another example, *z..?**, 2019 (fig.73), blue fields resembling sea and sky separated by a vertical horizon are covered in a dense build-up of paint, caked like plaster on the surface. It is not only the framing or structural mechanisms of the painting that contradict the idea that *z..?** is a replication of a computer or television screen. Rather, its tactility and materiality reveal the identity as screen to be inauthentic. Like the drips that are not drips after all, the painting could not be further removed, or beyond, the flat screen it supposedly reveals.

Humphries talks about linear perspective as magnetically pulling the viewer's eye to the vanishing point on the horizon. She claims the horizon is a projection of the viewer's eye: a subjective, imaginary space.[57] She does not elaborate on how this is transposed to her abstract paintings, because, of course, it is not. She references but never fully reveals the vanishing point because the painting pulls the viewer's eye back to the surface. No sooner have we recognised the reference to diminishing perspective than we are back looking at drips, marks, blurs, and scratches. Akin to the use of the diagonal in *Dark Star*, the game in the landscape paintings is transposed to a variety of gestural marks, stencilled layers, cuts through a differentiated field of coloured paint.

In the twentieth century, painters such as Kazimir Malevich, El Lissitzky, Piet Mondrian, and later Ad Reinhardt, used the canvas as a single space to create multiple layers within a square or rectangular frame. Ultimately, their intention was to place the viewer's body in a new relationship to space. Or better, to create a space through and around which the viewer was invited to move. Humphries goes beyond these experiments in modernist abstraction by inviting her viewer to immerse themselves into an image environment in which painting cohabits with other visual media. Humphries's painting-as-image is marked by ambiguity, competing and negating perspectives, dual images, and proliferating possibilities. Painting is filled with frames and windows, inside and beyond which the static of the cathode ray produces afterimages, and through which we recognise our consumerist behaviour before popular cultural screens. Inside the painted landscape, the viewer becomes conscious of seeing, feeling, and experiencing their body, reflecting on visual practices that are referenced in – but cannot be replicated by – painting. Humphries's creation and negotiation of space and the relationship between the canvas and the multitude of contemporary visual experiences undergird her reinvention of painting, from within the medium of painting. For Humphries, the limits and dimensions of painting pour over into the three-dimensionality of the gallery and beyond. Following the modernist tradition of revolutionary art, Humphries's abstract paintings are 'spaces' or frames, within which culture is reflected. Humphries's frames, edges, and structuring devices are barriers designed to be broken, stretching painting to new experiential limits. Such limits were never reached by viewers of Malevich's, Mondrian's, or Reinhardt's painting because they did not yet know the frames of twenty-first-century visual culture.

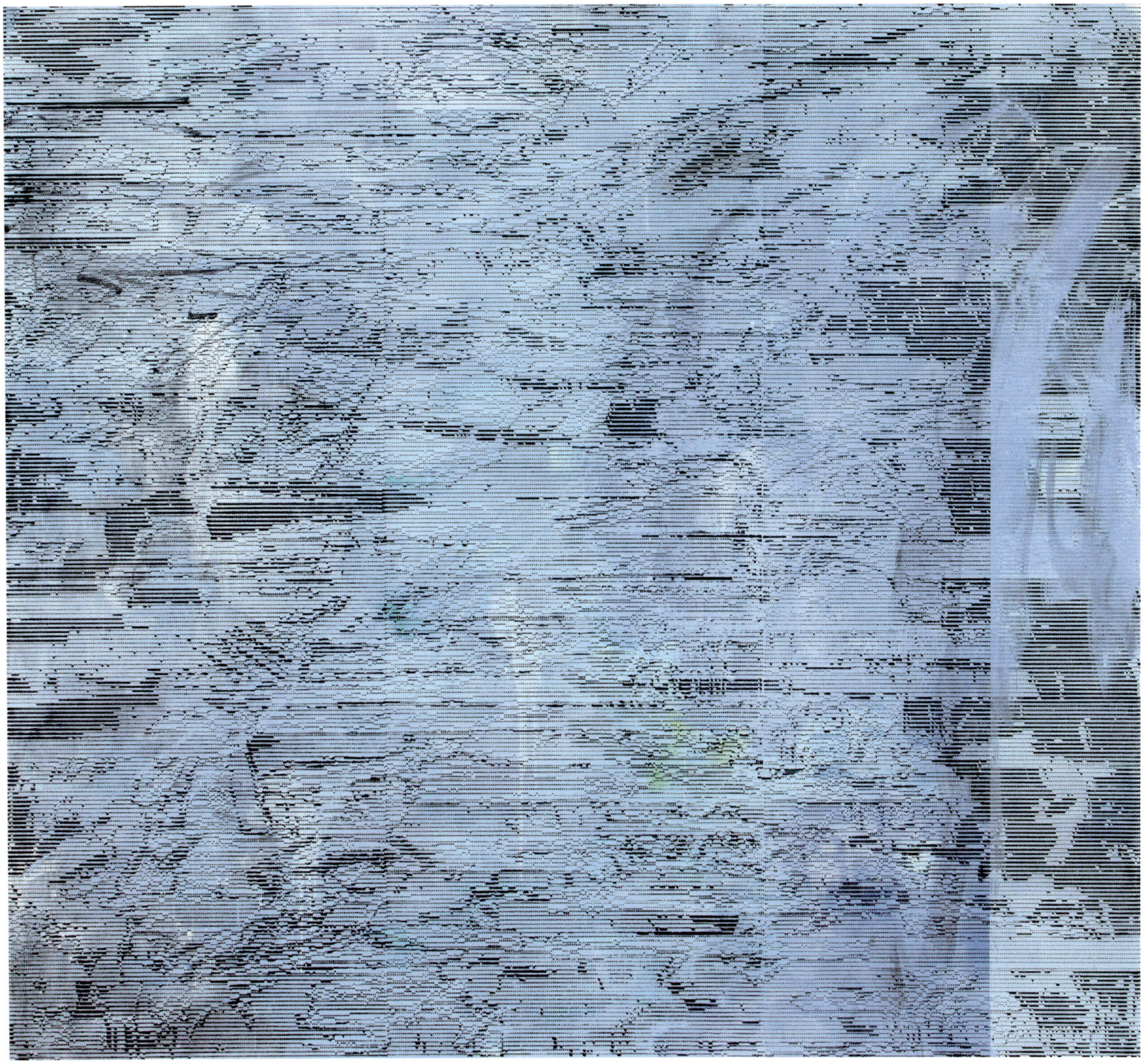

73. z..?* 2019

Oil and enamel on linen
254 × 281.9 cm (100 × 111 in)

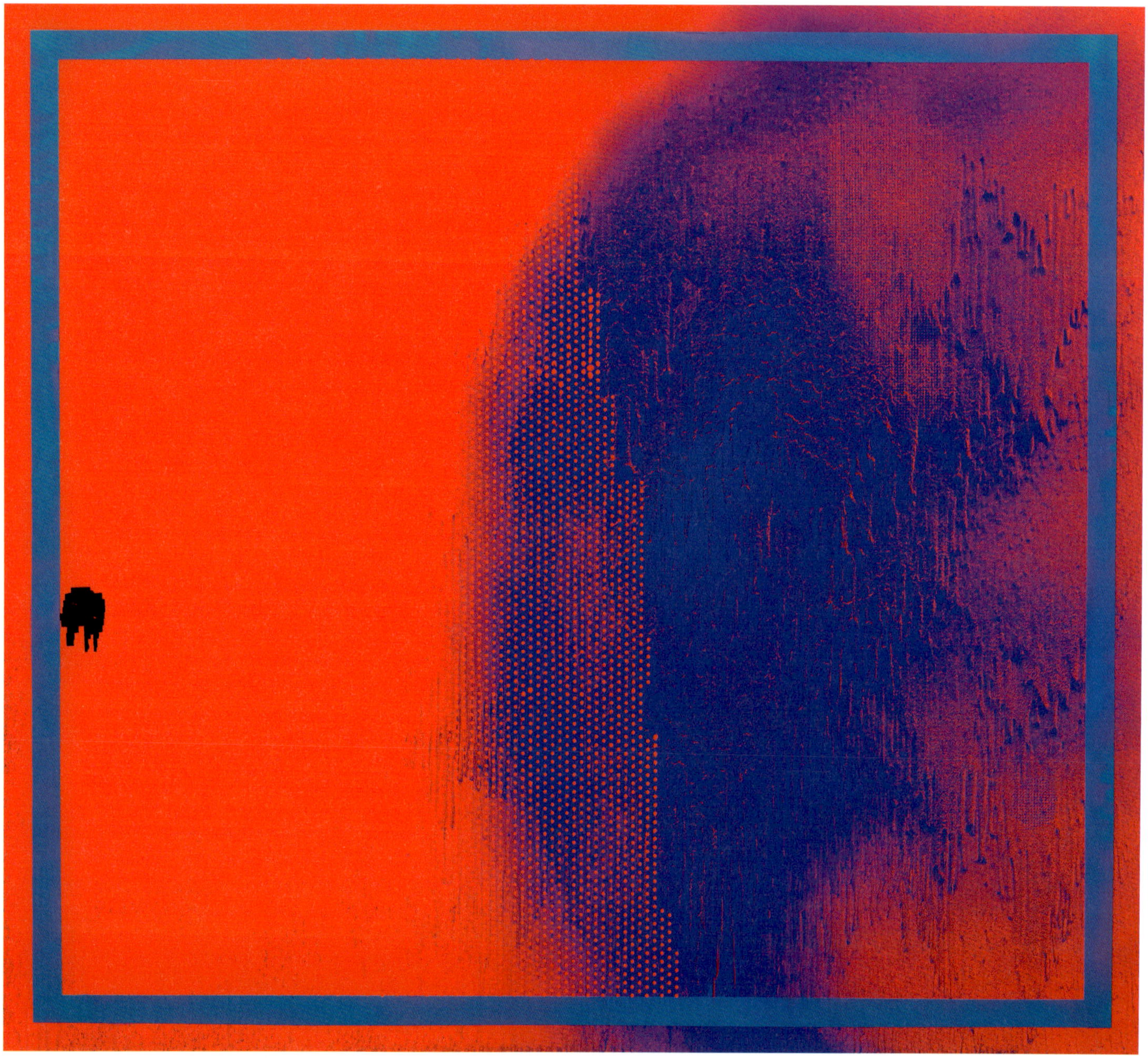

74. Untitled 2016

Oil and enamel on linen
289.6 × 322.6 cm (114 × 127 in)

4 Painting with Light

In a 2009 discussion with fellow American artist Cecily Brown, Humphries mentions her admiration for Goya's ability to 'channel' events in his midst into paintings.[58] In the same interview, Humphries talks about the resonance between her paintings and Caravaggio's, particularly his evocation of something physically absent from the painting.[59] She calls it a ghost, a not-quite-dead being lurking inside the painting. Humphries does not elaborate further, but she is obviously inspired by artworks that move painting beyond what was known in the artist's time. Her work then moves beyond what Caravaggio or Goya could have imagined: Humphries manipulates light as a way to take painting into new, uncharted landscapes.

Light has many different forms and personalities in Humphries's oeuvre. The black-light paintings from the 2000s are a source of illumination, while earlier works juxtapose silver and black pigments to create reflective, cinema-like screens. Still-earlier works remind the viewer of the cold light produced by the television's cathode tube or the hazy grey light of early computer screens. Humphries's scratching, dripping, and tracing on the surface of paintings such as *Materiel*, 2001 (fig.72) create a luminous space behind the surface as much as they shut out the light. Tim Griffin describes these light effects as 'the empty, ambient depth and disembodied light housed within monitors and their translucent casings'.[60] We could just as easily describe them as the fading luminescence of twilight familiar from Romantic painting. The point being that, across Humphries's oeuvre, light shifts unpredictably between natural and artificial. Within a single painting, luminescence can be both a

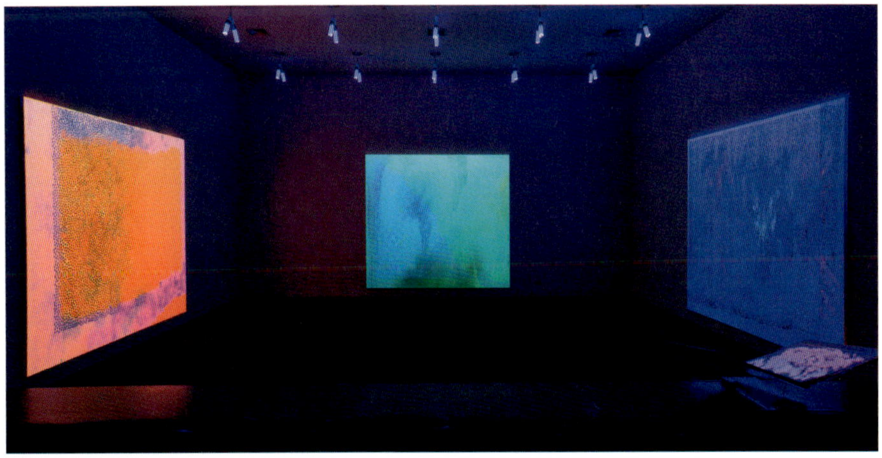

75. Installation view
Carnegie Museum of Art, Pittsburgh, Pennsylvania, 2015

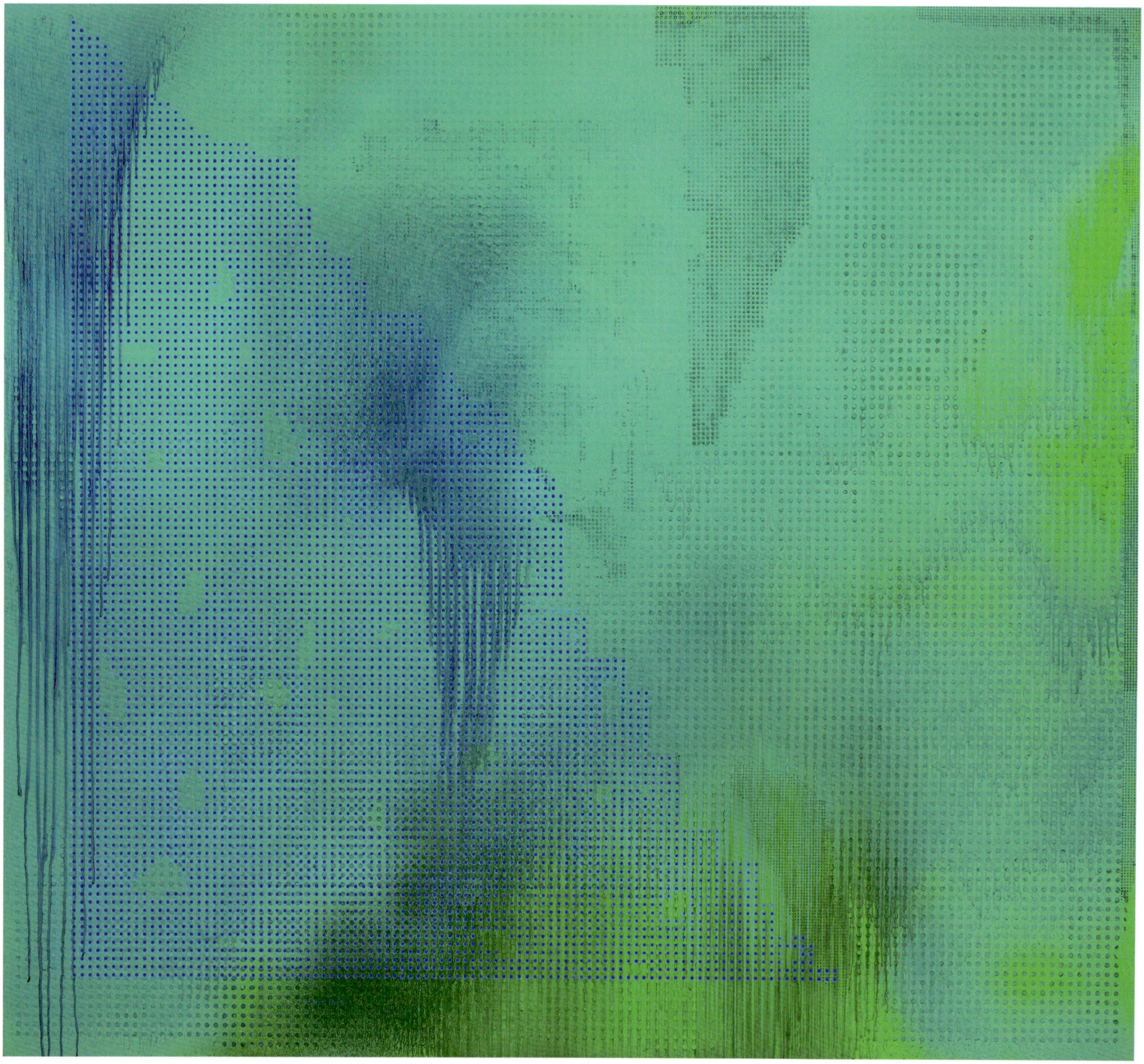

76. Untitled 2015

Enamel on linen
289.6 ×322.6 cm (114 × 127 in)

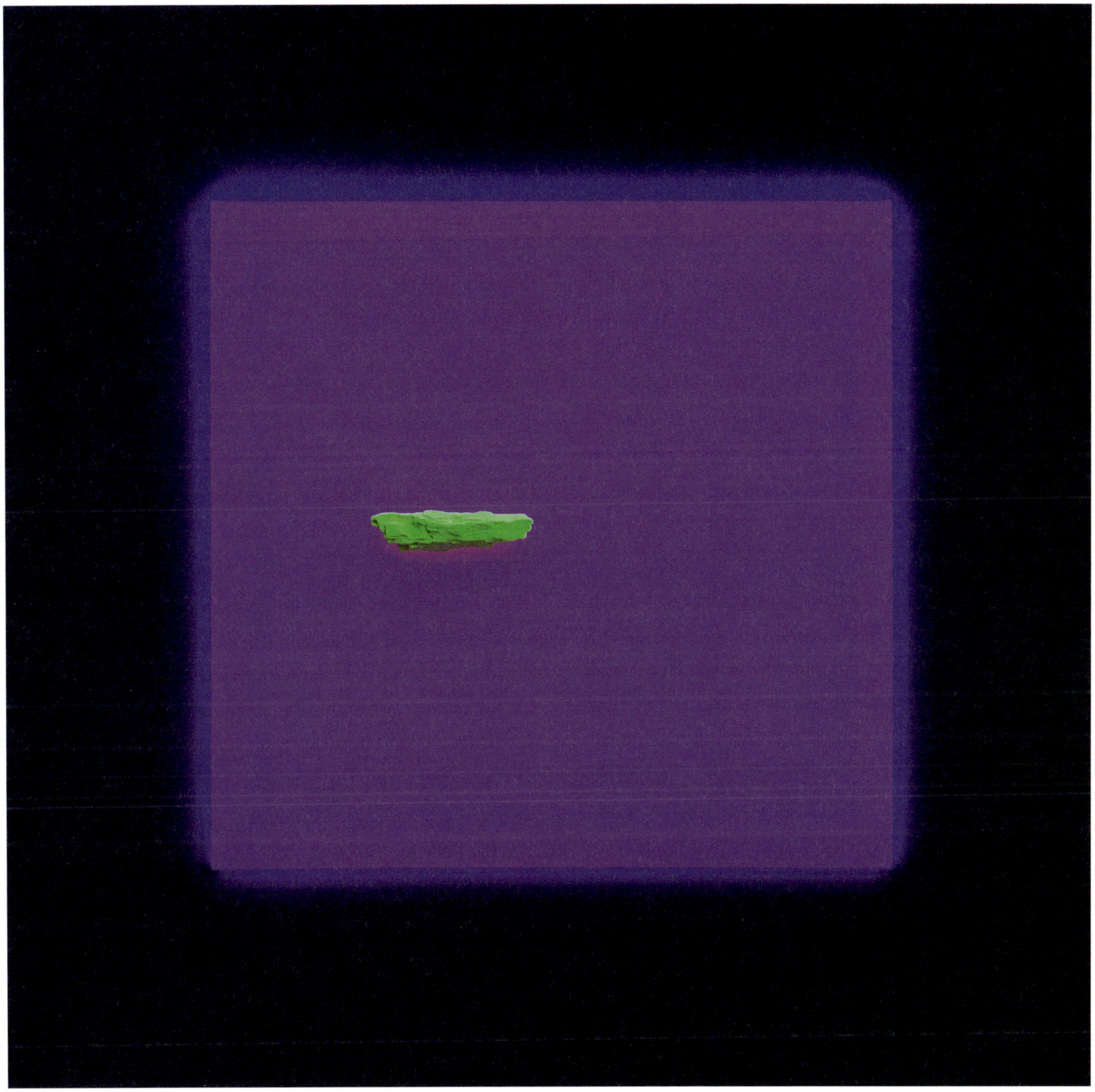

77. Painting 2019

Pigmented urethane resin and pigmented aqua resin
95.9 × 101 × 10.2 cm ($37\frac{3}{4} \times 39\frac{3}{4} \times 4$ in)

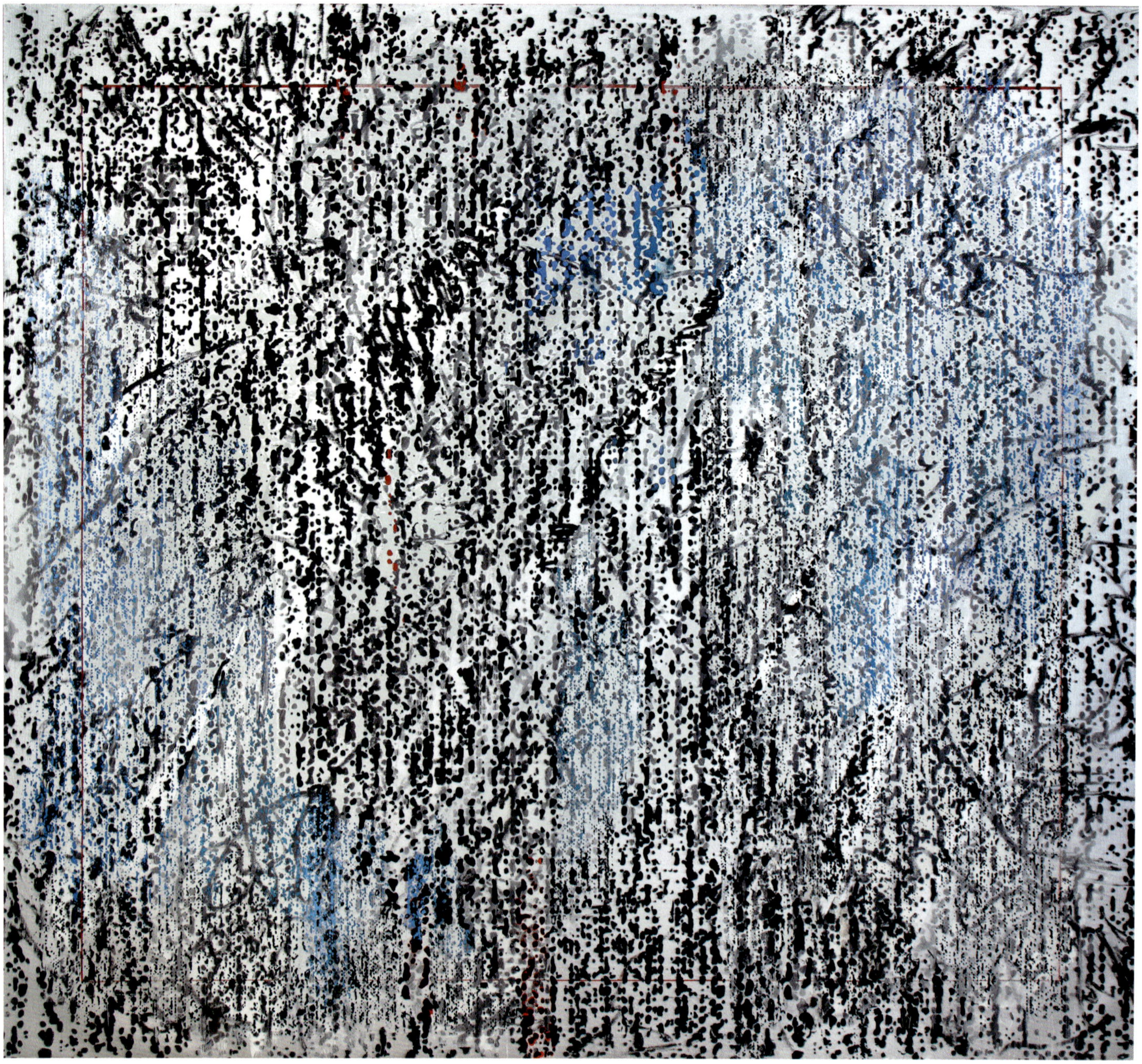

78. [\\] 2015

Oil on linen
254 × 281.9 cm (100 × 111 in)

response to the changing light of day and a fabricated source of interior illumination. The distinctions between darkness and light, artificial and natural, and in the case of Humphries's manipulation of painting as a light source, painting and installation, are often murky. Is this because these opposites are continuous, even interchangeable, in everyday life?

The light works are illustrative of Humphries's inhabitation of the art historical past as a place from which to push painting into the cultural present. Moreover, they are arguably the most vivid examples of the democracy of images thanks to their incorporation of the viewer in installation. Humphries insists that the tools she uses and the languages featured in her paintings are available to anyone because they begin in everyday usage.[61] The materials and mechanisms are familiar, making them as democratic as the works themselves. The same can be said of her recasting of painting as light. Across the oeuvre, paintings receive, mirror, produce, and reflect light such that viewers do more than simply look *at* a painting. They interact *with* the paintings in physical space. Thus, she uses familiar materials and subjects them to an innovative process to produce light paintings. Ultimately, in exhibition, the paintings require viewers to engage in a physical – bodily – experience of shifting light effects.

In the earliest works, Humphries used her tools to make pools of light, shimmering surfaces in which light dances around the painting as the viewer moves. From the 2000s onwards, the paintings became light sources bathing a room in gaudy colours and glittering effects reminiscent of a nightclub. Humphries thus introduced a further layer of democracy to her images: the viewer's physical interaction with light effects. If Caravaggio pulled people off the streets of Rome as models for his paintings, Humphries uses tools and languages from popular culture to create light, reflection, luminosity, and fluorescence in which everyone can bathe.

Soft illuminations

Despite their artificiality, Humphries's works verge into capturing the changing moods of daylight. In paintings such as *z..?** (fig.73), sky-blue clouds of different formations appear to blow in the wind, filling the image with a diffuse light. Meanwhile, in */\\/*, 2015 (fig.78), from a distance, we seem to look down through the clouds at a landscape filled with pockets of daylight blue. The appearance of light wavering on another level is then complicated, compromised by the thin red internal frame. This artificial – and somewhat random stamp of the painting's construction brings the viewer's eye back to the surface. Nevertheless, there are moments, when viewed from certain perspectives, that daylight appears to shimmer underneath the (stencilled) surface.

In *Black Sheep*, 1999 (fig.38), it is as if moonlight glows over a calm sea or cuts a path through pitch-black woods. In a surprise discovery, Humphries talks of how in exhibition at Greene Naftali Gallery, New York, in 1999, the paler section in the

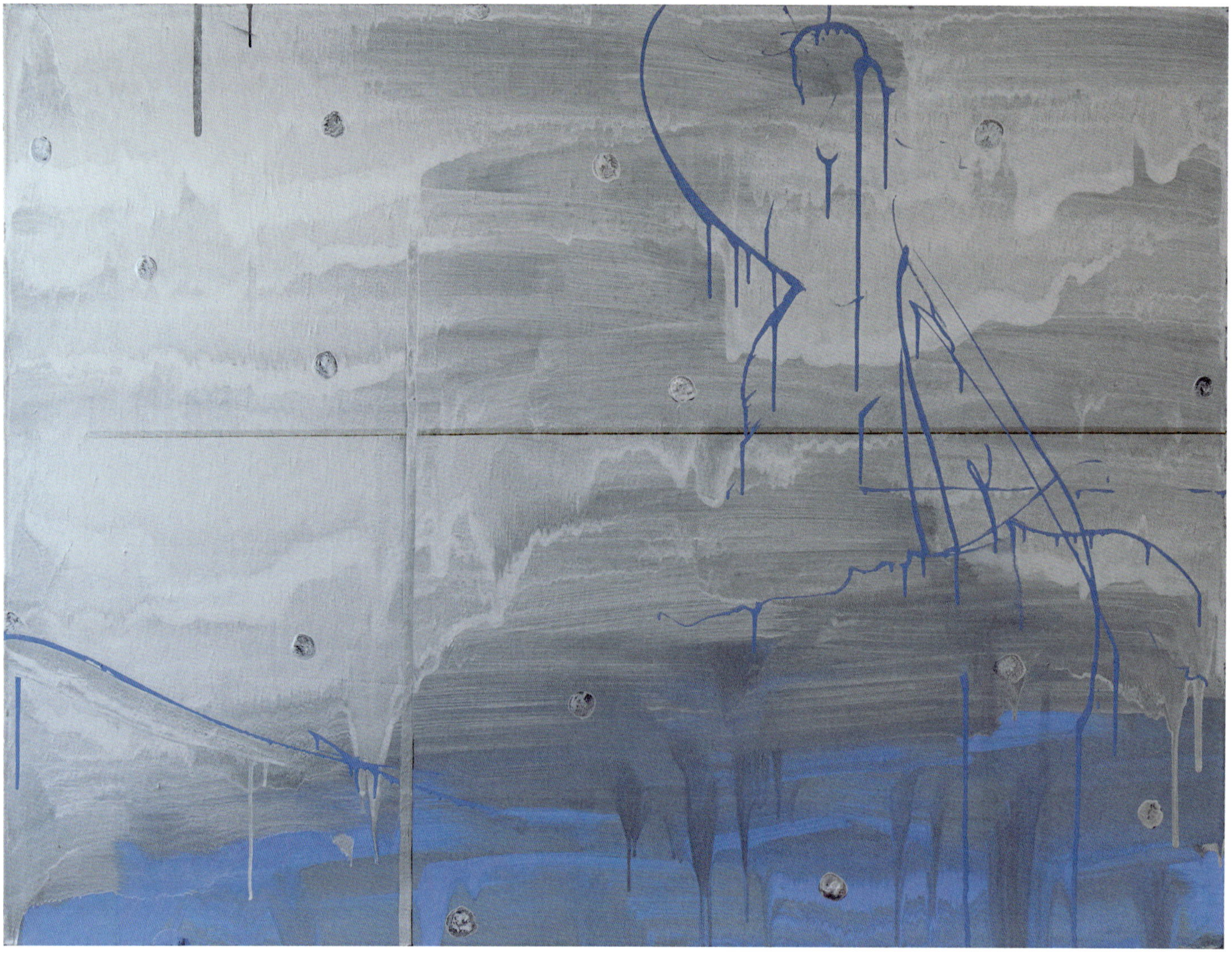

79. Untitled 2003

Oil and enamel on canvas
76.2 × 101.6 cm (30 × 40 in)

bottom of *Black Sheep* unexpectedly cast a pool of soft light onto the gallery floor.[62] Consequently, the viewer might no longer imagine themselves in nature, but standing in the pool of light from a lamp post. Light spills into our space, even though we are looking at a painting. Light shifts from natural to artificial, from deep in the woods to a lonely street, from illusion to representation, and back to reality when it shines on the gallery floor. Thus, light is propelled into a process of transformation and, with it, our vision moves through phases of deception and enlightenment. Ultimately, we are drawn to step into the pool of light on the gallery floor, reminiscent of our desire to pull up a seat in the empty place in the light at the tax collector's table in Caravaggio's *The Calling of Saint Matthew*, 1599–1600, as we step inside the Contarelli Chapel in the church of San Luigi dei Francesi, Rome.

Returning to the *Untitled* paintings from the early 2000s (for example, fig.71), shades of green and blue, diluted and made opalescent with the addition of white paint, create luminous landscapes. The paintings nod towards landscapes and seascapes seen from above or perpendicular to the shoreline, evoking the possibility of an ideal vision as might be experienced before a Caspar David Friedrich painting. The search for a vision beyond the everyday industrialised world is, after all, the use to which landscapes and seascapes have been put throughout the history of painting. Nevertheless, the daylight in Humphries's paintings is anything but lucid. The landscapes are seen through windows, frames, and screens scratched by the elements, or perhaps by a person. The promise of infinite horizons and the receding perspectives of Romantic painting might be heightened for some viewers when seen through dirty windows, but it remains unfulfilled.

In Humphries's land- and seascapes, vision is frustrated, expectations are redirected. The surface interruptions – the black horizontal line resembling barbed wire in *Untitled*, 2002 (fig.71) – render all illumination opaque. Such foreign details scramble the visual languages and thus our vision of the painting. Swathes of paint, graffiti-like scratches, and coloured drops are thrown together on the same canvas, creating tension among the different elements. The painted motifs (a broken grid, scratches, and blotches) on the surface of *Untitled*, 2003 (fig.79), could be dirt on the screens on which we customarily perceive reality. Even the silver paint falling down this work, resembling gently lapping waves on the shoreline, creates obfuscation. The scape or screen is in tension with the surface scratchings, hard-edged lines, punch marks, whimsical gestures, and interruptions. They collectively challenge what we think we are looking at, what we think we know about painting. We search without success for a coherent meaning. Humphries takes the viewer to an unexpected place in front of a painted canvas. In an oscillation between different visual languages, different types of natural and artificial light, we experience this new kind of presence. It is both a recognition of the artwork within a history of art and one that embraces the multiple 'non-art' media in circulation.[63]

Light belongs to everyone

In her early uses of stencils, the traces of actions made by Humphries's body were all but invisible. In the light works, her presence is ostensibly removed from the finished product while the viewer engages with the effects of light in the gallery space. The more distant Humphries's hand is from the work as we experience it, the more conceptually ambiguous the painting. Thus, questions about it – What is this painting? Where does it begin? Where does it end? What am I meant to be looking at? – are not clarified across the oeuvre. Rather, through an increasingly sophisticated use of different pigments and processes to create multiple types of illumination, the painting becomes more obscure, the painter more aloof, and the viewer more uncertain. This trajectory is underlined by Humphries's explorations in light. She exploits various visual possibilities in light that recall those created by windows, screens, billboards, gaming devices, mirrors, and gaudy disco lights. Artists have always used the visual possibilities in their immediate environment to create new worlds in the image. Think of the 1920s avant-garde photographers' engagement with the contemporaneous industrial world, producing images of reflections on the shiny body of recently manufactured automobiles and in side-view mirrors. Humphries is motivated by the same impulse to make images from the latest inventions. She works in a culture where reflections are newly seen on computer screens and in nightclubs as opposed to the bonnets of polished cars.

Silver paintings

In the mid-2000s, Humphries moved the relationship between painting and light to new levels through her unique pigments and techniques. The optical instability of the viewer's experience becomes literalised as the silver paint shifts – from reflective, to absorptive, to opaque – depending on the environmental conditions and the viewer's movement around the room. In the silver works, painting is a mirror that reflects the light of the room. It can be a window on which the surroundings are seen in reflection, or an opaque obstruction to image and vision. During the viewing experience, the painting transforms into a cinema screen in which the room is set in motion. Alternatively, if the silver paint catches direct sunlight, the reflection is so bright that the painting is replaced by a shining square surface of light. The variability of effects generated by the silver pigment makes the viewing experience visually akin to looking at screens. The painting has the capacity to obstruct vision, like the window on a computer screen blocks what lies behind. By turns, the painting offers an illusion only existing on the image's surface, an effect we know from the movies. Alternatively, the painting opens onto worlds to which the human eye has no access. At their most sophisticated, these paintings evoke the cinema's capacity to bring together multiple times and places into a single image passing before the viewer's eyes. They go further

80. 😟:) 2016

Oil on linen
96.5 × 101.6 cm (38 × 40 in)

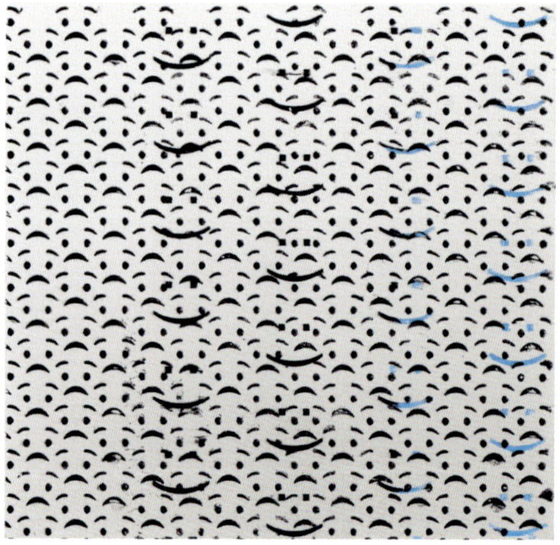

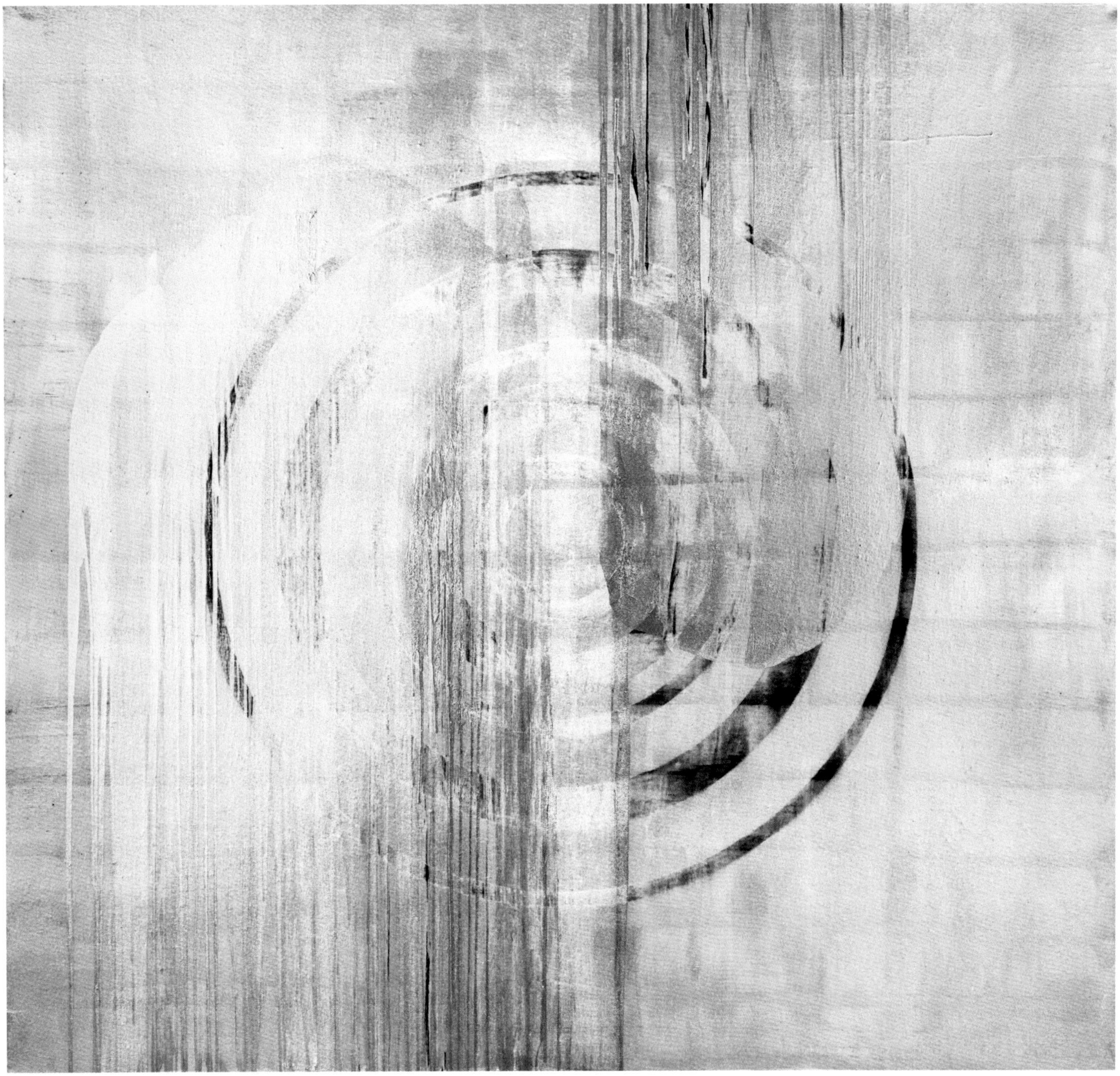

81. Aegis 2009

Oil on linen
228.6 × 243.8 cm (90 × 96 in)
Whitney Museum of American Art, New York; purchased with funds from the Painting and Sculpture Committee

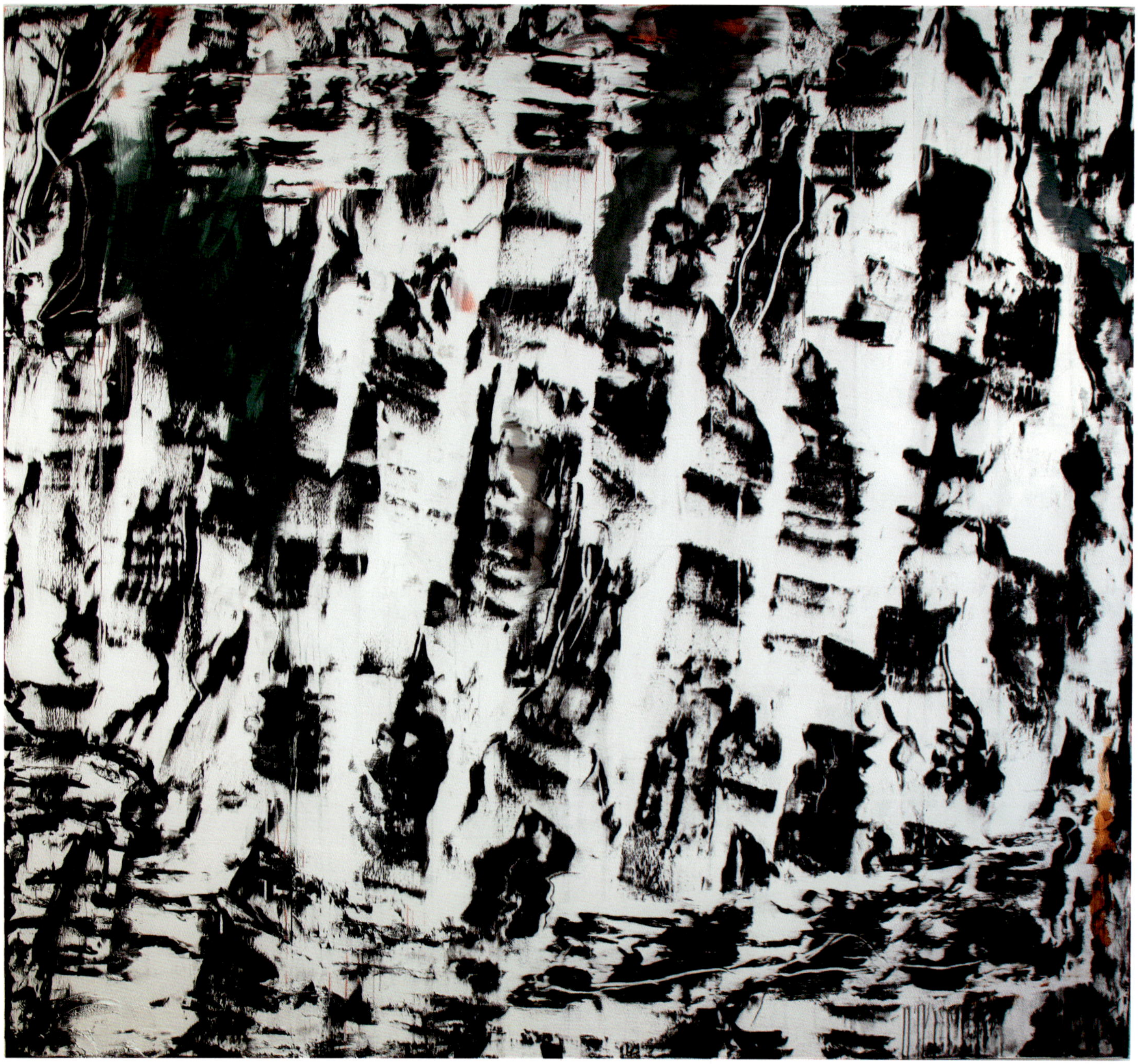

82. Untitled 2013

Oil and enamel on linen
254 × 281.9 cm (100 × 111 in)

when the digital world's opening into non-sequential, untethered times and spaces is splayed across the silver surface. The silver paintings shift from physical to analogue to digital images, appearing and disappearing. First, to their process of production.

Humphries makes the silver pigment herself by placing aluminium powder in a solvent and mixing it with oil. Depending on the proportions of each, the pigment will result in different textures, from light and fluffy to more liquid. Humphries pours the silver, brushes it, or applies it with a knife, depending on its viscosity. She claims to use 'whatever tools necessary to get it onto the canvas: sticks, knives, hands, sponges'.[64] She even uses a trowel or a hawk, tools otherwise employed to apply sheet rock and plaster. The silver's textures and material properties are quite different from the black paint she uses. Humphries must step on the paint tube to get the clay-like black out, forcing it onto the brush, scraping it from the canvas, stripping, washing, smoothing, sponging. As she describes it, the act of making and applying these paints is like mixing cement and building walls. In art terms, she sees her process as akin to building a sculpture.[65] Even before paint reaches the canvas, Humphries challenges the conventions of paint and painting. She does away with all assumptions that paint is a pigmented liquid or liquefiable substance applied to a support with a brush. That said, the traces of tools, materials, and processes are not left on the surface of the image because, following application, Humphries scrapes, layers, repaints, strips, repaints, removes, washes, and gouges at the painting. By the time we see the works in the gallery, they have an all-over smooth surface.

While the silver is the most visually striking element of these paintings, the black comes first.[66] Humphries applies a powdery black pigment to the canvas before laying on the silver. Next, she desecrates the painting by scraping away silver, revealing black underneath. If she adds colour on top of or underneath the silver, she re-scrapes to produce a flat democratic surface: she scours until all pigment belongs to the same layer. The levelling out of each painting's surface means that the familiar language of figure and ground is inadequate to describe the painting. Often, however, the human eye cannot see colour, black, or silver on the same level: we resort to looking as if at a conventional painting, refocusing to find the foreground and background. We might even search for precedents, recalling Josef Albers's experimentation with juxtaposed colours to alter the form and size of the coloured area as we visualise it. Thus, we see the olive-green gesture on the left side of *Untitled*, 2013 (fig.82) as if it lies on top of the silver paint, yet it was painted both underneath and over top and is now part of a contiguous surface. All painted elements contribute to a physically undifferentiated surface. If the language of classical painting is to be found in this work, it is envisioned, not actual. Figure and ground, foreground and background, distance and depth are projections of the limitations resulting from the acculturation of human vision. Such notions cannot describe Humphries's painting. When we are deceived by the organisation of space within the painting, we move around, in search of a stable position from which to view a fixed image. Face to face with Humphries's silver paintings, such a position does not exist.

83. Untitled 2013

Oil on linen
254 × 281.9 cm (100 × 111 in)

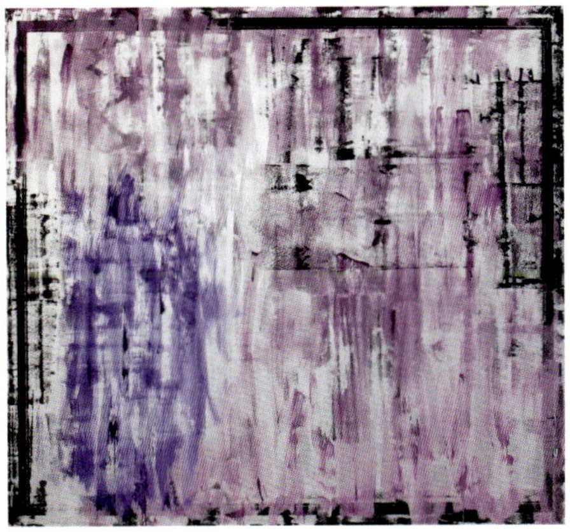

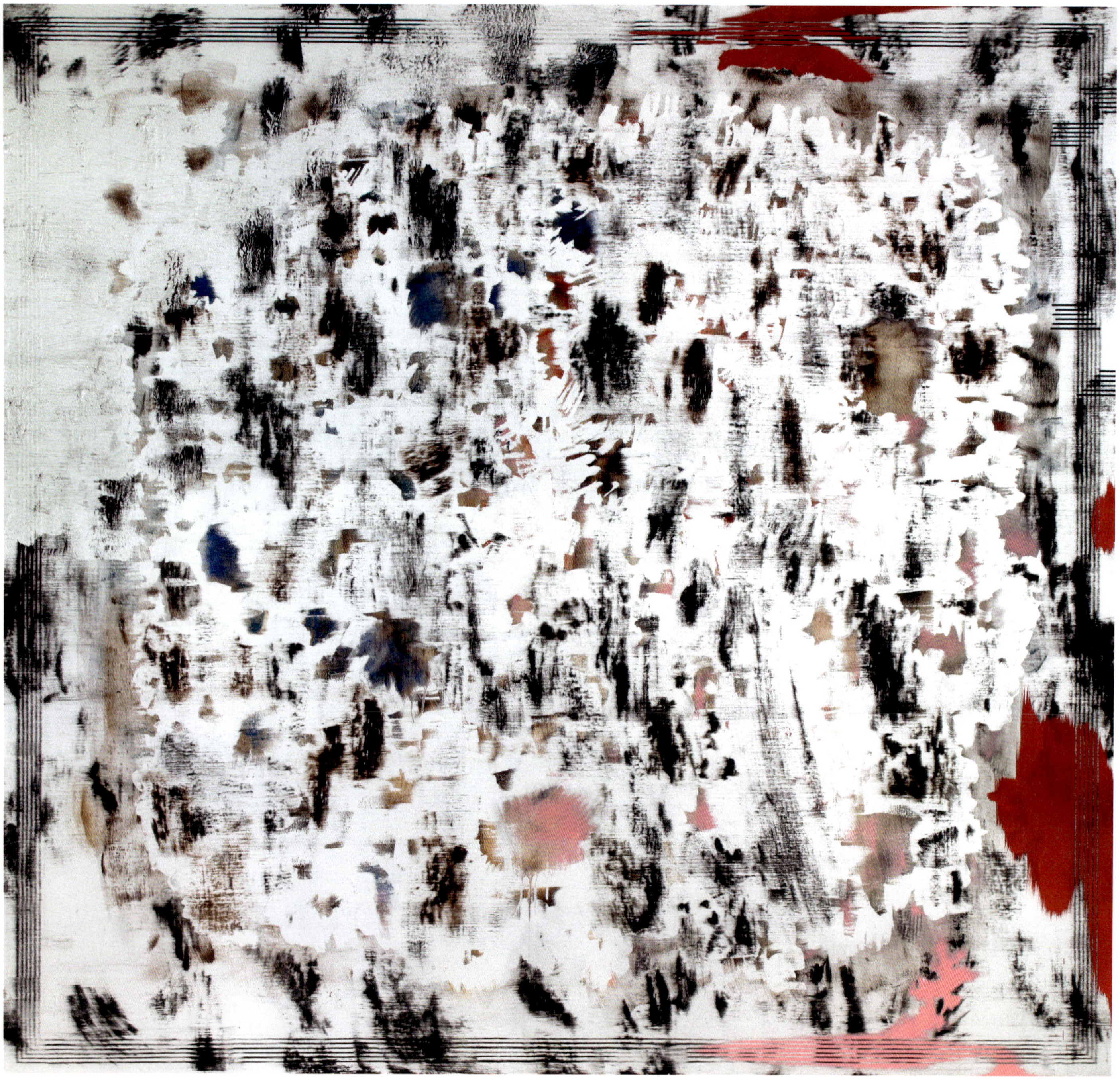

84. Untitled 2011

Oil on linen
228.6 × 243.8 cm (90 × 96 in)

With silver, light is added to this already complex use of paint to expand our vision. Consequently, the democracy of images extends. Anything goes in the shiny metallic world of Humphries's silver paintings. As we move around, looking for an ever-elusive certainty, the painting absorbs and reflects light, shifting from transparent to opaque, pushing us to keep moving and redetermining both the work's status and our relationship to it. Linda Yablonsky describes these paintings as amalgams of non-textured surfaces with the illusory appearance of a history. She says that the visual layering of silver and coloured pigments, together with the different types of markings, make the paintings look like walls from which posters have been torn off, leaving remnants of paper behind.[67] As Humphries points out, 'some are textured and some are flat. You get different kinds of light in a silver field, so it behaves like another kind of spectrum.'[68] Thus, even when we try to explain them through comparison to static everyday visual surfaces, we fall short. Even when the surface of Humphries's paintings is historically vibrant, it is also an anachronistic, sheer presence. This constant unsettledness is more usually found in experimental moving images – in the cinema, not on a painting.

The silver paintings do not represent scenes from films; rather, their effect is cinematic. The flickering light of a clandestine haunt casting shadows from behind louvre blinds comes alive on Humphries's kinetic, two-dimensional surfaces. They may also remind one of the view outside: wet streets, rain falling across the light of a solitary streetlamp. Whether the chiaroscuro effects of the silver and black remind viewers of the underground world of 1940s film noir or the presence of a disgruntled ghost refusing to die, the silver creates mood, effect, and a narrative unfolding in time. Like the cinema, the paintings replicate – or claim to – the experience of looking through windows in the real world.

While the silver canvases invite light-generating narratives, time and space are also flattened. We have already seen this in the similarity to stacked open windows on a computer screen, one behind the other, existing on the same plane. *Untitled*, 2011 (fig.84) demonstrates how time and space are simultaneously erased from the silver paintings. The flattened surface, the frequent imposition of frames, transforms the painting into a window. It is unclear, however, whether it is an open window on a screen or a framed glass image. The frame within the frame effectively announces, 'These are the limits of this two-dimensional object, which, in case you haven't noticed, is a painting.' The static object existing in space is, however, unsettling. For Humphries, frames invite transgression. Like a spaceship or a shark from a Steven Spielberg film, the painting finds a way to fly out of its space and into ours. Yet it sits on the wall, simultaneously expecting to be looked at as a painting.

I invoke the Spielberg film analogy because the viewer's experience of the silver paintings is closer to that of watching a film than looking at pigment on a canvas. Humphries transforms the experience of high art into one mimicking our experience of popular culture. Akin to Spielberg's introduction of velocity and dynamism to the

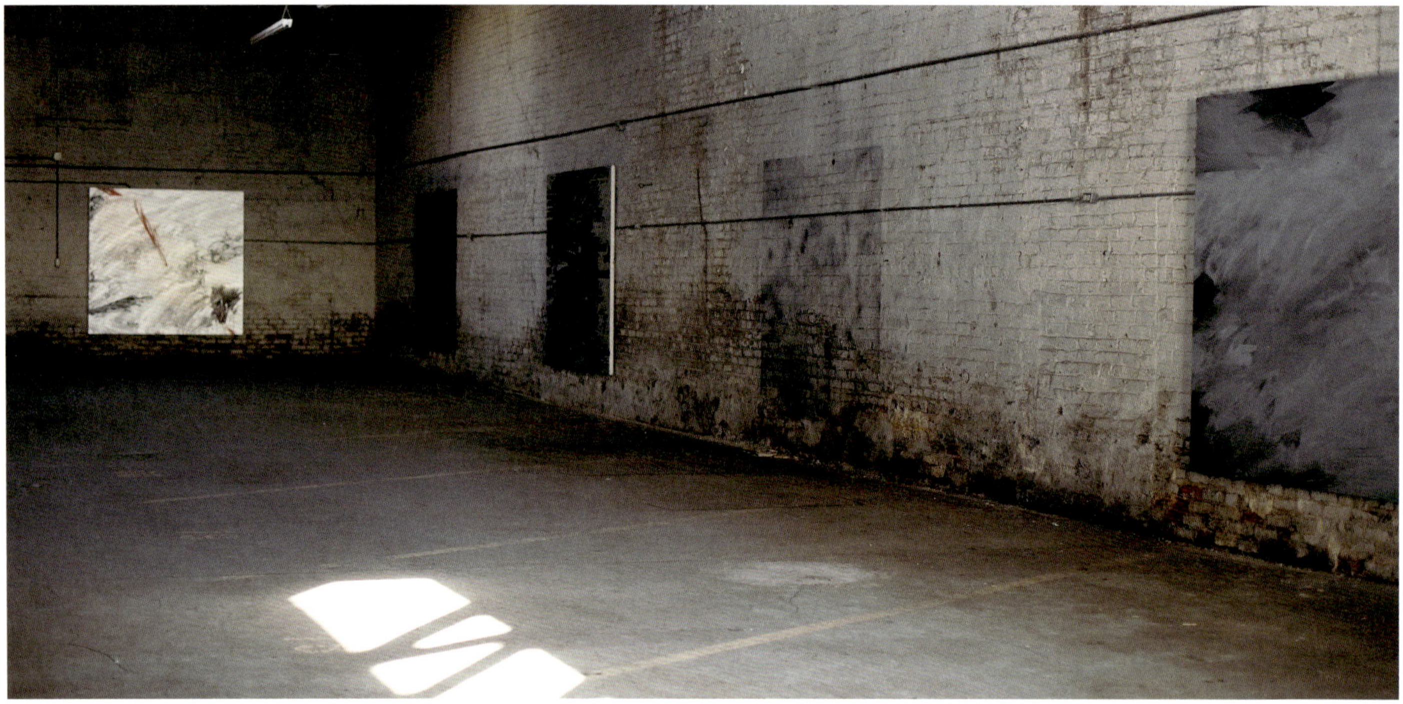

85. Installation view
Prospect.1 New Orleans, 2008

cinema in the 1970s, Humphries brings new dimensions to painting. In the ultimate transgressive gesture, Humphries makes paintings that refuse to identify as paintings.

From November 2008 to January 2009, Humphries exhibited five large silver paintings in the Prospect.1 biennial in the Warehouse District of New Orleans. On the walls of a vacated industrial space – the former Ideal Auto Repair shop – *In the Back*, 2008 (fig.86) and *Beat the Devil*, 2008 (fig.87), shimmered in the changing light that streamed through high windows and flooded through the front roller door as it would have through giant windows of cathedrals from the Gothic period onwards. The light fell onto Humphries's silver surfaces as if hitting metal car parts. The paintings came alive through light, not dissimilar to how Caravaggio's *The Calling of Saint Matthew* might appear at certain times of the day in its sixteenth-century Roman chapel. However, at Prospect.1 the shiny silver finishes of car parts, not precious paintings, were the reference point. Humphries included a series of 'non-paintings' in the space: black squares, mimicking the shape and size of her canvases, were sprayed directly onto the worn industrial walls. The question they begged was clear: 'Where does the wall end and the painting begin?' The artist's paintings were the same as patterns on the brick walls of a workshop. The traces left by an artist were likened to those of a mechanic.

We see this continuity between painting and non-painting, painting and work, in *In the Back*: the orange lines at the top and bottom could be a continuation of the bricks on which it hung. At Prospect.1, the black squares looked like ghosts, memories left

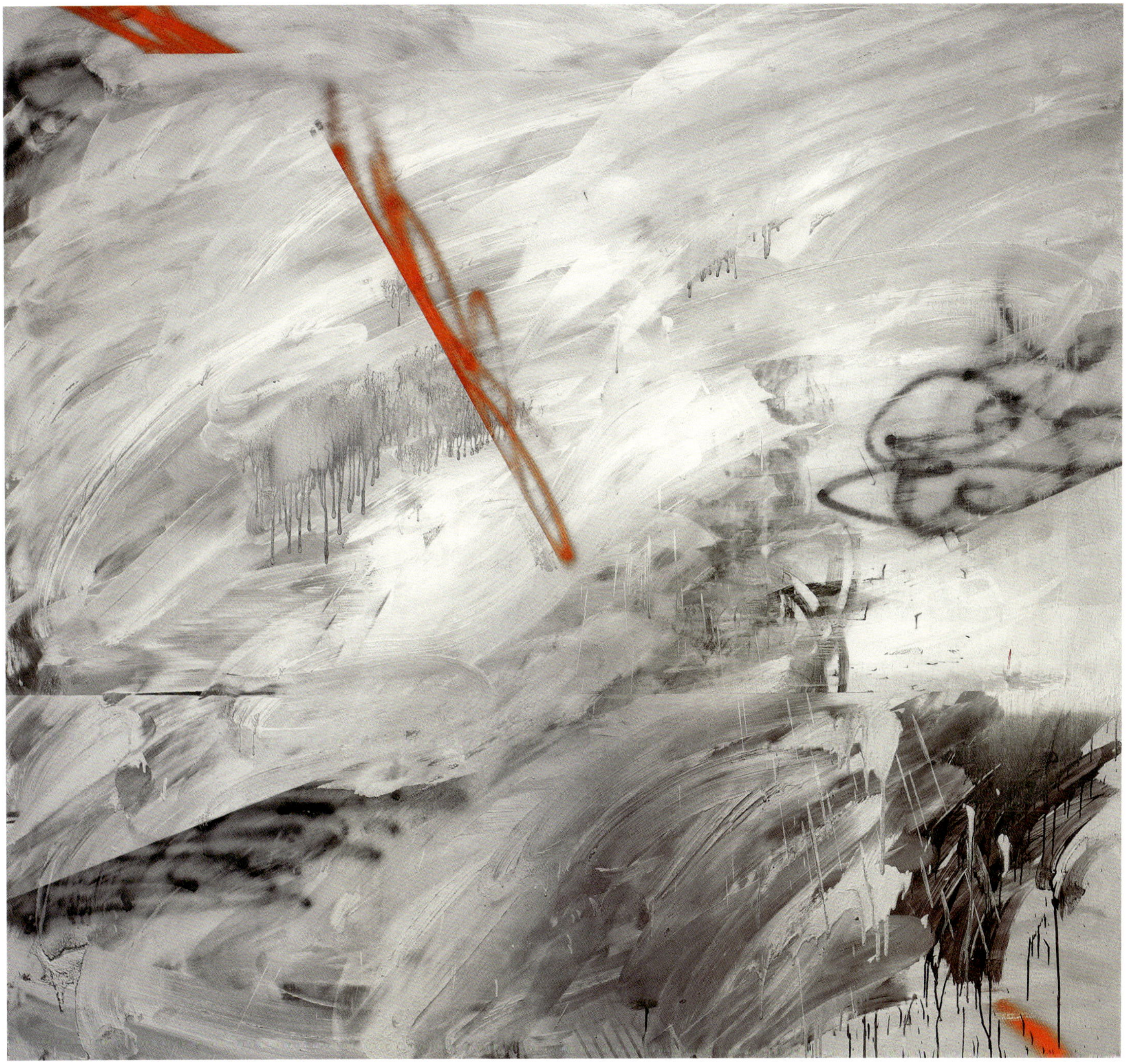

86. In the Back 2008

Oil and enamel on linen
203.2 × 221 cm (80 × 87 in)

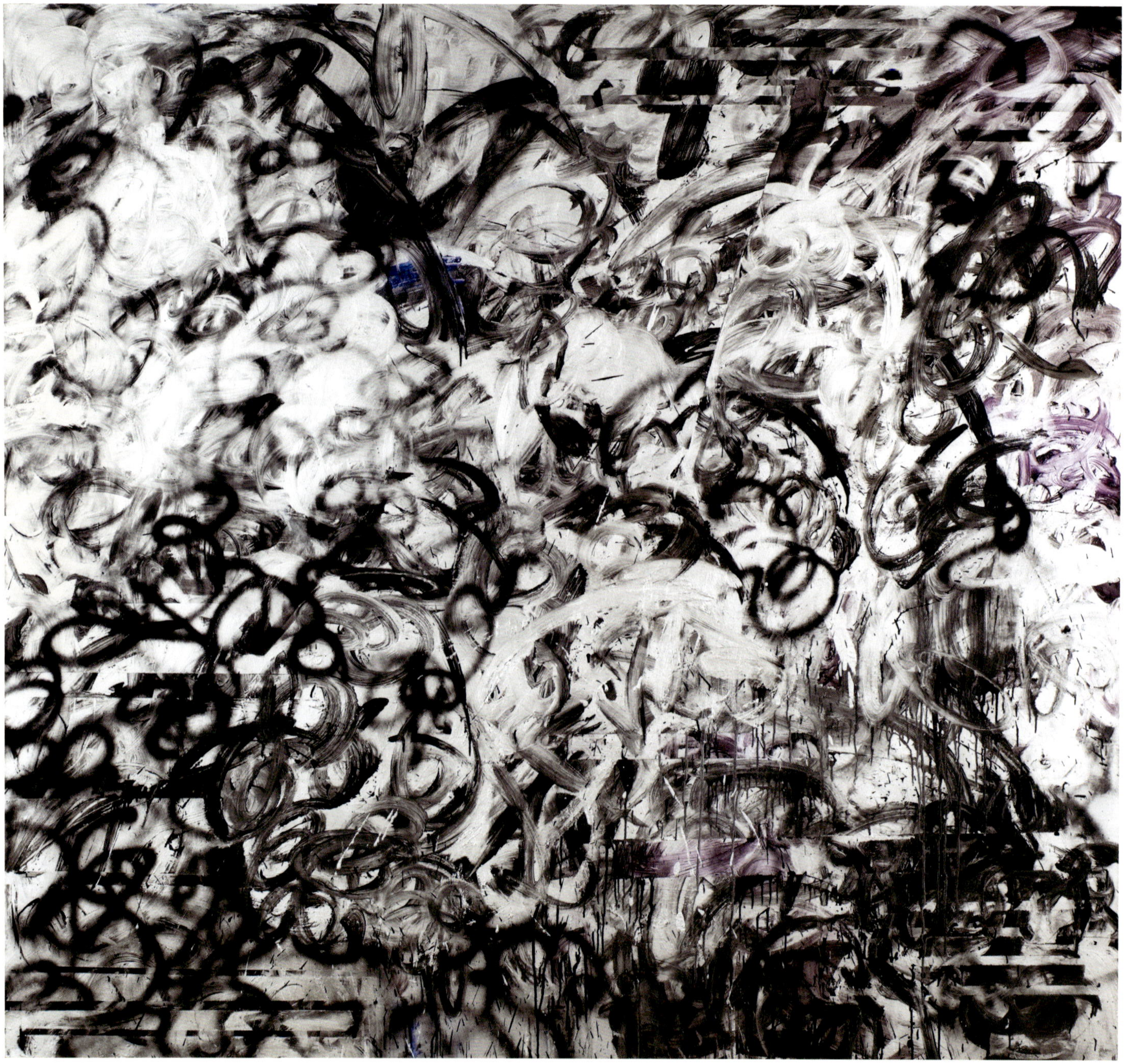

87. Beat the Devil 2008

Oil and enamel on linen
203.2 × 221 cm (80 × 87 in)
Museum of Modern Art, New York;
gift of Jerry I. Speyer and Katherine G. Farley

by the previous users of the space. This highlights another dimension of Humphries's paintings: their dependence on the space of exhibition. The significance of context and its extension of the democracy of painting becomes underlined when considering the protest signs, in the back room. These signs were sprayed in situ, the paint invading the frame and bleeding onto the wall. When the sign is removed from its position against the wall, another non-painting appears.[69] Humphries's non-paintings resemble stains left after something has been taken away, the residue of a vanished past.

The Russian painter Kazimir Malevich comes to mind when looking at the black 'non-paintings'. While Humphries talks about 'mak[ing] endless last paintings' and the finality of painting, the resonance with Malevich adds another layer.[70] When she paints a black square on the wall of an auto-repair shop, it brings with it, via Malevich, a revolution. The black square is a place from which to begin. It is the beginning of pure abstraction. Humphries's works are present where the past is now absent. Black has become the illumination where the light has been turned off in the auto-repair shop. Nevertheless, Humphries's silver paintings are in their world, not Malevich's. In this building, the paintings speak directly to the weathered walls and small windows inviting the sunlight. Thus, in the context of the auto-repair shop, 'non-paintings' relate to the material and industrial world. They mark a revolution that may have happened, but since then, the workers have laid down their signs. In their place, painting revivifies. Humphries might call the anonymous black squares 'non-paintings', but they show the power of painting to begin again.

As such, at Prospect.1 silver and non-paintings are flags of hope. The ghosts might be dead, but they are brought back to life in the silver paintings, protesting the past seen by these walls. The exhibition was hung a few years after Hurricane Katrina had decimated Humphries's birth city of New Orleans. Painting has taken over where natural disaster and other injustices took place.

Humphries describes the physics of the silver pigment: 'It picks up light in unpredictable ways, sometimes coming forward very aggressively, at other times going more dead gray and giving way for the color to advance. So, at times they look really gaudy and crass, and at other times quite sedate.'[71] The metallic paint tells a complex, moving story. For Humphries, silver does not reference value or precious metal. It has none of the sparkle of a capitalist fantasy seducing a viewer. Silver is about pop. It is about heavy-metal music and the movies, about bringing light into the darkened space of an auto-repair workshop in the wake of a deluge. Light beams into the heart of everyday life to create new beginnings. At first glance, Humphries is not interested in what black and silver symbolise, but in channelling the events in her midst into paintings that unsettle through their unpredictability. She breaks all the rules by using abstraction to create the ultimate revolution. She puts painting where it is not meant to be, on the walls of an auto-repair shop, shining a light on the culture of power within those walls, in that city, in that historical moment. However, this does not mean that viewers will not interpret the works in other ways.

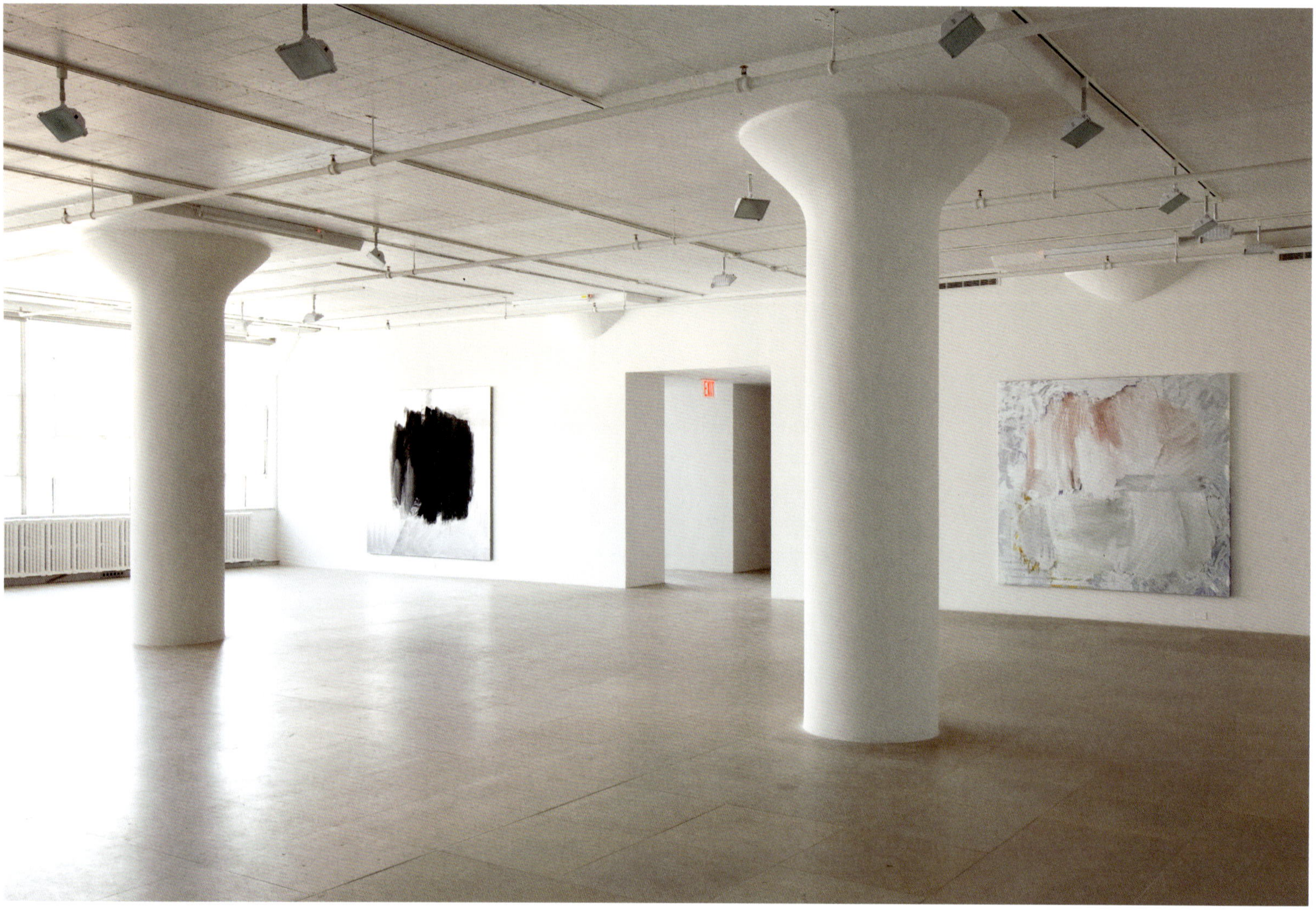

88/89. Installation views
Past Out, Greene Naftali, New York, 2006

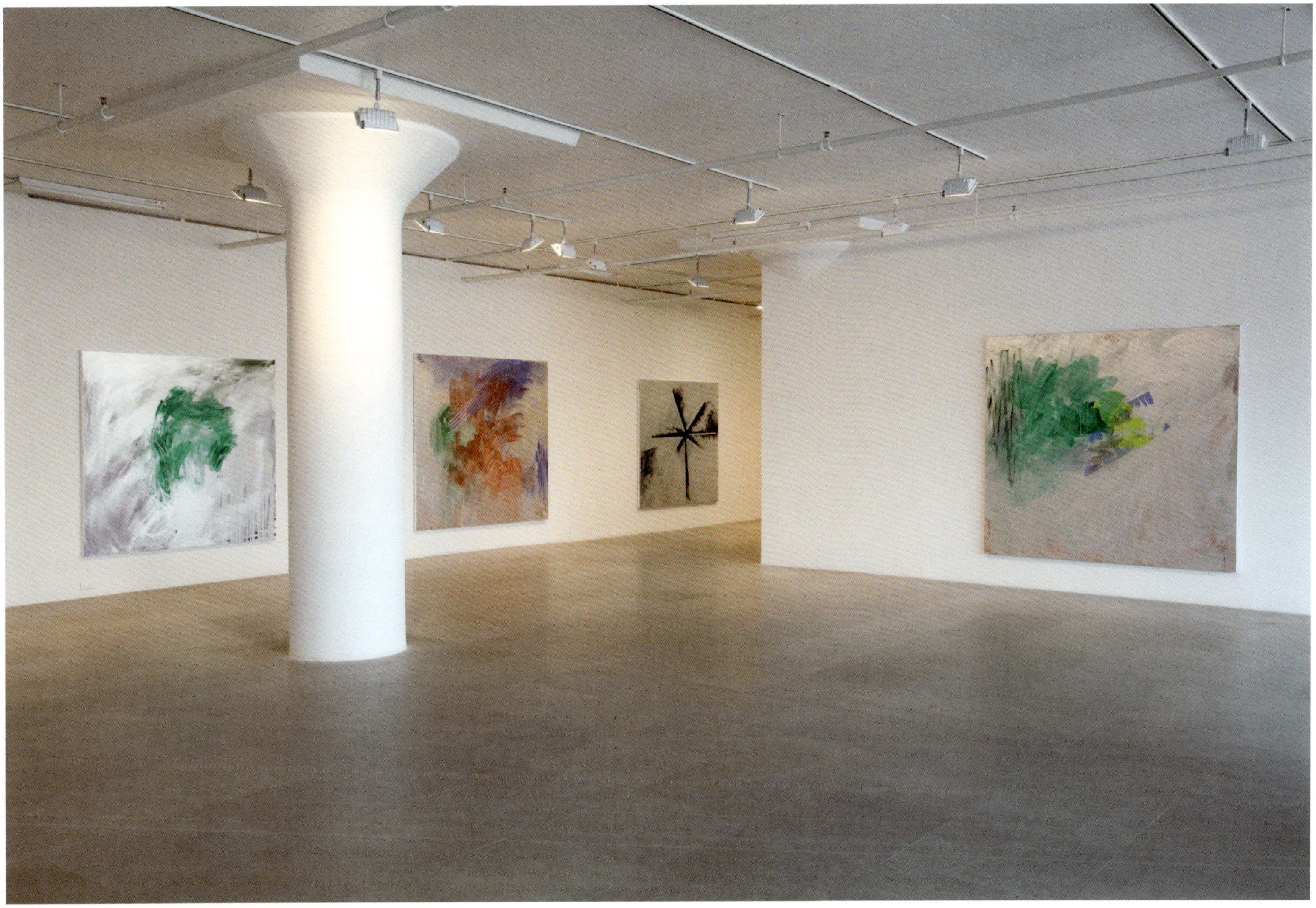

The silver paintings remind one of frescoes, mutating, transfiguring in the light. For example, Andrea del Sarto's cycle of the life of Saint John the Baptist (1513–26) painted on the walls of the Chiostro della Scalzo, designed for the Confraternity of Saint John the Baptist in Florence. Different panels of a narrative in a rainbow of greys are illuminated at different times of the day depending on the position of the sun in relation to the walls. Humphries calls the silver paintings gaudy and vulgar, but they also point towards an oblique relationship to the long history of religious art that might be read into her work. The paintings are mesmerising, enticing us into motion, emotion, and reverence, until they frustrate our attempts at enlightenment. To reiterate, this type of ambivalence is familiar from the great works of modernist abstraction.

Black-light aesthetics

In Humphries's 2019–20 exhibition at Dia Bridgehampton, the small ground-floor gallery space was filled with the serene glow of black-light sculptures. An interesting conversation emerged between Dan Flavin's sculptures in the upstairs galleries and Humphries's on the lower floor. Most notably, like Flavin's, Humphries's fluorescent light works defined the space around them. A handful of objects, some on the floor, others hanging on the walls like paintings, and one resembling a billboard sitting on an easel, were strategically placed around Dia's intimate downstairs space. The objects were put under black light and became fluorescent light sources, saturating the space in artificial illumination.

A table of flotsam and seashells and the odd piece of neon-green driftwood were not, in fact, the objects we thought they were. Rather, they were resin casts of 3-D prints. The objects, fashioned from digital files that Humphries found on the internet, were infused with fluorescent pigments in the printing process. When they were placed under black light, their invisible ultraviolet light made visible the phosphorous pigments infusing the objects. The results were glowing patches of vibrant luminosity emanating from garishly coloured objects and flooding Dia's dark gallery space. More like light installations, sculptures made to look like paintings changed the colour and appearance of visitors' faces and bodies. Depending on where we, the viewers, stood in relation to individual works, anything white – eyes, teeth, and clothing – glowed in the dark. The luminous objects under black light transformed us into ghouls. Inside the exhibition, translucent paintings without origin resembled natural objects and made spectres out of human bodies. Black-light technology had the effect of creating democratic spaces like the bedrooms, bars, discos, and funfairs in which the same lights are found.

In their connection to the nearby Long Island coastline, Humphries's objects merged the technological and the natural detritus that litter our physical and memory landscapes. A small, fluorescent green fragment attached to a violet panel of *Painting*,

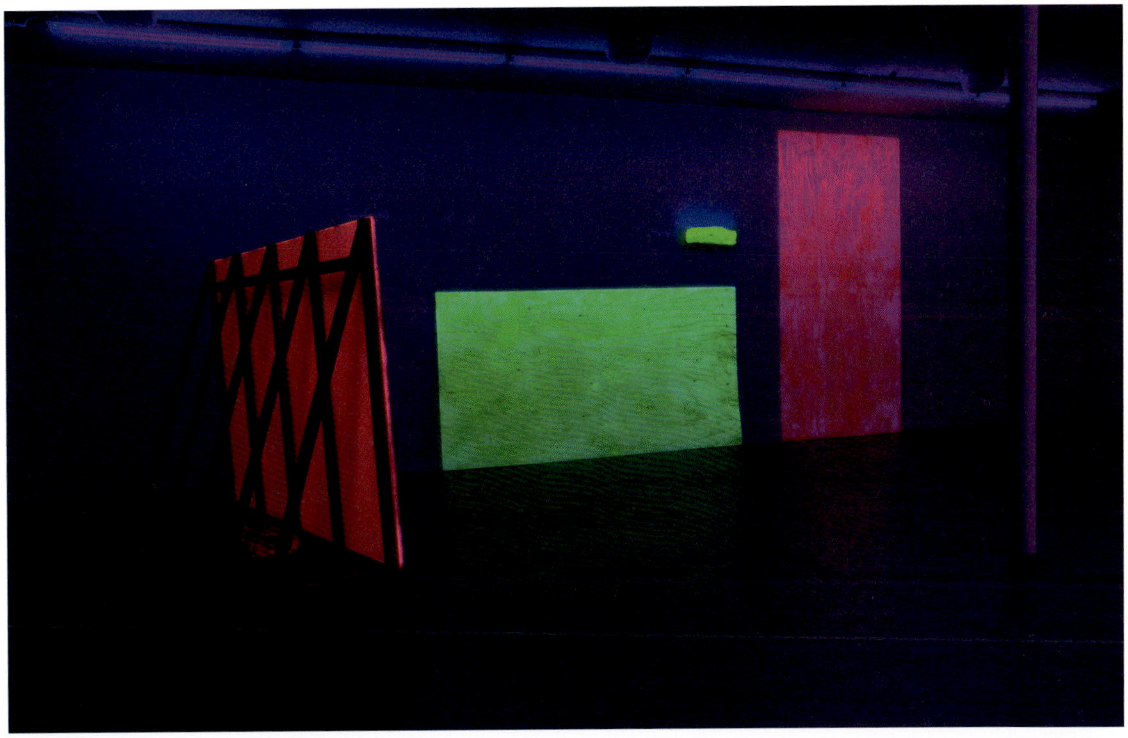

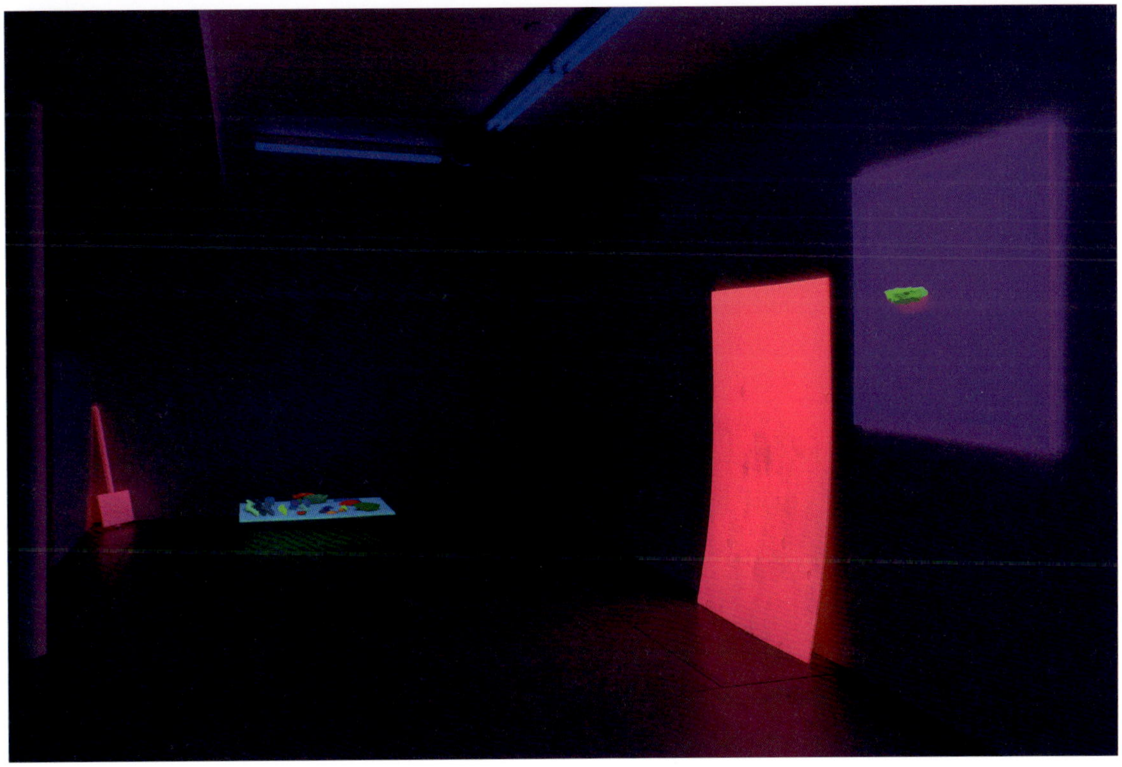

90/91. Installation views of *Jacqueline Humphries*
Dan Flavin Art Institute, Bridgehampton, New York,
2019

2019, and various seashells and flotsam laid on a table titled *Collection*, 2019, were technologically produced to mimic what are recognised as natural objects that might have washed up on the shore. Moving closer to the objects raised questions even though we were told they were digital productions: What are these objects? Does light emanate from the sculpture, or is it being directed onto the works from elsewhere in the gallery?

Other cultural references surfaced while inside the exhibition. The imitation remnants of driftwood visible above *Full Sheet Green*, 2019, and tucked behind *Billboard*, 2019, suggested they had a former life. The word 'Dia' lurked under the glowing surface of *Billboard*, and the obvious question was whether Humphries found the piece of plywood – which is really a resin cast of plywood – in the trash on site. Had it been used to transport the previous artist's work? Even though the objects were fabricated with a 3D printer in time for the exhibition, we gave them a history. Was Humphries playing a joke on us? The game of looking at and searching for understanding images and objects that are not what we think they are, despite knowing that we are being deceived, is the ultimate – or Omega – artist statement.

The pieces remind us of lava lamps and stick insects glowing in the dark. They also suggest scientific discovery, particularly given their dependence on the behaviour of light and its interaction with chemical substances. Yet Humphries's art objects are ephemeral. The fabricated ephemera remind us of Cy Twombly's sculptures made of driftwood, painted white. Twombly made random debris washed up on the beach into something precious and beautiful. Humphries's works are likewise aesthetically pleasing, objects to look at over time, objects that are not what they appear to be, but worthy of display. They incorporate everyday technologies – fluorescent pigments, laser printers, light – but they are simultaneously aesthetic creations.

Looking at the works, fully aware of their deceit, we wonder if the history with which they engage is also an illusion. In their play with the interstice between scientific object and artwork, natural and digital, authentic original and fully manufactured object, Humphries manipulates the history of art by alluding to everyday contexts. The line between reality and illusion as it has been established, questioned, reinstated, critiqued, and rejected over centuries is reignited in Humphries's use of the digital. Humphries takes the familiar attestation of representation as always being an illusion and pushes it to new levels of irony. Our inability to determine the line between real and illusory reproduction is irrelevant. What matters is our experience of the art, falling in and out of seeing and blindness, knowing and not-knowing, certainty and doubt.

The experience of having our expectations aroused and assumptions disproven is further exaggerated in photographs of the black-light works. In the flesh, they glow, and their substance as light floods into a three-dimensional space. We walk around the exhibition, examine the works from different distances. In photographs, the objects appear to float in an expansive gallery space. In the flesh, the same space is surprisingly small and cosy. Photographs show entirely different artworks.

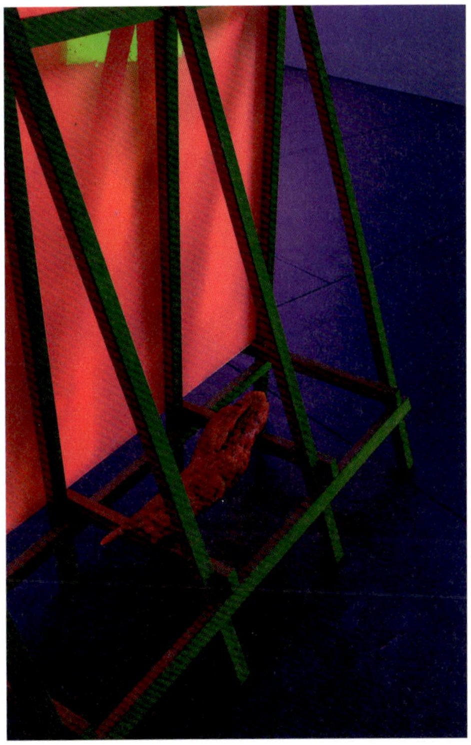

92. Installation view of *Jacqueline Humphries*
Dan Flavin Art Institute, Bridgehampton, New York, 2019

Immersed in this sanctuary of light, awash with iridescence, we are reminded of our ongoing relationship with screen worlds. Humphries raises the stakes of twenty-first-century technology in painting to a new level. At Dia Bridgehampton, the revelations do not take place visually through our altered distance from the canvas. Rather, they are had through immersion, reminding of the sensuous overload of the screen image. It is as though involvement in the screen world is writ large in the three-dimensional gallery space. The effect reminds of sitting in a darkened room on a video call, texting, or gaming after lights out. With our eyes focused on smartphones, tablets, and computers, our faces are bathed by the internal illumination of a screen. We are no longer observers of the technologically produced image, we are inside it. Moreover, inside this proto-phosphorescent den of consumption, our physical state mutates. We are spectres of our human selves. Humphries invites a performance of what Vivian Sobchack warns will be the result of the 'electronic presence' of technological media. We have been reduced to 'ghosts in the machine', without corporeality or agency.[72] True to the contradiction of being inside Humphries's exhibition spaces, we nevertheless experience our bodies in a world of wonder, seeing (ourselves) differently.

Billboard uses individually developed pigments that are not as bright as those typically seen in blacklight settings. Thus, the incandescent orange object with traces of text under the surface, covering over what it once advertised, is recognisable as a billboard. That is, it draws attention to itself through a different means. *Billboard* is also placed on an easel-like stand, thus likened to a painting in process. Ironically for something resembling a billboard or a painting, this is an image of obfuscation, not illumination. Frani O'Toole interprets *Billboard* in relationship to the question it asks about art. She writes, 'In advertising, a lot of things that claim to be honest are obfuscations – is art so different?'[73] While *Billboard* speaks about the illusions and deceptions of the image on its face, it is also the opposite. *Billboard* is painting as sculpture, even as it parades the consumption of images.

Billboard also reflects the superficiality and elan of life in the Hamptons. Dia's Bridgehampton space is, after all, on the opposite side of Long Island to the house that inspired F. Scott Fitzgerald's *The Great Gatsby* (1925). The reference prompts us to question the process of a billboard convincing us we need possessions. In turn, our thoughts lead to the inflated value of art as an object to be bought, sold, consumed, reproduced, and further commodified. And yet Humphries's objects are also individually made, original artworks, even if they are pure fabrication. The works embody the contradiction of optical printing as a technological process not yet available to the masses. Moreover, the fluorescent pigment that gives them the appearance of painting is embedded within the cast object. Thus, in another strategy, the works' colour further removes the 'painting' from what we assume we are looking at. We nevertheless react to them as though they are paintings. There is no paint involved in these works, and yet they are about painting. Unless, of course, they are

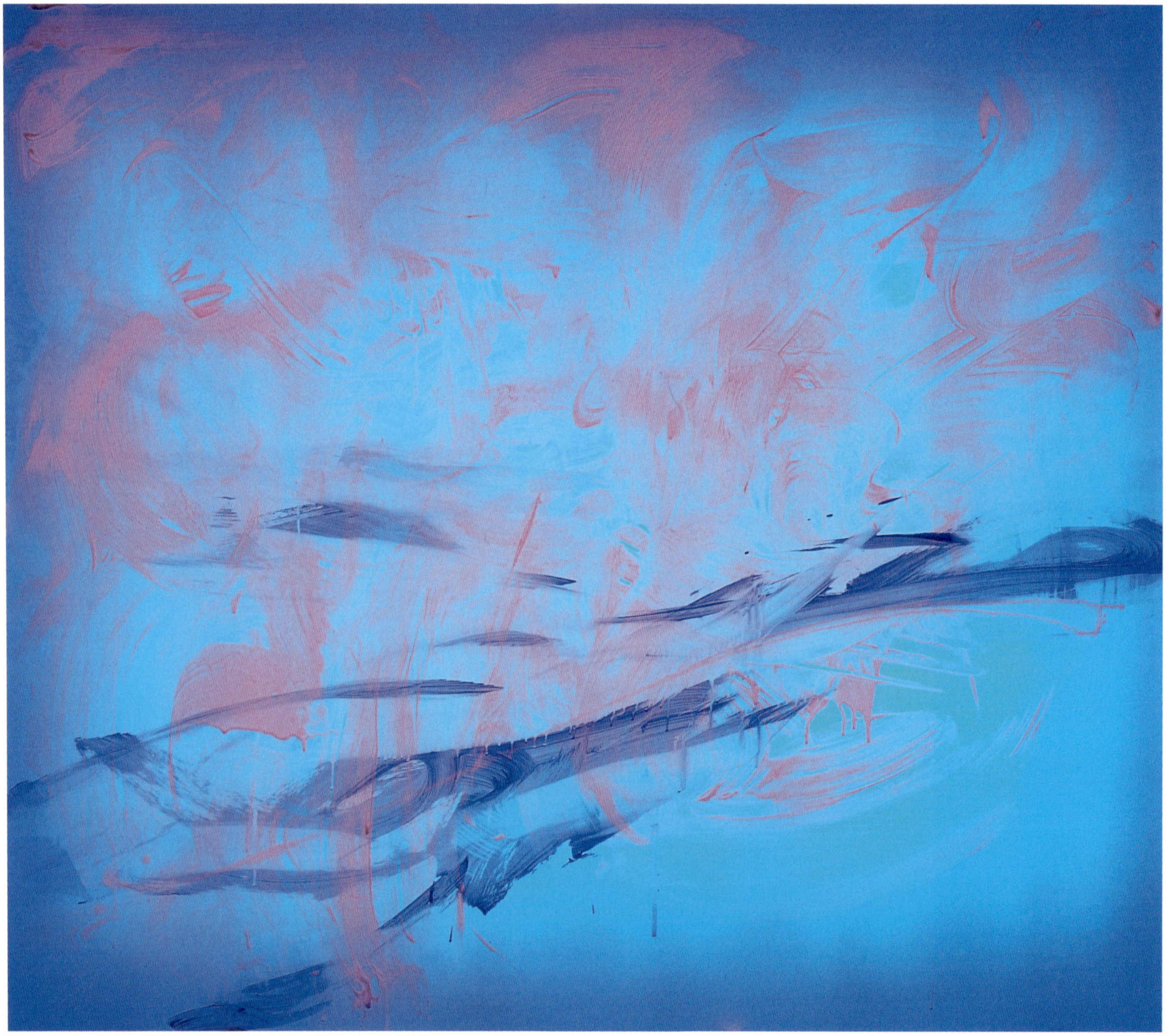

93. Untitled 2005/2008

Acrylic and oil on fabric on black light box
132.1 × 152.4 cm (52 × 60 in)

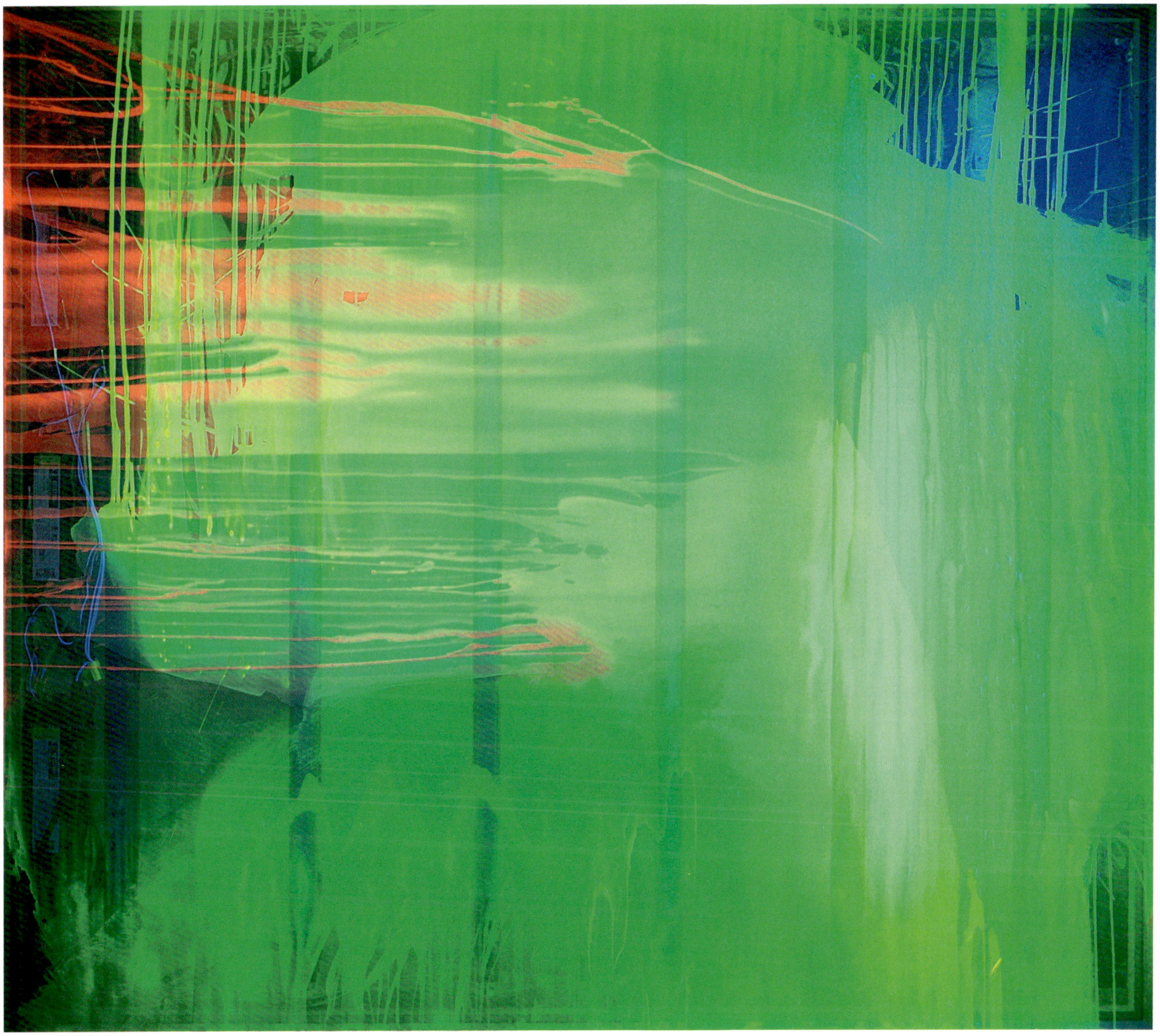

94. Untitled 2005

Oil and acrylic on silk screen on fluorescent black light box
132.1 × 152.4 × 10.2 cm (52 × 60 × 4 in)

about light. Humphries creates objects that go beyond what art history has seen. A self-reflective object posing as a painting that comes alive in the light and physically changes the viewer in order to make a claim for the consumption of art. This is a radical use of light as painting and painting as light.

Profanity in light

Humphries began using pigments that fluoresce under black light in the early 2000s. She painted in the same conditions under which we are required to experience the works: in the dark with the invisible black lights turned on. From the start, she used her materials promiscuously. She talks about painting in the dark and having no idea of how the paintings will look. She is much like an early filmmaker or photographer having to wait for their images to be processed in a laboratory. Humphries explains that the paintings emerge as each layer of a medium is applied.[74] That is, paintings made in darkness under black-light conditions are transformed into fluorescence, appearing quite different from paintings in natural or incandescent light.

In the mid-2000s, Humphries also made light-box paintings. She painted on sheer and translucent fabric, then lit the image from behind. The lighting technology is thus part of these paintings. The black-light tubes and wiring are visible through the fabric onto which she has painted, sometimes faintly and sometimes clearly. In another layer of complexity, a reflective polyester film is placed behind the light tubes, amplifying the light. Humphries explains the illusions and distortions that result: 'the painting then reflects in the Mylar and does a kind of funhouse thing with the reflection, like what I painted, but out of control. You can also see the room and yourself.'[75] Thus, the light-box works are a genre unto themselves, made of incompatible and inappropriately matched materials. Again, similar to modernist abstract photography or cinema, Humphries engages her historical context in the making of the work. Paint, fabric, electrical cords, black light, and thermal insulators result in a range of images. We recognise the technology of illuminated advertising billboards, early glass-plate photography, dioramas. When looking in the Mylar at our own deformed image overlaid with coloured paint, interrupted by fluorescent light tubes, we see ourselves as if in a funhouse mirror. The journey of discovery with the light-box works is not what we anticipate in the presence of a painting.

By contrast, the black-light paintings are made with fluorescent paint. 'They are not natural pigments, they are dyes mixed with resins and then ground into pigment, so they're totally artificial, created by the Switzer brothers in the 1930's [sic].'[76] In a blacked-out room, ultraviolet light is activated to 'excite' colours individually, transforming the pigment into patterns of light glowing in the dark. Nothing about these works resembles what we think painting is supposed to do and be. Their effects are more commonly experienced in a nightclub. They are visions reminding us of

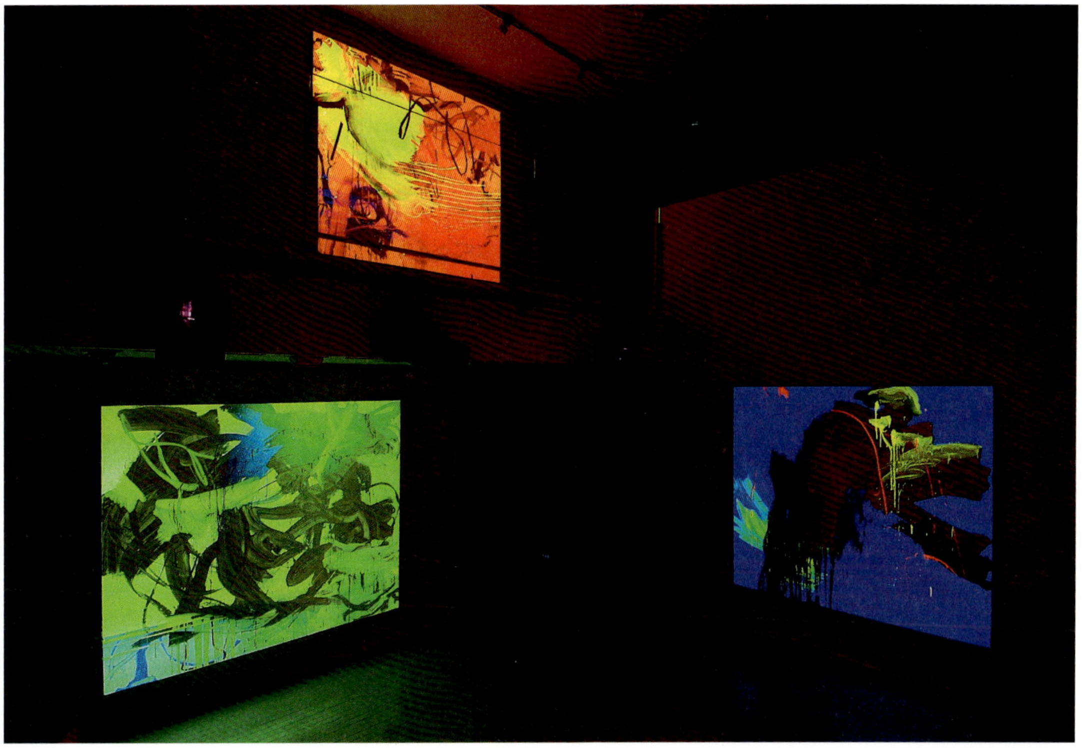

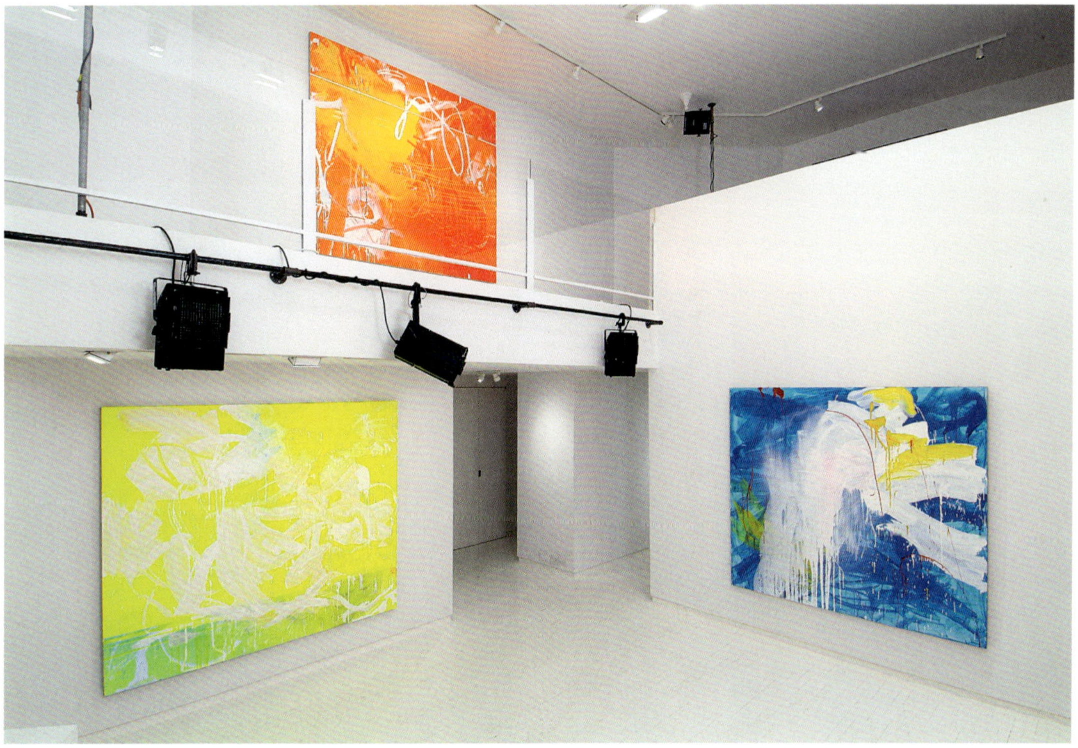

95/96. Installation views
Black Light Paintings, NYEHAUS, New York, 2005

what we might see having taken magic mushrooms or LSD, or over the rainbow. While these types of looking were respectable and edgy in the 1960s, today they are marginal. Psychedelic drugs designed to alter perception, to give out-of-body experiences, are frowned upon. In typical Humphries fashion, she mismatches and provokes through her materials and their use and exhibition. In an interview with Tony Oursler, Humphries likens the source materials for these paintings to landscapes in a Garden of Eden.[77] Being with them is a thrilling and scary escape from reality. The anarchy of painting reaches its most exciting (or egregious) levels with the recognition that visitors are in an environment that encourages screaming, laughter, joy, and fear. In the amusement park or the cinema – places Humphries might refer to as landscapes – we indulge in the disorientation of alternative realities. This is not how art is supposed to behave. This is not how we are supposed to behave in an art gallery.

Humphries's black-light paintings also remind of other cultural phenomena: fireflies glowing in the dark, the release of energy in nuclear fusion, the vision enabled by night goggles in military reconnaissance operations. Painting is no longer the revered object, an image to be venerated above others in the gallery as shrine. Painting has become, as Wilfried Dickhoff asserts, 'profane illumination'.[78] As Walter Benjamin did in his original use of that term, Humphries uses the 'secular' and seductive illumination of popular (drug) culture to move past traditional ways of seeing.[79] Like the surrealists in Benjamin's time, so Humphries culls the effects of consciousness-altering substances to create unexpected ways of looking in painting.

The chemical process attracting or luring phosphorescence out of paint creates a shining object where previously there was nothing to see. Like images produced through night-vision technology, converting what is invisible to the human eye into visible light, Humphries's paintings use science to bring light into darkness. But the use of phosphorescence also tells us that we must approach with caution, reminding us of the deadly annihilation caused by a nuclear reaction. Light in Humphries's art can destroy, blind, obfuscate, as well as illuminate. These paintings break all the rules of form, function, and the etiquette of painting. Like the surrealists a century ago, Humphries brings inappropriate – or obscene – ingredients to the artwork. The result of this daring are works which maintain the appearance of painting but are made through the medium of light. And with it, Humphries pushes past abstraction to reshape the viewer's experience of painting.

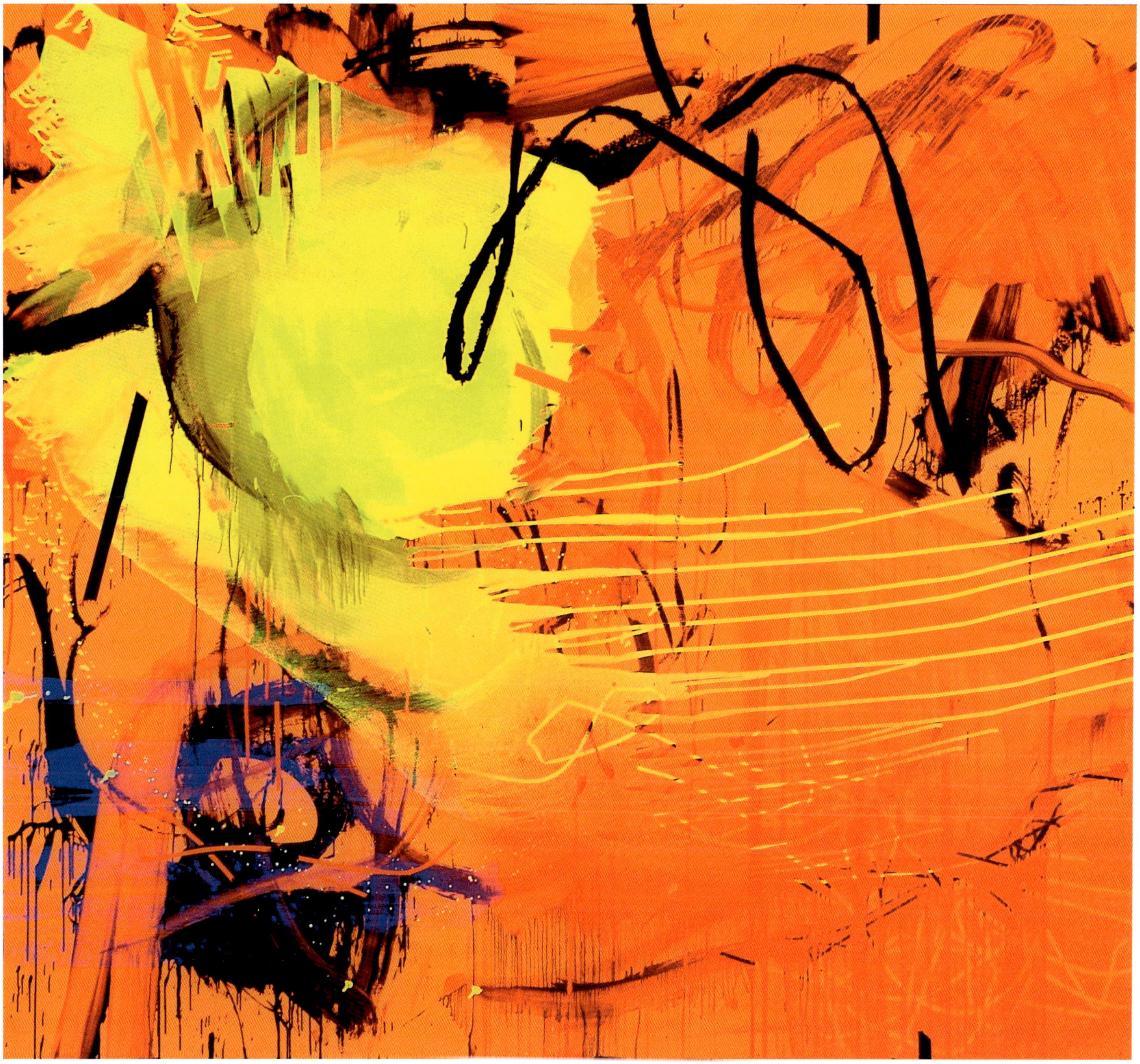

next spread

98. Installation view of *Jacqueline Humphries: jHΩ1:)*
Wexner Center for the Arts, Columbus, 2021

97. Note to Self 2005

Oil on linen
193 × 213.4 cm (76 × 84 in)
Museum Brandhorst; acquired 2013, Udo and Anette Brandhorst Collection

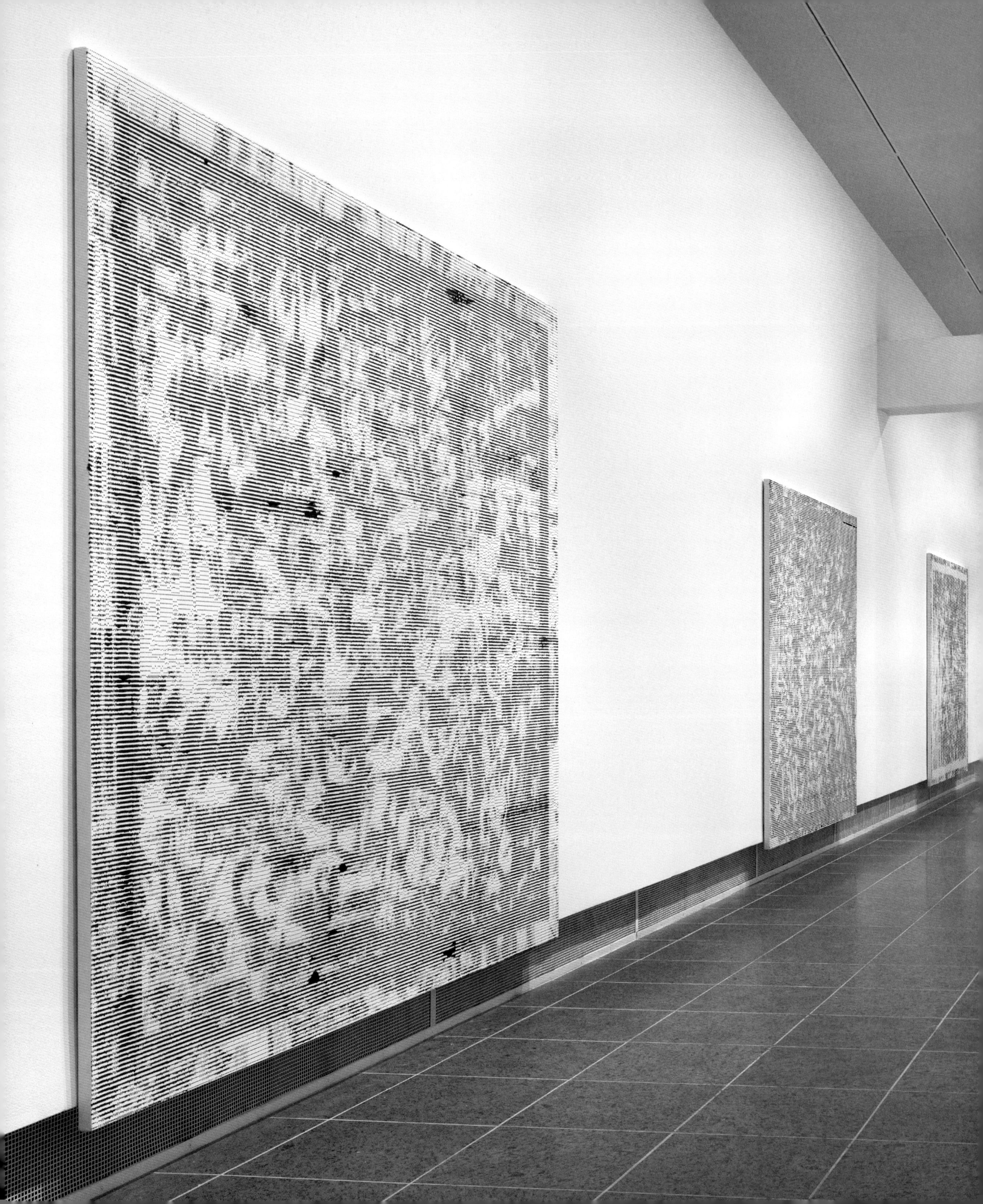

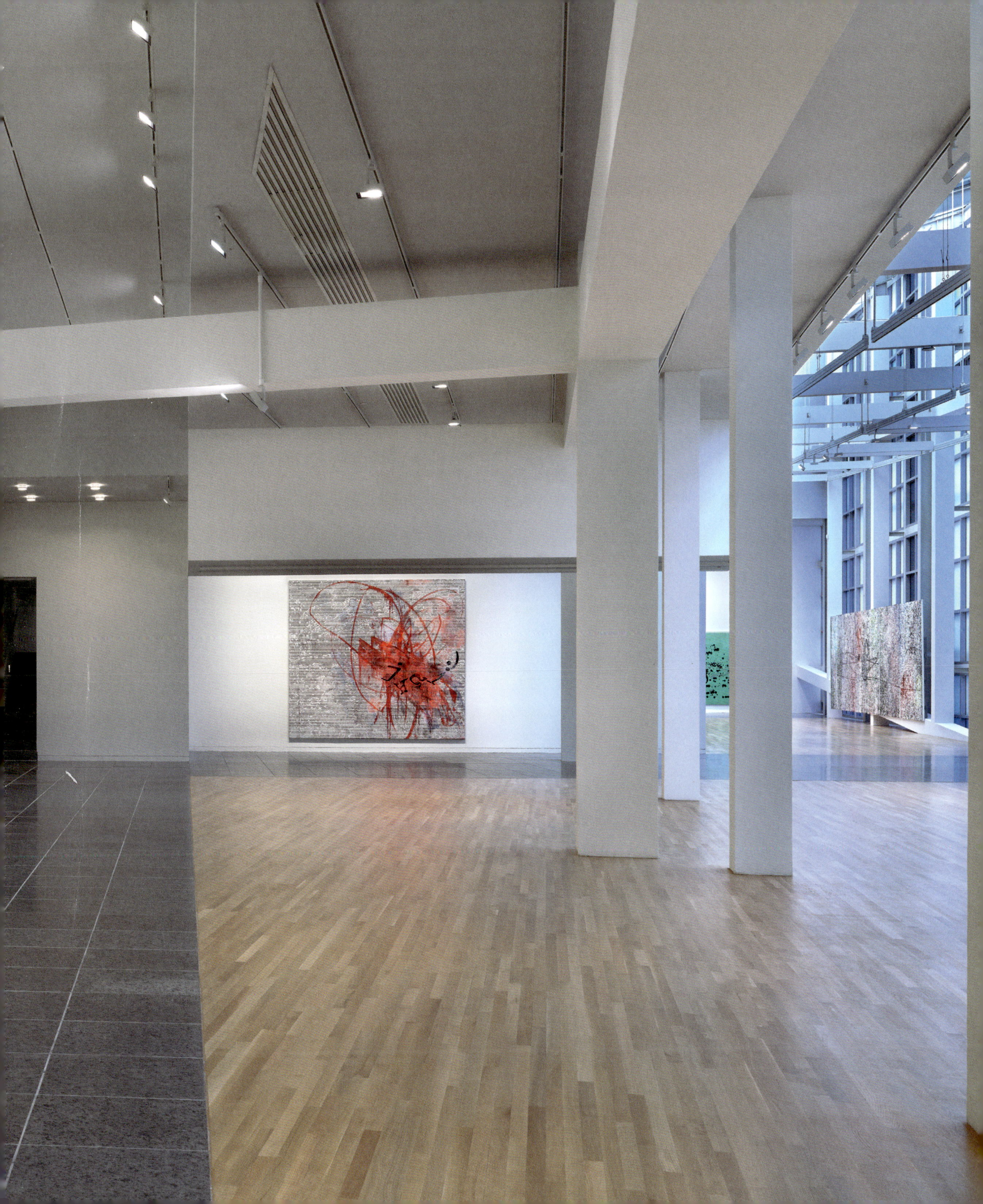

Notes

1. Jacqueline Humphries quoted in 'Interview with Jacqueline Humphries', Cecily Brown, *BOMB Magazine*, no.107, Spring 2009,p.31: https://bombmagazine.org/articles/jacqueline-humphries/ (accessed January 2021).
2. Humphries claims her work is anti-abstract expressionism: see 'Interview – Jacqueline Humphries: "I am painting last paintings all the time"', Museum Brandhorst, https://www.museum-brandhorst.de/en/interviews/jaqueline-humphries-i-am-painting-last-paintings-all-the-time/ (accessed January 2022).
3. David Joselit, Suzanne Hudson, and Angus Cook variously posit her work in relation to minimalist, expressionist, post-minimalist, and high modernist artists: *Jacqueline Humphries*, Walther König, Cologne, 2014.
4. See Clement Greenberg on the trajectory of abstract art: Clement Greenberg, 'Modernist painting' [1965], reprinted in Francis Frascina and Charles Harrison (eds), *Modern Art and Modernism: A Critical Anthology*, Harper & Row, London, 1982, pp 5–10.
5. Quoted in Linda Yablonsky, 'Artifacts: not like a man', *The New York Times Style Magazine*, 6 April 2012, https://tmagazine.blogs.nytimes.com/2012/04/06/artifacts-not-like-a-man/ (accessed 30 June 2021).
6. Ann Landi, 'A minimalist maximalist', *ARTnews*, Summer 2011, p.104.
7. Conversation with the artist, 15 July 2021.
8. Jacqueline Humphries quoted in 'Painting as event: an interview with Jacqueline Humphries', David Ryan, *Journal of Contemporary Painting*, vol.4, no.1, April 2018, p.47.
9. On Humphries and her contemporaries, see Mark Godfrey, 'Statements of intent: the art of Jacqueline Humphries, Laura Owens, Amy Sillman, and Charline von Heyl', *Artforum*, May 2014, https://www.artforum.com/print/201405/statements-of-intent-the-art-of-jacqueline-humphries-laura-owens-amy-sillman-and-charline-von-heyl-46327 (accessed 29 June 2021).
10. Jacqueline Humphries quoted in 'A romantic and sublime threshold state: Jacqueline Humphries – Jacqueline Humphries in conversation with Felix Bernstein', *Mousse Magazine*, 30 May 2019, www.moussemagazine.it/jacqueline-humphries-interviewed-felix-bernstein-2019/ (accessed 12 January 2021).
11. See, for example, ibid.; Ryan, 'Painting as event', op.cit., p.47.
12. The 2013 exhibition at Cheim & Read *Reinventing Abstraction: New York Painting in the 1980s* presented artists such as Mary Heilmann, Thomas Nozkowski, and Jonathan Lasker, who made their most significant contributions to abstraction in the 1980s: see https://www.cheimread.com/exhibitions/2013-06-27_reinventing-abstraction-curated-by-raphael-rubinstein (accessed 10 August 2021).
13. See also the work of Humphries's near-contemporary Moira Dryer. Dryer exhibited at John Good Gallery in the mid-1980s where Humphries also showed before moving to Greene Naftali in 1995. See also Barry Schwabsky, 'Playful and philosophical: the paintings of Moira Dryer', *New York Review of Books*, 25 April 2020: https://www.nybooks.com/daily/2020/04/25/playful-philosophical-moira-dryers-paintings/ (accessed 24 January 2022).
14. Conversation with the artist, 25 January 2021. Mention of these late Manet paintings is also quoted in Andrew Russeth, '"The thrilling feeling of creating light": Jacqueline Humphries on her recent work', *ARTnews*, 7 October 2015, https://www.artnews.com/art-news/artists/the-thrilling-feeling-of-creating-light-jacqueline-humphries-on-her-recent-work-5092/ (accessed 28 June 2021).
15. Michael Fried, 'Art and objecthood' [1967], reprinted in *Art and Objecthood: Essays and Reviews*, University of Chicago Press, Chicago and London, 1998, pp 148–72.
16. ibid.
17. David Joselit, 'Painting time: Jacqueline Humphries', in Joselit, Hudson, and Cook (eds), *Jacqueline Humphries*, op.cit., pp 15–30.
18. David Joselit, 'Reassembling painting', in Manuela Ammer, Achim Hochdörfer, and David Joselit (eds), *Painting 2.0: Expression in the Information Age*, exh.cat., Museum Brandhorst, Munich, 2016, p.172.
19. Joselit, 'Painting time', op.cit., p.30.
20. See Fried, 'Art and objecthood', op.cit.
21. See Godfrey, 'Statements of intent', op.cit., especially pp 301–3. See also 'Artist talk: Jacqueline Humphries', Aspen Art Museum 25 July 2019', https://www.youtube.com/watch?v=kl6YydkDQDI (accessed 22 June 2021).
22. Conversation with the artist, 17 July 2021.
23. See Kirk Varnedoe, *Pictures of Nothing: Abstract Art Since Pollock*, Princeton University Press, Princeton, New Jersey, 2007.
24. Alexander R. Galloway, *The Interface Effect*, Polity, London, 2012, p.vii.
25. 'L'Almanach 18: Jacqueline Humphries', Consortium Museum, 2018, https://www.leconsortium.fr/en/en/lalmanach-18-jacqueline-humphries (accessed 15 May 2021).
26. Some of Humphries's paints are custom-made and she makes her own stencils.
27. Conversation with the artist, May 2021.
28. On ASCII process, see Lloyd Wise, 'Feelings aren't facts', *Artforum*, Summer 2019, p.262.
29. See Galloway, 'Are some things unrepresentable?', in *The Interface Effect*, op.cit., pp 78–100.
30. '4/18/2017 Jacqueline Humphries', https://vimeo.com/216330883, quotation at 57 minutes.
31. In interview with Felix Bernstein: 'A romantic and sublime threshold state', *Mousse Magazine*, op.cit.
32. ibid.
33. Wise, 'Feelings aren't facts', op.cit., p.263.
34. Conversation with the artist, January 2020.
35. '4/18/2017 Jacqueline Humphries', op.cit.

36. Paul Schrader, 'Notes on film noir', *Film Comment*, vol.8, no.1, Spring 1972, pp 8–13 (p.11).
37. Quoted in Nicolas Trembley, 'Comment Jacqueline Humphries transforme le code informatique en peinture', *Numéro*, 15 October 2020, https://www.numero.com/fr/art/jacqueline-humphries-artiste-du-mois-peinture-code-informatique (accessed 16 May 2021).
38. Verity Platt and Michael Squire (eds), *The Frame in Classical Art: A Cultural History*, Cambridge University Press, Cambridge, 2017.
39. Erving Goffman, *Frame Analysis: An Essay on the Organization of Experience,* Harvard University Press, Cambridge, Massachusetts, 1974.
40. See Slavoj Žižek, *The Parallax View*, MIT Press, Cambridge, Massachusetts, 2006.
41. Donald Kuspit focuses on Humphries's relationship to the grid as a postmodern emptiness: see Donald Kuspit, 'On the mannerist cutting edge: Jacqueline Humphries' neo-pure painting', in Ute Riese and Donald Kuspit (eds), *Jacqueline Humphries: Malerei / Paintings*, exh.cat., Kunsthalle Wilhelmshaven, Kerber Verlag, Bielefeld, 2000, pp 6–15.
42. See Nicholas Mirzoeff, *How to See the World*, Penguin, London and New York, 2015.
43. Fried, 'Art and objecthood', op.cit., p.151.
44. See Anne Friedberg, *The Virtual Window: From Alberti to Microsoft*, MIT Press, Cambridge, Massachusetts, 2006.
45. In interview with Felix Bernstein: 'A romantic and sublime threshold state', *Mousse Magazine*, op.cit.
46. On German expressionism, see Peter Selz, *German Expressionist Painting,* University of California Press, Berkeley and Los Angeles, 1974.
47. Quoted in Godfrey, 'Statements of intent', op.cit.
48. Joselit discusses Pollock as a precursor to Humphries in Joselit, 'Painting time', op.cit., pp 15–20.
49. On the use of drips in automatic painting, see Karin Wimmer, 'From automatic drawing to American abstract art: André Masson, Jackson Pollock and Cy Twombly', *Kunstgeschichte*, 26 March 2015, https://www.kunstgeschichte-ejournal.net/445/ (accessed 14 April 2021).
50. Pollock used an industrial paint to avoid run-off once the painting was vertical.
51. Claire McConaughy, 'Collapsing the surface: Jacqueline Humphries runs with the drip', *Cover Magazine*, May 1994, p.17.
52. See Godfrey, 'Statements of intent', op.cit. He writes: 'their canvases are populated by uncertain, fake, or unlocatable gestures' (p.298).
53. 'Interview with Tony Oursler', *Jacqueline Humphries: Black Light Paintings*, exh.cat., Foundation 20 21, NYEHAUS, 2005, pages unnumbered.
54. Yve-Alain Bois, 'Perceiving Newman', in *Painting as Model*, MIT Press, Cambridge, Massachusetts, 1993, pp 187–214.
55. Kenneth R. Allan, 'Barnett Newman's The Wild': painting as spatial intervention', *October*, vol.143, December 2013, pp 71–94.
56. See Barry Schwabsky, Todd Bradway et al., *Landscape Painting Now: From Pop Abstraction to New Romanticism*, Thames & Hudson, London and New York, 2019.
57. 'Artist talk: Jacqueline Humphries', Aspen Art Museum, 25 July 2019, op.cit.
58. Brown, 'Jacqueline Humphries', op.cit., p.26.
59. ibid., p.28.
60. Tim Griffin, 'Jacqueline Humphries', *Time Out New York*, June 2001, pp 7–14.
61. 'Artist talk', Aspen Art Museum, 25 July 2019, op.cit.
62. ibid.
63. See Vivian Sobchack, 'The scene of the screen: envisioning cinematic and electronic presence' [1994], reprinted in John Thornton Caldwell (ed.), *Electronic Media and Technoculture*, Rutgers University Press, New Brunswick, New Jersey, 2000, pp 137–55.
64. Conversation with the artist, 22 July 2021.
65. ibid.
66. See Godfrey, 'Statements of intent', op.cit., p.301.
67. Yablonsky, 'Artifacts', op.cit.
68. ibid.
69. See Joselit, Hudson, and Cook (eds), *Jacqueline Humphries*, op.cit., p.147.
70. Quotation from interview with Felix Bernstein: 'A romantic and sublime threshold state', *Mousse Magazine*, op.cit.
71. Brown, 'Jacqueline Humphries', op.cit., p.29.
72. Sobchack, 'The scene of the screen', op.cit.
73. Frani O'Toole, 'Seeing is not believing in the art of Jacqueline Humphries', *Apollo*, 1 August 2019, https://www.apollo-magazine.com/jacqueline-humphries-dan-flavin-art-institute-review/ (accessed January 2022).
74. 'Interview with Tony Oursler', *Jacqueline Humphries: Black Light Paintings*, exh.cat., Foundation 20 21, NYEHAUS, 2005, pages unnumbered.
75. 'Ultra violet: an interview with Tony Oursler', *Sleek*, no.8, Autumn 2005, pp 52–61 (p.56).
76. ibid., p.52.
77. ibid., p.56.
78. Wilfried Dickhoff, 'Shining: abstraction as profane illumination', in *Jacqueline Humphries: Black Light Paintings*, op.cit.
79. Walter Benjamin, 'Surrealism: the last snapshot of European intelligentsia', in *Reflections: Essays, Aphorisms, Autobiographical Writing*, Schocken Books, New York, 1986, p.64.

Select Bibliography

Selected Articles

Anon., 'Seven Sisters: new work by artist Jacqueline Humphries'. *ArtDaily*, 7 September 2006: Web.

Bankowsky, Jack. 'Painting 2.0: expression in the Information Age'. *Artforum*, July 2016: 384–87, 442.

Barron, James. 'A metal-gate makeover'. *The New York Times*, 2 May 2011.

Bookhardt, D. Eric. 'Abstraction's unlikely attractions'. *New Orleans*, June 1995.

Bookhardt, D. Eric. 'Beyond the modern and back again'. *Inside Art*, New Orleans, May 1996: 215.

Brown, Cecily. 'Interview with Jacqueline Humphries'. *BOMB Magazine*, no.107, Spring 2009: 22–31.

Burton, Johanna. 'Jacqueline Humphries'. *Artforum*, February 2007: 292.

Cala, Terrington. 'Gesture & allusion'. *The New Orleans Art Review*, March–April 1999: 2–5.

Calas, Terrington. 'Notes on virtuosity'. *The New Orleans Art Review*, November–December, 1993: 20.

Calas, Terrington. 'Some New York hedonists'. *The New Orleans Art Review*, May–June 1995: 36.

Chaiklin, Amy. 'Studio visit: Jacqueline Humphries', *NY Arts Magazine*, January–February 1998: 15.

Coomer, Martin. 'Reviews: Jacqueline Humphries'. *Art Review*, no.42, Summer 2010: 134.

Cotter, Holland. 'Art in Review: Assume Vivid Astro Focus, "Knowing When to Stop"'. *The New York Times*, 21 June 2002: 37.

Cotter, Holland. 'Art in Review: Superimposition'. *The New York Times*, 7 July 2001: 33.

Cyphers, Peggy. 'New York in review, Jacqueline Humphries'. *Arts Magazine*, October 1989: 105.

Damianovic, Maia. 'Jacqueline Humphries'. *Tema Celeste*, January–February 2000: 131.

Farago, Jason. 'Jacqueline Humphries's digital paintings, aglow in the dark'. *The New York Times*, 6 September 2019: C14.

Gilson, Nancy. 'Visual Arts: Humphries exhibit at the Wexner Center an experiential event'. *The Columbus Dispatch*, 3 October 2021: https://eu.dispatch.com/story/entertainment/2021/10/03/humphries-exhibit-wexner-center-presents-art-new-light/5829008001/.

Godfrey, Mark. 'Statements of intent: the art of Jacqueline Humphries, Laura Owens, Amy Sillman, and Charline von Heyl'. *Artforum*, May 2014: 294–303.

Griffin, Tim. 'Jacqueline Humphries'. *Time Out*, June 2001: 7–14.

Griffin, Tim. 'Jacqueline Humphries'. *Artforum*, December 2015: 224–7.

Herbert, Martin. 'Jacqueline Humphries'. *Frieze*, September 2014: 173.

Hudson, Suzanne. 'Besides, With, Against, and Yet'. *Artforum*, February 2010: 201.

Humphries, Jacqueline. Interview with Kunstforum Editors. 'Malen ist etwas Öffentliches'. *Kunstforum International*, January–February 1999: 324–5.

Humphries, Jacqueline. Interview with Tony Oursler, in Annie Dufour, *Tony Oursler, Gustave Courbet*, 2004. Paris: Musée d'Orsay / Hazan: 18–49.

Humphries, Jacqueline. Interview with Paul Soto. 'Painting in silver and noir: Q + A with Jacqueline Humphries'. *Art in America*, 30 April 2012: Web.

Humphries, Jacqueline. 'The artists' artists'. *Artforum*, December 2015: 119.

Humphries, Jacqueline. 'Nice talking you David :)'. *Journal of Contemporary Painting*, vol.4, no.1, April 2018: 29–44.

Humphries, Jacqueline. 'Not dripping, but pouring: Jackson Pollock: Blind Spots'. *Tate Etc.*, 2019: Web.

Humphries, Jacqueline. 'Jacqueline Humphries in conversation with Felix Bernstein'. *Mousse* 66, 2019: 135–36.

Humphries, Jacqueline. Interview with Nicolas Trembley. 'L'artiste du mois – Jacqueline Humphries'. *Numéro*, no.217, October 2020: Web.

Humphrey, David. 'Jacqueline Humphries'. *Tema Celeste*, October–December, 1989: 73.

Humphrey, David. 'The abject romance of low resolution'. *Lusitania*, vol.1, no.4, Winter 1993: 155–9.

Hunt, David. 'Editor's Choice: Jacqueline Humphries, new paintings'. *Bomb*, Summer 2001: 16.

Huzenis, Ella. 'Wade Guyton and Jacqueline Humphries want to renovate an NYC Art Venue and not change a thing'. *Interview*, 19 February 2021: Web.

Johnson, Ken. 'Begetting art, and social commentary, too'. *The New York Times*, 6 July 2012: C23.

Kelsey, John. 'The best of 2005'. *Artforum*, December 2005: 252.

Kan-Sperling, Olivia. 'Venice Dispatch: From the Biennale'. *The Paris Review*, 29 April 2022: https://www.theparisreview.org/blog/2022/04/29/venice-dispatch/

Kimmelman, Michael. 'Art in Review: Jacqueline Humphries, Nyehaus'. *The New York Times*, 27 May 2005: E34.

Kreimer, Julian. 'Jacqueline Humphries at Greene Naftali'. *Art in America*, April 2007: 142–3.

Kuo, Michelle. 'Acting out: the AbEx effect'. *Artforum*, Summer 2011: 351.

Kuspit, Donald. 'Jacqueline Humphries'. *Artforum*, September 1992: 94.

Kuspit, Donald. 'Sublime negative'. *Artnet*, 30 November 1999: Web.

Landi, Ann. 'A minimalist maximalist'. *ARTnews*, Summer 2011: 100–105.

Larson, Kay. 'We've come a long way . . . maybe'. *ARTnews*, May 1997: 138.

Levy, Matthew L. 'Jacqueline Humphries, Carnegie Museum of Art, Pittsburgh, 11 June–5 October 2015'. *Journal of Contemporary Painting*, vol.2, no.2, 2016: 322–6.

MacAdam, Alfred. 'Jacqueline Humphries'. *ArtNews*, January 1991: 154.

Maloney, Martin. 'Young Americans: Parts I & II'. *Flash Art*, May–June 1996: 109.

Masciere, Christina. 'Critical mass: Jacqueline Humphries pours it on'. *New Orleans Magazine*, vol.30, no.8, May 1996.

McConaughy, Claire. 'Collapsing the surface: Jacqueline Humphries runs with the drip'. *Cover Magazine*, May 1994: 17.

McDonough, Tom. Review, *Art in America*, March 2000: 127–8.

McHargue, Keegan. 'Best of 2009: artists' artists – Jacqueline Humphries (Greene Naftali, New York)'. *Artforum*, December 2009: 90.
McQuaid, Kate. 'Pollock, Humphries exhibits make splash by stressing paint'. *Boston Globe*, 1 August 2006: C5.
Nixon, Bruce. 'Jim Campbell, Jeanne Dunning, and Jacqueline Humphries at Rena Bransten Gallery'. *The Guide/San Francisco*, February 1995: 17.
Noor, Tausif. 'Critics' Picks: Jacqueline Humphries'. *Artforum*, November, 2017: Web.
O'Rourke, Marguerite. 'Jacqueline Humphries'. *Tema Celeste*, March–April 1992.
Rimanelli, David. 'Jacqueline Humphries'. *Artforum*, Summer 2012: 312.
Rubinstein, Meyer Raphael. 'Jacqueline Humphries'. *Flash Art*, November–December 1990: 156–7.
Rubinstein, Raphael. 'Provisional painting'. *Art in America*, May 2009: 123–35.
Russeth, Andrew. '"The thrilling feeling of creating light": Jacqueline Humphries on her recent work'. *ARTnews*, 7 October 2015: Web.
Ryan, David. 'Painting as event: an interview with Jacqueline Humphries'. *Journal of Contemporary Painting*, vol.4, no.1, April 2018: 45–58.
Schjeldahl, Peter. 'Get with it: the Whitney Biennial'. *The New Yorker*, 17 March 2014: 76–7.
Schjeldahl, Peter. 'Jacqueline Humphries'. *Artforum*, November 2017: Web.
Schwabsky, Barry. 'Jacqueline Humphries'. *Artforum*, January 1998: 100–101.
Schwartzman, Allan. 'A new age in painting (at last)?'. *Art Agency, Partners*, 9 November 2017: Web.
Schwendener, Martha. 'Jacqueline Humphries'. *The New York Times*, 1 December 2017: C19.
Scott, Andrea K. 'Behind the scenes'. *The New Yorker*, 23 November 2020: Web.
Siegel, Jeanne. 'The real meaning of the work'. *Tema Celeste*, Autumn 1992: 83.
Smith, Roberta. 'Jacqueline Humphries'. *The New York Times*, 14 July 1989: 22.
Smith, Roberta. 'A luscious journey, exhaustively annotated'. *The New York Times*, 20 August 1999: 35.
Stillman, Nick. 'Painting abstraction: new elements in abstract painting by Bob Nickas'. *Res*, March 2010: 150–58.
Vogel, Carol. 'The Whitney's 2014 Biennial starts taking shape'. *The New York Times*, 15 November 2013: C26.
Wise, Lloyd. 'Feelings aren't facts'. *Artforum*, Summer 2019: 258–65.
Yablonsky, Linda. 'Artifacts: not like a man'. *The New York Times Style Magazine*, 6 April 2012: https://tmagazine.blogs.nytimes.com/2012/04/06/artifacts-not-like-a-man/.
Young, Geoffrey. 'Putting on the dot'. *Arts Magazine*, October 1990: 68–73.

Catalogues

2022
Burton, Johanna, Mark Godfrey, Courtney J. Martin, and Jenny Nachtigall. *Jacqueline Humphries: jHΩ1:)*. Columbus, Ohio: Wexner Center for the Arts / Gregory R. Miller & Co.

2014
Joselit, David, Suzanne Hudson, and Angus Cook. *Jacqueline Humphries*. Cologne: Walther König.

2005
Nye, Tim, ed. *Jacqueline Humphries: Black Light Paintings*. Foundation 20 21. New York.

2000
Riese, Ute, and Donald Kuspit, eds. *Jacqueline Humphries: Malerei / Paintings*. Bielefeld, Germany: Kerber Verlag.

Selected Group Exhibition Catalogues

2017
Colacello, Bob. *The Age of Ambiguity*. St Moritz: Vito Schnabel Gallery.
Manné, Jamie G. *Unpacking: The Marciano Collection*. Los Angeles: The Maurice and Paul Marciano Art Foundation.

2016
Alemani, Cecilia, and Massimiliano Gioni, eds. *Good Dreams, Bad Dreams – American Mythologies*. Beirut: Aïshti Foundation, Skira.
Ammer, Manuela, Achim Hochdörfer, and David Joselit, eds. *Painting 2.0: Expression in the Information Age*. Munich and Vienna: Museum Brandhorst, Munich; mumok, Vienna; and DelMonico.
Fine Young Cannibals. New York: Petzel.

2015
Delahunty, Gavin, ed. *Jackson Pollock: Blind Spots*. London: Tate.

2014
Comer, Stuart, Anthony Elms, and Michelle Grabner, eds. *Whitney Biennial 2014*. New York: Yale University Press.

2012
Burton, Johanna, ed. *Anti-Establishment*. Annandale-on-Hudson: Center for Curatorial Studies, Bard College.
EDITOR, ed. *Eagles: artistas contemporáneos americanos*. Madrid: Galería Marlborough.

2011
Aguirre, Peio, and Negar Azimi, eds. *Vitamin P2: New Perspectives in Painting*. London: Phaidon Press.

2009
Nickas, Bob, ed. *Painting Abstraction: New Elements in Abstract Painting*. London: Phaidon Press.

2008
Bloemink, Barbara, et al., eds. *Prospect.1 New Orleans*. Brooklyn: Picturebox, Inc.

2003
Riese, Ute, and Gerhard Finckh, eds. *New Abstract Painting: Abstraktion in der neuen Malerei / Painting Abstract Now*. Leverkusen: Museum Morsbroich.

1998
Poetter, Jochen, ed. *I Love New York: Crossover der aktuellen Kunst*. Cologne: Museum Ludwig.

1996
Deitch, Jeffrey, ed. *Young Americans: New American Art in the Saatchi Collection*. London: Saatchi Gallery.

1995
Rub, Timothy, ed., *A Decade of Collecting, 1985 – 1995: Contemporary Prints*. Hood Museum of Art, Dartmouth College. Hanover, New Hampshire: Trustees of Dartmouth College.
Thomas, Lew, ed. *New York Abstract*. New Orleans: Contemporary Art Center.
Yau, John, ed. *Abstraction from Two Coasts*. Houston: Doug Lawing Gallery.

1993
Jacqueline Humphries. New York: John Good Gallery.
The Louis Comfort Tiffany Foundation: 1991 Awards in Painting, Sculpture, Printmaking, Photography, and Craft Media. New York: Louis Comfort Tiffany Foundation.
Cappuccio, Elio, ed. *Verso Bisanzio, con disincanto*. Prato: Sergio Tossi Arte Contemporanea.
O'Rourke, Marguerite, ed. *Behind Bars*. New York: Thread Waxing Space.
Smith, Joshua P., et al., eds. *Drawn in the 90s*. Katonah, New York: Katonah Museum of Art.

1991
King, Elaine A., ed. *New Generations: New York*. Pittsburgh: Carnegie Mellon Art Gallery.

1990
Green, Nancy E., and Nancy Allyn Jarzombeck, eds. *Cornell Collects*. Ithaca, New York: Herbert F. Johnson Museum of Art, Cornell University.
Nye, Tim, and Miguel Abreu, eds. *Three Painters: Hyun Soo Choi, Jacqueline Humphries, Paul Pagk*. New York: 470 Broome Street.

Biography

1960
Born in New Orleans, USA
Lives and works in New York

1984
Yale Summer School of Art, Norfolk, Connecticut

1985
Parsons School of Design, New York

1986
Whitney Independent Study Program, New York

Awards and Fellowships

1989
Edward F. Albee Foundation Fellowship

1992
Louis Comfort Tiffany Award

1995
Joan Mitchell Foundation Grant

1999
Pollock-Krasner Foundation Grant

2001
American Academy of Arts and Letters Purchase Prize

Exhibitions

Selected Solo Exhibitions

All titled *Jacqueline Humphries*, unless otherwise stated

2021
Jacqueline Humphries: jHΩ1:), Wexner Center for the Arts, Columbus, Ohio

2020
Galerie Gisela Capitain, Cologne

2019
Dia Bridgehampton, Bridgehampton, New York

2018
Stuart Shave / Modern Art, London

2017
Greene Naftali, New York

2016
Crown Point Press, San Francisco
Galerie Gisela Capitain, Cologne

2015
Contemporary Art Center New Orleans
Greene Naftali, New York
Carnegie Museum of Art, Pittsburgh

2014
Stuart Shave / Modern Art, London

2012
Greene Naftali, New York

2011
Galerie Forsblom, Helsinki

2010
Stuart Shave / Modern Art, London

2009
Greene Naftali, New York

2007
Jacqueline Humphries, Mercury's Moon, Jensen Gallery, Auckland

Albert Merola Gallery, Provincetown, Massachusetts
Stuart Shave / Modern Art, London

2006
Jacqueline Humphries, Past Out, Greene Naftali, New York
Seven Sisters: New Work by Jacqueline Humphries, Williams College Museum of Art, Williamstown, Massachusetts

2005
Jacqueline Humphries: Black Light Paintings, NYEHAUS, New York

2002
Lawing Gallery, Houston, Texas

2001
Greene Naftali, New York

2000
Kunsthalle Wilhelmshaven, Germany

1999
Greene Naftali, New York
Galerie Heinz Holtmann, Cologne
Galerie Simonne Stern, New Orleans

1997
Greene Naftali, New York

1996
Mario Diacono, Boston, Massachusetts
Galerie Simonne Stern, New Orleans
Rena Bransten Gallery, San Francisco

1995
Greene Naftali, New York
Rena Bransten Gallery, San Francisco

1994
John Good Gallery, New York
Universal Fine Objects, Provincetown, Massachusetts

1993
Angles Gallery, Los Angeles
Galerie Simonne Stern, New Orleans

1992
John Good Gallery, New York
Thomas Segal Gallery, Boston, Massachusetts

1990
John Good Gallery, New York
Galerie Ryszard Varisella, Frankfurt

1989
John Good Gallery, New York

Selected Group Exhibitions

2022
Milk of Dreams, Venice Biennale
Invitational Exhibition of Visual Arts, American Academy of Arts and Letters, New York
White Columns Annual, New York

2021
Infinite Games... 2, Capitain Petzel, Berlin
Greene Naftali Gallery at Galerie Chantal Crousel: Arrangement in Gray, Galerie Chantal Crousel, Paris
Recent Acquisitions: Modern and Contemporary Drawings and Prints, Morgan Library and Museum, New York

2020
Ice and Fire: A Benefit Exhibition in Three Parts, co-organiser, The Kitchen, New York
Structures of Feeling, Galerie Maria Bernheim, Zurich
Drawing 2020, Gladstone Gallery, New York
50th Anniversary Benefit Exhibition, The Kitchen, New York
Overwrite, Greene Naftali, New York

2019
Feel the Sun in Your Mouth: Recent Acquisitions, Hirshhorn Museum and Sculpture Garden, Washington, DC
Rosebud, Matthew Marks Gallery, Los Angeles
7 Painters, Greene Naftali, New York
Painters Reply: Experimental Painting in the 1970s and Now, Lisson Gallery, New York
Forever Young – 10 Years Museum Brandhorst, Museum Brandhorst, Munich
Sun Women: A Tribute to 8 Women Artists in the USA, Charles Riva Collection, Brussels
Collection Exhibition, Art Institute of Chicago, Chicago

2018
Burn It Clean, 1301PE, Los Angeles
We the People: New Art from the Collection, Albright-Knox Art Gallery, Buffalo, New York
L'Almanach 18, 3rd International Biennial of Contemporary Art, Le Consortium, Dijon, France
The Mechanics of Fluids, Marianne Boesky Gallery, New York
Abstraction Today – Mapping the Invisible World, Tobias Mueller Modern Art, Zurich
'Au diapason du monde' ('In tune with the world'), Fondation Louis Vuitton, Paris
The Whole Drum Will Sound: Women in Southern Abstraction, Ogden Museum of Southern Art, New Orleans
Crossroads: Carnegie Museum of Art's Collection, 1945 to Now, Carnegie Museum of Art, Pittsburgh
My So-Called Reality, Marciano Art Foundation, Los Angeles

2017
The Electric Comma, V-A-C Foundation, Palazzo delle Zattere, Dorsoduro, Venice
Social Surfaces: A Fundraising Exhibition, Artists Space, New York
Unpainting, Art Gallery of New South Wales, Sydney
The Age of Ambiguity, Vito Schnabel Project, St Moritz, Switzerland

2016
A Slow Succession with Many Interruptions, San Francisco Museum of Modern Art, San Francisco
Fine Young Cannibals, Petzel Gallery, New York
Good Dreams, Bad Dreams – American Mythologies, Aïshti Foundation, Beirut
Tales of Ratiocination, Campoli Presti, London
Making Traces, Tate Modern, London

2015
Painting 2.0: Expression in the Information Age, Museum Brandhorst, Munich
Surface Matters, Museum of Fine Arts, Boston, Massachusetts
My Wife Does the Dishes, I Do the Revolution, Kimmerich, Berlin
The Triumph of Love: Beth Rudin DeWoody Collects, Norton Museum of Art, West Palm Beach, Florida
Made in USA, V-A-C Foundation, Moscow
Painting After Technology, Tate Modern Collection Show, London

2014
Some Artists' Artists, Marian Goodman, New York
Loveless, Greene Naftali, New York
Whitney Biennial, Whitney Museum, New York
Pouring It On, Herter Gallery, University of Massachusetts, Amherst, Massachusetts

2013
LAT. 41° 7' N., LONG. 72° 19' W., Martos Gallery, East Marion, New York

2012
Eagles, Galeria Marlborough, Madrid
Inside Out and From the Ground Up, MOCA Cleveland, Cleveland, Ohio
Painting in Space, an exhibition to benefit CCS Bard Center for Curatorial Studies, Luhring Augustine, New York

2011
Contemporary Galleries: 1980–Now, Museum of Modern Art, New York
If You Lived Here, You'd Be Home by Now, CCS Bard Hessel Museum of Art, Annandale-on-Hudson, New York
New Silver, Kunsthalle Gießen, Giessen, Germany
Provisional Painting, Stuart Shave / Modern Art, London

2010
Painting Extravaganza, Cardi Black Box, Milan
Re-Dressing, Bortolami, New York
The Big New Field, Dallas Museum of Art, Dallas

2009
Besides, With, Against, and Yet: Abstraction and the Ready-Made Gesture, The Kitchen, New York

2008
Prospect.1 New Orleans, New Orleans

2007
Affinities: Painting in Abstraction, CCS Bard Hessel Museum, Annandale-on-Hudson, New York

2006
Under Pressure, Art Concept, Paris

2005
POST-MoDERN, Greene Naftali, New York

2004
Selections from the Collection of the Museum of Fine Arts, Boston, Nagoya Museum, Japan

2003
New Abstract Painting – Painting Abstract Now: Abstraktion in der neuen Malerei, Museum Morsbroich, Leverkusen, Germany

2001
Against the Wall: Painting Against the Grid, Surface and Frame, Institute of Contemporary Art, Philadelphia
Superimposition, New York American Academy Invitational Exhibition of Painting and American Academy Invitation Exhibition of Painting and Sculpture, American Academy of Arts and Letters, New York
New Paintings, Kevin Bruk Fine Arts, Miami

2000
The Berardo Collection, Fundação Centro Cultural de Belém, Lisbon
Painting Abstraction, New York Studio School
Trailer, Greene Naftali, New York

1999
Free Coke, Greene Naftali, New York

1998
I Love New York: Crossover of Contemporary Art, Museum Ludwig, Cologne
Painting: Now & Forever, Part I, Pat Hearn & Matthew Marks Gallery, New York

1997
Alive & Well: New Painting, Elizabeth Harris Gallery, New York

1996
Young Americans: American Art in the Saatchi Collection, Saatchi Gallery, London

1995
Degrees of Abstraction: From Morris Louis to Robert Mapplethorpe, Museum of Fine Arts, Boston, Massachusetts

1994
Fall Group Exhibition, John Good Gallery, New York

1993
Summer Group Exhibition, John Good Gallery, New York
Jessica Stockholder, Jacqueline Humphries, Karin Davie, John Good Gallery, New York
Sailing to Byzantium, With Disenchantment, Sergio Tossi, Prato, Italy

1992
Jacqueline Humphries, James Balla, Universal Fine Objects, Provincetown, Massachusetts
Baziotes to Basquiat . . . and Beyond, Bellas Artes, Santa Fe, New Mexico

1991
New Generations: New York, Carnegie Mellon Art Gallery, Pittsburgh
Young American Painters, Tavelli Gallery, Aspen, Colorado

1990
Cornell Collects, Johnson Museum of Art, Ithaca, New York
Untitled, John Good Gallery, New York
Hyun Soo Choi, Jacqueline Humphries, Paul Pagk, 470 Broome Street, New York

1989
Galerie Ryszard Varisella, Frankfurt
Methods of Abstraction, Gallery Urban, New York

1988
Numerators, John Good Gallery, New York
Living in New York, Aubes 3935 Galerie, Montreal

1985
The Non-Objective World, Kamikaze Gallery, New York

Selected Public Collections and Foundations

Aïshti Foundation, Beirut
Albright-Knox Art Gallery, Buffalo, New York
Art Institute of Chicago, Chicago
Blenheim Palace, Woodstock, UK
Carnegie Museum of Art, Pittsburgh
Cincinnati Art Museum, Cincinnati
Columbus Museum of Art, Columbus, Ohio
Dallas Museum of Art, Dallas
Fondation Louis Vuitton, Paris
Glenstone Foundation, Potomac, Maryland
Hessel Museum of Art, Annandale-on-Hudson, New York
Hirshhorn Museum and Sculpture Garden, Washington, DC
Hood Museum, Dartmouth College, Hanover, New Hampshire
The Metropolitan Museum of Art, New York
mumok, Vienna
Museu Coleção Berardo, Lisbon
Museum Brandhorst, Munich
Museum of Fine Arts, Boston
Museum of Modern Art, New York
New Orleans Museum of Art, New Orleans
New School University Art Collection, New York
Norton Museum of Art, West Palm Beach, Florida
Ogden Museum of Southern Art, New Orleans
Orlando Museum of Art, Orlando, Florida
Parrish Art Museum, Water Mill, New York
The Saatchi Collection, London
San Francisco Museum of Modern Art, San Francisco
Semler Collection, Portland Museum of Art, Portland, Oregon
Solomon R. Guggenheim Museum, New York
Tate, London
Whitney Museum of American Art, New York
Zabludowicz Collection, London

Acknowledgements

I am grateful to Barry Schwabsky for his invitation to write this book, and for his support throughout the process. Dore Bowen and Joe McElhaney offered careful readings of the manuscript and helped pull it into shape. Regina Fiorito at Galerie Gisela Capitain made it possible to visit the 2020 Cologne exhibition, against all odds, mid-pandemic. I also want to thank Lucy Clark, Rochelle Roberts, and their colleagues at Lund Humphries, who were a pleasure to work with from proposal to publication. A big thank-you to all at Greene Naftali Gallery for their unreserved support of the book. Particular thanks go to Jeffrey Rowledge, Martha Fleming-Ives, and Zhiwei Chen for supporting the book and their furnishing of every request, from texts to images, recommendations to introductions. Taylor Walsh also provided helpful edits on the manuscript. My most profound thanks go to Jacqueline Humphries for her generosity, time, and enthusiasm for conversing with me about her painting over oceans, time differences, and Mexican food. Her extraordinary body of work has opened doors and led me to places I did not know existed.

Image Credits

Index

Page numbers in *italics* refer to illustrations

First published in 2022 by Lund Humphries

Lund Humphries
The Alphabeta Building
18 Finsbury Square
London
EC2A 1AH
www.lundhumphries.com

ISBN: 978-1-84822-472-8

A Cataloguing-in-Publication record for this book is available from the British Library.

Copy-edited by Abigail Grater
Designed by Mark Thomson
Set in Custodia (Fred Smeijers)
Printed in Belgium

Frontispiece: Jacqueline Humphries in her studio, 2021.
Photo: Martha Fleming-Ives.
Cover: ???~, 2017, oil on linen, 254 × 281.9 cm (100 × 111 in).